T0276420

LIVE!

In Search of the Crack
Spain: A Portrait After the General
The Way We Wore: A Life in Threads
London Made Us: A Memoir of a Shape-Shifting City

LIVE!

Why We Go Out

Robert Elms

unbound

First published in 2023

Unbound
c/o TC Group, 6th Floor King's House, 9–10 Haymarket, London sw1y 4bp
www.unbound.com

While every effort has been made to trace the owners of copyright material reproduced
herein, the publisher would like to apologise for any omissions and will be pleased to
incorporate missing acknowledgements in any further editions.

Typeset by Jouve (UK), Milton Keynes

A CIP record for this book is available from the British Library

ISBN 978-1-80018-282-0 (hardback)
ISBN 978-1-80018-283-7 (ebook)

Printed in Great Britain by CPI Group (UK)

1 3 5 7 9 8 6 4 2

Bobby, Russell, David, Stanley, Alfie and all the fellow
sufferers in G Block

'Without music, life would be a mistake'
Friedrich Nietzsche

Contents

Chapter 1

Dead

The contagion raged and ripped, a plague upon all our houses, rendering us housebound, trapped. Mostly it was fine, for most of us, most of the time, a time perhaps for reflection, a slowing down, a taking stock. Long days spent pretending to work from home and escaping home by walking, walking, walking, alone or in our sanitised bubbles, segregated from the mortal danger of others, avoiding proximity with humanity as we wandered the silent streets.

But silence is not peace. Those muted thoroughfares were not tranquil – they were agitated and cacophonous with a deathly hush, which by night became oppressive and fractious, the deafening disquiet amplified by piercing sirens ferrying the breathless and by the occasional cries of the tormented and the lost. I dreaded those silent nights.

Cities – my city – are not meant to be still or serene; they should jump and jive, rock and roll, skank and twist and pogo. Pop is the onomatopoeic sound of the city. They are massive mosh pits for agglomeration, for get-togethers, parties, raves, sing-alongs, they thrive on crowds and the clamour of glamour. The metropolis is made for noise and song.

Seeking respite, I would walk the sullen shell of my home town – Camden Town – a barrio famed for teenage ebullience, punk rock and hip-hop, reggaeton and speed metal, usually a bubbling Babylon of global musics flowing from every car window, doorway and boozer, to see only vacant tarmac, closed shutters and shut-up shops, to hear nothing. Dead.

I even missed the god-awful buskers who usually make the station and the market such an aural affront: the skinny white dreads with bongos and dogs on string, and the 'Smoke on the Water' two-bob guitar heroes. I craved human creativity of any kind, but playing was banned, music was outlawed, live performance a forbidden pleasure, and congregation a serious crime. This cursed virus made sure we were living in days with no dancing. Cheek to cheek a potential death sentence. Bass players delivered pizzas.

At least we could all find solitary solace in our favourite tunes – the blues seemed especially apt – this was downtime. Distracted by the silence and the science, the daily death tolls and the graphs, those horribly compelling five-o'clock briefings from bullshit politicians and shellshocked statisticians, my concentration was shot. Despite all those empty hours, I could barely watch a film or read a book during lockdown, but I could devour the sleeve notes to the first Roxy Music album: 'Piccadilly, 1972: taking a turn off main street . . .' My box sets for bingeing were by Miles Davis and Johnny Cash. My solace was song, as loud as possible.

I developed a haphazard plan to work my way through my record collection, pulling LPs out at random and putting on whatever fate proffered, never saying no and never playing the same album twice. Long-buried treasures emerged: Little Feat and Dr Feelgood, Kip Hanrahan and Astor Piazzolla, listening to side two of *Mingus Ah Um* and Bowie's *Low* for the first time in years, gorging on the gorgeousness of the Abyssinians or the thump of the Flamin' Groovies, reacquainting myself with Albert Ayler's tender chaos, falling back in love with Pere Ubu and Perry Como. Music, music, music.

Time became fluid, unfathomable; days rolled together, hours dragged remorselessly, yet months just vanished. And just as Covid changed people's perception of taste, so I believe it altered our aural receptors too. Music sounded especially potent and almost unbearably poignant in those stilled and troubled times; a vital reminder of the human spirit suffocated by the pandemic. Dear dead David Bowie now made me weep in the same inexplicable way that a room full of Rothko paintings can reduce me to tears; something to do with vibrations and associations, emotional muscle memories of better times. Like whistling in the dark.

But listening and whistling was not enough. I was craving the company of strangers. I'd had enough of me and a sufficiency of my own family, cooped up in our lovely Georgian cell, held hostage with my wife and kids. House arrest. I kept dutifully, if digitally, in contact with ancient mates via all the modern methods. Enthusiastically group-Zoomed for the first few weeks until that fizzled out, scant replacement for human interaction.

We could all keep in touch with those we knew, even if we daren't actually touch anybody. But there was no chance of chance encounters or the serendipity of adventure, no possibility of new places, new people, of making new, even if only fleeting, friends, as you venture forth into the night. For me life's greatest pleasure is to be hijacked by the streets, to be whisked away to where music plays. I knew what I really wanted was to go to a gig or a game.

To come alive, I craved live performance. I needed to be out there among the heaving masses bound to see people play. The fact that we 'play' music and we 'play' sport is an indication that they are both expressions of the primal, childlike urge to enjoy ourselves, to have fun, to engage in an activity for its own joyous sake. Music is the most important pointless thing of them all.

Listening to live music; the human voice in exaltation, the clapping of hands, the banging of drums, rhythm and melody, must surely be the original performance art, the purest expression of our shared humanity. Running, jumping, chasing, throwing, catching and kicking are also basic instincts. I've never been good at any sport and couldn't be less dextrous or more musically maladroit. But watching others who are good, who can really play, who can charm and enthral with their skill is an unalloyed delight. A delight denied.

I longed to be amid the throng of like-minded souls with tickets in their pockets (or on their phones in this digital age) and hope in their hearts, heading for an assignation with a football stadium, a cricket field or a music venue. It is the community and communality of the live event, the unifying sense of purpose, the way that strangers are not truly strangers, because we all have Queens Park Rangers or Ry Cooder in common, shared sorrow or joy.

I like crowds. Not the slow, shuffling throng of the aimless masses on Oxford Street nor the avaricious bustle of an airless shopping mall, but any crowd where there is a mass movement of the like-minded. I relish rowdy political demonstrations, cinema queues self-consciously discussing tropes and auteurs, the cultured and fanciable lines that form in cool art galleries, and the air of febrile expectation outside the red rope of a nightclub. I particularly love the acoustically sonorous tiled tunnels of the London Underground when they are full and fast-moving, echoing with people on a mission. We know where we are going.

It's even more marked at football, of course, wearing colours on the Tube, a four-deep-in-the-bar buzz in the pubs, shoulder to shoulder in the narrow streets around the ground, singing the tribal songs, the expectation building with every yard progressed, inching forward in line towards the ultimate goal. The end result will often be a bitter disappointment, but the journey is always a joy.

With my distinctly metropolitan tastes and my urgent, restless need for stimulation, there was precious little joy, pleasure or excitement to be found in those locked-down, fed-up months. Some claimed to love the serenity and the calm, the streets without cars, the skies without planes, the return of nature. But not for me; bugger birdsong.

If it was trying for a music lover, it was near fatal for musicians trying to make a living. A deep despair settled over the community of players. The poor ones – which is most of them – faced an existential threat. The wealthy ones could chill out and use the time to write, but even they got agitated at the inability to do what they do, be who they are.

Gary Kemp told me he was crawling up the walls of his elegant Regency abode because of his elemental need to get back on the road. Nick Lowe, a great singer-songwriter and a good friend who had entered his eighth decade just before the pandemic hit, said with resigned sadness that after a lifetime on stage stretching back to Brinsley Schwarz and pub rock, through 'Breaking Glass' and heartbreaking balladry, he genuinely feared he might have played his last-ever concert. Such was the black hole of silence into which we had fallen.

But of course, musicians are creative souls, and many found ways to perform. In the earliest, sunshine-filled, yet scarily dark days of the pandemic, it literally meant singing and playing in the garden or on the balcony for their neighbours. But as with so much of our experience of this thoroughly modern plague, technology provided a way forward.

Solo shows from living rooms or kitchens broadcast via smartphones became commonplace, and there was a certain voyeuristic pleasure in watching such intimate displays. Then, once the rules had softened a little and musicians could gather, even if audiences could not, clubs and venues got in on the act. Watching a live feed from Ronnie Scott's in my own hermetically sealed home was – a little like those soon-abandoned Zoom friendship groups – a fun novelty at first.

Just seeing a drum kit set up opposite a piano on a stage was exciting, a double bass lying on its side, waiting in repose. I would happily stare at the screen trying to place myself in that darkened Soho space where I have sat enraptured so many times. And once the musicians entered my computer and the first notes flowed, it was a sweet relief to know that music still existed. But I wasn't there. And it is all about being there.

This did not feel like being part of the event, sharing, experiencing the hot breath of live music; you couldn't feel it at all. It was porn, not sex. A great concert will take you out of yourself, became a transcendental experience, but a concert online will not even take you out of your own living room. Ultimately, watching live music online only served to remind me of what I was missing. It was OK at first, but that soon wore off. As Chet Baker once sang on that very stage in Frith Street, 'The Thrill is Gone', and soon so was I. Returned to my vinyl, a worried man.

Again, there were links between my two abiding loves of football and music. The people's game rushed back to business as soon as possible, without any people present whatsoever. Playing the Premier League in vacuum-packed stadia was supposedly a tonic to the nation, a moral boost in tough times, but just how much of a fillip the nation got from watching Burnley draw with Brighton in a deathly quiet ground, stripped of all atmosphere and context, devoid of passion or purpose, I'm not so sure. Is this a library, or maybe a mortuary?

One of the most dispiriting days I've ever spent was at my beloved Loftus Road on a Monday afternoon mid-pandemic, high up in a near-empty stand, watching Queens Park Rangers (QPR) draw nil-nil with Stoke, less than 1,000 people present in total, all wearing masks, all separated from each other, whole areas taped off, bars shut, away fans banned, home fans making no noise, sharing no emotion, no contact, no connection, no point.

It surely became apparent to anybody who has ever been to a match that this was the ghost of the great game, a pale apparition drained of all zest and meaning. Yes, I'll watch it because there's bugger all else to do, but you can't call this entertainment. Going to a ground to see sport, to cheer on your team, to hear the thud of leather on willow or studs on shins, the curses from the crowd, the humour and the anger, the despair and the elation, is the ultimate shared experience; you are an intrinsic, indeed indispensable, part of the event, not a mere consumer of it. The comfiest sofa is a pretty poor seat compared to the lowliest terrace in the rain. A day at the cricket with some mates will always beat a day in an armchair with some Hobnobs.

But in this age of global brands and billion-pound broadcast deals, relentless marketing and merchandising, the distant millions peering at Harry Kane on phones in Bangkok or Bahrain are more important than the few thousand 'heritage fans' traipsing through the turnstiles. He who pays the piper calls the tune, so games are rescheduled at ridiculous hours at short notice, rules are changed, the whole spectacle is tailored to suit the armchair, arm's-length spectator.

We have allowed the pernicious idea to take hold that sport is primarily viewed via a screen. Boxing, once experienced in all its bruising, blooded glory up close in sweaty halls in Bethnal Green or amid the roar of raucous football stadia, now gives its greatest nights to distant deserts. Cricket and golf tournaments too are shunted to empty quarters for cash: inaccessible, inhospitable, in the pay of sheikhs and potentates. A FIFA World Cup in a corrupt, autocratic and sparsely populated dust bowl, anybody? Sport has sold its soul to the highest bidder. Who can get excited about a 'franchise'? Is 'brand' the ugliest word in the sporting lexicon, or would that be 'product'?

Something similar seems to be happening with movies, where watching at home or even on your phone via Netflix or Amazon is rapidly replacing the act of buying a ticket for the multiplex or the art house. And as more and more gigs went online, so I fretted over the fact that the exigencies of the pandemic could mean the same thing would happen to live music.

There was definitely an idea afoot that this was the way of the future and maybe, sadly, it is. Promoters saw a new revenue stream suddenly materialise. If you could flog a video link to a worldwide audience, why worry about the chumps who come out in the cold? Or else introduce a performance 'apartheid'. Ratchet up the prices yet again for the 'premium' tickets for the actual live experience, while creaming off a fortune from the distant digital fans.

And what's more, would punters who had settled for the sanitised, atomised experience of lard-arsed vicarious viewing in sweatpants ever bother to go out again? Would we all be too scared to venture forth among other pestilential human beings? I became a worrier.

It felt to me that the pandemic was speeding up the collective retreat into an online existence. So much of what we do has been reduced by its digitisation, life lived at one remove, experienced through the blurring veil of binary numbers, as we have bought into the lie that online is a valid alternative to real life, that a text message is a conversation, that Instagram is a community, that virtual reality is the equivalent, or maybe even better than, real reality. That playing *Company of Heroes 2* on your laptop is just like fighting in the Ardennes. Good luck telling that to my uncle Jack, the Desert Rat.

At least I had my analogue records. Then one day, chance presented me with *Overture and Beginners,* a disc which has lain untouched and unplayed in my collection for decades. The full title is *Rod Stewart/Faces Live – Coast to Coast – Overture and Beginners.* A 1974 album, which I bought from a shop on the Edgware Road, as a fifteen-year-old lad in love with London's finest ever band of tousle-haired rock'n'roll roustabouts and have had as part of my collection ever since.

I put it on with some trepidation: this was an album which received a critical mauling when it first came out for being slapdash and sloppy, the sound of a band falling apart, destroyed by

Rod's ego and Ronnie Lane's departure. And it's all true; this is not the best of the best little rock'n'roll band in the world. It is indeed rough around the edges, yet lazy to the core, a sprawling stadium show a long way from home and close to the end. The band were about to break up and it shows. But. But.

As the needle caressed the groove and the crowd roar rose from my speakers, I was hit square by Ian McLagan's rolling barrel-house piano intro, so like the sound of parties at my grandad's in Shepherd's Bush, when the joanna came alive as crates of light ale would be carried in and the furniture pushed to the edges of the room when I was but a small boy. Followed by Ronnie Wood's instantly recognisable guitar twang, chiming yet grating, like a much-loved old motor running through the gears and then, finally, Rod comes in, my first musical love and still probably my favourite ever singer, because he swaggered like a likely lad from the local estate but sounded like Sam Cooke: one of us, but one of a kind. I was transported.

This was instant time travel, lifting me out of this room in this damn pandemic and back to Kilburn High Road in 1974, when I spent the night camped out on the pavement with some mates in front of the Gaumont State, a vast old art deco cinema turned rock venue, where we queued aged fifteen to be in the front row for a Faces gig. I don't know if I have ever been quite so excited since as at that moment, after those freezing, sleepless, aching but thrilling hours, when we made it to the box office and secured the best seats in the house.

Then on the night of the gig itself, draped in tartan and perched on platform soles, feather cuts to the fore, we swaggered along the Edgware Road. This was the epicentre of Irish London at a time when the bombs of the Troubles were exploding all around us. That evening was to be incendiary in every sense.

This turned out to be the Faces' last ever live London gig,

before Rod swanned off to LA superstardom wearing Britt
Ekland's clothes and Ronnie Wood joined the Stones, playing
second fiddle (well, guitar) to Keith Richards, who cheekily
turned up on stage to jam with his new bandmate that night.
Nothing would ever be quite the same again, especially me.

In a crowded, darkened auditorium thronging with fans and
drenched in expectation and perspiration, the frisson of anticipated revelry, from the opening note they were magnificent,
the very essence of a real good time. But it wasn't just a good
time, not just a fun night out. I realised from the off, from that
first riff, that this was my culture, the collective culture of our
grimy, glamorous youth; this was my future. Not just Rod and
rock'n'roll, but the whole rowdy shebang.

Queuing up all night was about commitment, allegiance,
wearing the schmutter, buying the records, learning the songs, a
badge of pride, a statement of intent. We were part of something,
and this was my first proper taste of the sweet treats adult life
might proffer. It felt dangerous and thrilling and cool, and I felt
part of it. The true high point of a seismic evening was a searing,
rollicking version of 'Stay with Me', probably my favourite ever
rock'n'roll song, which has done just that ever since.

And listening to *Overture and Beginners* in a pandemic, I was
there again, fifteen and full to the brim of life's hedonistic and
artistic possibilities. I was a young North London boy on the
brink, but I was also simultaneously and bizarrely at a polo
ground in Surrey, on a sunny Saturday afternoon more than
forty years later, older and, sadly, wiser. The fifth of Septem-
ber 2015, to be precise, to see Rod and Ronnie and original
Faces drummer Kenney Jones up on stage together for the first
time since that last time in Kilburn.

Roderick, having always been reluctant to go back to the
Faces – perhaps because many saw these as his true glory days –
had finally agreed to perform because it was a charity event for
prostate cancer, of which Kenney and he were both survivors. I

suspect many of the men present had felt their insides probed; it was not a teenage audience.

I'd been invited to the show by the showman himself, whom I had got to know via my radio programme, to discover with some relief that he is charm personified. Rod Stewart, an unrepentant Jack the Lad made very good indeed, but still with a beguiling hint of devilment in those smiler eyes. I loved Rod's company, so I was also slightly wary about revisiting what had been a pivotal experience; like bumping into your first love to find you've both gone to seed.

I have been to thousands of gigs since and know that live music has played an extraordinary part in my life and career. I wouldn't be where I am now and all that. But this one, in a manicured Surrey field scattered with 4x4s and full of well-groomed middle-aged groovers seemed somehow portentous. I was nervous.

Under-rehearsed and overhyped, what remained of the Faces was never going to be that legendary bunch of tearaways of yore, but the sheer delight of seeing them up there in front of microphones was enough to make grown blokes, and plenty of women too, terribly excited and a little emotional. It meant a lot.

Then about half an hour into a truncated but terrific set of classic Faces numbers, Rod stepped forward to do one of his cheeky-chappie intros, that voice now equal parts Archway Road and Laurel Canyon, speaking over a ringing, rolling guitar intro that everybody spread out over the grounds gleefully recognised. And suddenly I was ten feet tall.

As the opening bars of 'Stay with Me' rang out, Rod dedicated the tune I'd first fallen in love with four decades earlier 'to Robert Elms, for all he's done for the Faces'. I stood in that field honoured and amazed, thrilled, cocksure and just a tad humbled. Blimey, I thought, that's a bit of a journey.

*

Once the ravages of the plague had diminished and we were allowed out again, I went to a whole host of gigs in the first few weeks. I saw Van Morrison, majestic and grumpy, moaning about lockdowns and speaking in tongues in the Electric Ballroom in Camden Town. I DJ'd and MC'd for Stone Foundation with a snappy soul review in the Jazz Café. I returned in real life at last to Ronnie Scott's for some wonderfully jagged jazz from some young London tyros blowing the house down. I hosted a lusty neckerchief rock sing-along at a tiny Clerkenwell boozer called the Betsey Trotwood and sat in a fancy box to see Gregory Porter with a stirring gospel revue at the Royal Albert Hall.

Every one of these shows was sold out and greeted with a rapture which went way beyond: more than pleasure, more than joy, it was a deeply felt, emotional outpouring, a form of communion from people intensely relieved to be there. We had overcome. Live is back, so life is back.

I also ventured way out west to a small club in West Ken called Nell's, to see none other than Mr Nicholas Lowe, the bard of Brentford, perform a flowing and moving set of his greatest almost-hits. His fifteen-year-old son Roy guested on drums, while his wife Peta sported an understandably proud smile; it was a family affair. And there was indeed something familiar and familial about being crowded together into that room to hear those songs. You've got to be cool to be kind.

It was a room full of grins, where people who did not know each other were connected by the melodies and the stories and where a palpable sense of togetherness prevailed. We were there to witness the affirmation of this lovely little very big gig. Thankfully Nick Lowe and I were both wrong. Live music was back.

Chapter 2

ABC

I have a photographic memory, but it only takes Polaroids.

Memory teases and plays tricks; it illustrates and obfuscates in equal parts, giving me glimpses of who and where and what and when, but hiding details and telling lies. The musical memories, the long-gone, once-live events revealed in this tome are deeply untrustworthy but entirely true. That really is how I remember it. And maybe how it actually was.

I'm not good on facts. I can never invoke stats or set lists, I'm dodgy on dates, couldn't tell you who scored the goals away at Sheffield Wednesday that secured promotion, or which Ashes series it was when we beat them in the last test at the Oval. I can't remember which songs the Pistols played at Brunel or whether Curtis Mayfield sang 'Superfly' at Dingwalls, even though I know I was there and there and there. But then, these days the ether can usually provide those details.

My memory is faulty but full. I was never a keeper of memorabilia, no ticket stubs, programmes or photos, no aide-mémoires. But I am pretty good at recalling how I felt on any given occasion – the sensations, emotions, the thrills, the dis-appointments. Live entertainment for me has always been about the visceral response. And as this book has progressed, I have been able to access more and more of my own mental and emotional archive. The muscle memory of elation and ecstasy.

The process of writing is itself revelatory; it turns keys opening hidden doors, cracks codes, leads you sequentially through the maze of your mind, revealing stuff you thought was long lost. Those blurry mental Polaroids become a point of departure for a journey back to neon nights in seedy clubs, grand concerts in high style and scuzzy bars in far-flung towns, thrilling highs and occasional lows. Vomiting on the floor of a Cricklewood boozer while interviewing Shane MacGowan was a particularly high low.

The old adage about if you can remember it, you weren't really there has some veracity. And I really was there, and it really was wild, a brilliant hedonistic blur of a well-misspent youth. But somehow much more of the detail has been retained than I first feared, though I cannot in all conscience deny that hindsight may have played a part in some of these recollections.

I can only recall Madonna prancing on a downtown disco dance floor because she went on to be the biggest-selling female artist of all time. It was infinitely forgettable at the time. But I can summon up the exact sensation, the sound and smell of emerging from an Eastside dive just before dawn on a humid Manhattan evening with the sound of James White and the Blacks ringing in my ears and I can summon the clinking sound of cocktail glasses at Dr Buzzard's Original Savannah Band's last ever concert. But can't tell you the venue. 'Cherchez La Femme'.

I can taste the sweet, heady, floral air, which floats past the Guadalquivir on a night before an impromptu flamenco performance in a Betis bar, even if I cannot recollect the name of *el cantor*. I know all too well the uniquely bitter chill that invades the marrow on the away end at Craven Cottage after another shaming defeat for the Hoops, because it seems to happen every season.

It's similar with my memory bank of close encounters. I have been lucky to have met and interviewed so many interesting characters over the years (and Ginger Baker), but when people ask me for details, they are largely blank. I shocked myself by seeing an interview I did with David Byrne quite recently, but which I had completely forgotten about. Didn't think I'd ever met the man. Though I can still feel the electric jolt of the opening bars of 'Psycho Killer' as it reverberated round the Roundhouse in the summer of 1977.

So when I first dive head first into the mosh pit of musical memory, it is always just a moment and a feeling, an echo of a frisson, which surfaces. Dates disappear, whole events can vanish, recollection and recall sketchy, no set list, no encore, no overview, no chance. But still there is a ghost of a glimpse, a shimmer of a sensation relived, a fleeting second of sound and vision.

Suspended in time.

A crumbling old art deco fleapit in grim and grotty 1970s Harlesden, plush but ruined, brimming with brilliant anger. Me enthralled and anxious in brand new bondage, a wrap of sulphate in my socks, an overdose of desire in my veins. Paul Simonon svelte and angular, handsome and lissom, low-strung, high-style cool. Mick Jones urgent, marching on the spot, marking the beat, head bobbing, plectrum chopping. Joe Strummer all sinew and swagger, his right knee pumping, his fists clenching, his guitar swaying, a thin foam forming round his contorted mouth, taut with anticipation, those dumdum words just waiting to explode. London's burning. Wasn't it just.

A decade later in an esteemed Soho room, me suited and booted, playing cool watching Wynton Marsalis immaculately attired, like perhaps a fancy southern lawyer about to take the stand, august and arrogant, unleashed on London for the very first time. He was still a kid, but word was out. Mr Art Blakey holding time tight at the back, rimshots snapping as this pristine young fellow steps forward, all history and precision, his gilded horn gliding past the Windsor knot of his tie, towards his hard-won embouchure, about to blow the bloody house down. The new messenger, delivering jazz as righteous justice.

Or Bruce Springsteen, also first time in town, not yet The Boss but bossing this house, tearing it up then taking it down, taking it down, his palms suppressing the sound, his eyes beneath that beanie hat darting across the East Street, their collective quietude mesmerising, his charisma shining. You can hear the gleam in those peepers as he prepares one of his misty boardwalk tales, maybe the one about the pretty flamingo. Enraptured, enthralled, everybody present on that Odeon night knows we have just seen and heard the future.

So many notes on so many nights, so much music, so many moments which stay with me still. Some so far away.

Handsome chaps in fine guayaberas, deep in the rich Havana dark, *ritmo* and *clave*, the aroma of rum, the scent of sex and the rhythm of son cubano. Further south still, bandoneons as sharp as stilettos in elusive Buenos Aires backstreets, all danger and lust on a terrible tango mission. Or jagged Manhattan memories: punk on the Bowery, funk on Broadway, drunk on New York's over-proof late seventies music scene, powders and pushers and *Taxi Driver* demons. What a buzz; there's people spinning on their heads while my head spins.

Some memories are almost too potent to recall. I'm quick to tears these days, an emotional man, and this one makes me sob. Camarón de la Isla, the very embodiment of *gitano* joy and anguish, his tiny, wracked and wrecked flamenco frame contorted with generations of pain and abuse, his white shirt barely touching skin, billowing like a sail, his voice guttural and beautiful, ululating like a muezzin, reaching back across continents and ages, filling a dowdy Madrid sports hall with gorgeous despair, filling us all with chills and visions. Little did we know he was about to die. Or maybe we did.

Tom Waits showboating with an umbrella, Grace Jones vogueing with a mannequin, Gil Scott-Heron rapping with a conga drum, Madonna spinning on a Camden Town dance floor, all dirt and desire, Van entering a stuttering trance, talking in tongues, summoning demons, Toots convulsing, Chet whispering, Amy shimmying shamelessly like a little girl at a wedding. Dylan, Miles and Bowie, the Pogues, the Pistols, the Crusaders, the Jam, Nubya, and Gillian and Gregory . . . and the beat goes on.

And it all began with 'ABC'.

Because everything is now recorded in the know-it-all ether, I can tell you that this event took place on Sunday 12 November 1972, which makes me thirteen, a year younger than Michael. He was part of the coolest collection of singing siblings on earth (please don't dare mention the Osmonds). I was a pupil in form 3B at Orange Hill Grammar School for Boys in Burnt Oak, which happened to be a twenty-minute bus ride away from Wembley, where the Jackson 5 were appearing at the still pompously named Empire Pool.

Somebody, probably my classmate Danny Stern, who had an older brother with a bass guitar, went along to Wembley, as was the way in those days, and bought four tickets from the box office to see the Jackson 5's first ever British tour and my first ever live gig. Four third-form herberts let loose on a Sabbath night.

I came from a Tamla household. My two elder brothers had a pretty good collection of singles, usually inscribed with the name Reg on the labels so that they could be reclaimed at parties, and they were almost all either soul or reggae. Detroit's finest dominated, and pale-skinned pop music didn't get a look-in. As far as albums went, it was compilations: *This Is Soul*, the deep Atlantic one with the jigsaw sleeve, *Tighten Ups* for the latest ska and rocksteady from Jamaica, and of course *Motown Chartbusters* volumes one to six inclusive, including the Jackson 5 and Junior Walker & the All Stars, who were the support act at the Wembley show.

I immediately started telling people I was really going to see Junior Walker, whose 'Road Runner' was a particular favourite of mine, which proves that I was a pretentious poseur from a very early age. Saying you prefer the support act has always been a hipster's trick. But of course, truth be told, I was super-excited to see some cartoon characters come alive.

The idea that famous musicians are real flesh-and-blood human beings was still hard to comprehend. In the way that schoolkids find it difficult to imagine their teachers with lives away from the classroom or the staffroom until they see them drinking and smoking in the pub on the last day of term, so pop stars existed only on *Top of the Pops*. And given that the Jackson 5 were also animations, it made their sudden appearance just up the road from the Blackbirds pub, where my parents would occasionally stop for a pint and a port and lemon, even more miraculous.

Yet here I was, putting on my best clobber, including my maroon shirt with the lollipop lapels, my new stripy tank top and my channel-seam trousers with the French flare, to go and see them. In person, in real life. Live.

Wearing the correct attire for a concert has been a paramount concern ever since: tartan for Rod, bondage for the Pistols, always a whistle at Ronnie's. Getting dressed up to party down is a big part of the build-up to an event, a statement of intent, but on this night, it seemed even more important because of course there would be girls present. Going to an all-boys' school, with only brothers at home, meant that the proximity of females of a similar age was a rare and terrifying treat and they had to be treated to my most fashionable garms. Going to gigs was already sexy.

Quite why I thought anybody would notice me, a skinny ginger kid in a crowd of thousands, I have no idea, but I can still feel the visceral rush, the tsunami of sound ricocheting around that big echoing hangar as the audience whipped themselves into a frenzy. I don't think anybody noticed Junior Walker either, including me, because it was all about those five funky Jackson boys. There was an MC helping to foment the fervour, but it didn't take much to get this particular crowd going, an excitable cross-section of North-West London's first truly multicultural generation. Black and white unite and scream.

The loudest crowd noise ever recorded in the UK came from just over the road at Wembley Stadium, for a women's international hockey match in the 1970s, with a higher decibel count than Concorde in full flight. The girls can certainly make some noise. We used to go as a gang of local lads and stand outside the stadium for those hockey matches, just to hear the hormones at work and get a glimpse of the young ladies in a state of high excitement. But to be in among this maelstrom of teenage pandemonium was somewhere between exhilarating and terrifying.

I was used to the crush and rush of football; I'd been going to games with mates from about the age of ten or eleven and could navigate my way round the often unruly and occasionally downright dangerous terraces of London's ramshackle grounds. If you've been to Cold Blow Lane and lived to tell the tale, you already feel battle-hardened. But this was different; suddenly I was deep in the independent republic of Teenlandia, where grown-ups played no part and juvenile rules applied.

The girls were vocally ferocious, singing, chanting, screaming, some waving banners, many professing undying love for Michael, Marlon or Jermaine. But it was the boys present, although outnumbered and certainly out-shouted, who were throwing the funky shapes, doing their best *Soul Train* impressions, flares flapping furiously, legs spinning, arms weaving as the DJ played Motown classics between sets. Boys at gigs like to get physical, from mosh pits to pogoing, they make their presence known with movement and motion. Me, I stood and watched, transfixed by the carnival of the crowd.

Michael, already the star, was somewhere between a phenomenon and an automaton, a marvel, and in retrospect perhaps a tragedy. I actually remember very little of the concert – it was a beautiful musical blur – but I distinctly recall the moment. I have no idea where it came in the set, but it was one of those frozen-in-time fragments, which I can still summon at will. That brief pause between numbers, when a sharp, expectant silence reigns and the five up on stage were all potential kinetic energy, the audience all 'what comes next' anticipation.

And then it happens; Jermaine's bass swoops and Michael's afro bobs down in perfect time to the opening chord and that introductory boom boom boom boom b-boom and immediately everybody present can name that tune in one. A roar fills the air and a whoosh of unfettered pleasure sweeps through the mass of people present. A collective outpouring, a communal exaltation, orgasmic and fantastic.

'ABC', as perfect as anything I've ever witnessed up until that point in my tiny little life. Three minutes of divine or maybe diabolical delirium. That was the moment it all began.

Chapter 3

Simply the Best

What's the best concert you've ever been to?

It's the kind of question you ask or get asked after the third drink with a group of mates, or, if you're a famously inveterate gig-goer, all the time by people who know you've seen lots of live shows and want to test your knowledge and veracity, and maybe hear an anecdote or two about the Sex Pistols or The Boss. It's primarily a parlour game for blokes (and it is usually blokes) who know far too many album catalogue numbers and want to show off a little about all the great bands they've seen along the way. I know I'm one. But I also know it is a vexed and vexing question.

For some perhaps it is an easy one to answer, there really is one shining night, one perfect set which still rings in the ears and remains vivid in the memory. It tends to be particularly clear-cut for zealots and true believers, those faithful souls who are steadfast fans of one group or artist. These are people who've seen the Stones forty-seven times in nine countries, in three continents, or those who just know, with absolute certainty that the Jam are the best live band of all time and have barely been to a gig since they disbanded, or maybe that Barbra

Streisand is the single greatest entertainer ever to stalk the stage. (She's pretty good, but not that good.) But for most, or certainly for me, it is an almost impossible one to answer.

Far easier for me to tell you about the best gig I didn't go to. And we'll get there soon.

I am a gadfly. I've been an honorary member of every passing trouser tribe, sported every silly haircut imaginable and enjoyed almost every style of music, bar heavy metal and opera. (Both of which strike me as horribly bombastic and painfully tuneless, but then I love free jazz.) I've been a skin-head, a suedehead, a glam rocker, a soul boy, a punk and a New Romantic and enjoyed the music to match. I was an occasional zoot suiter and a very unconvincing rockabilly. I'm a life-long jazz nut as well as a dedicated reggae head, though thankfully my ginger nut has never ever sported dreadlocks. My taste is broad.

While I never trusted the lazy catch-all phrase 'world music', which reeked to me of hippy-dippy condescension and trusta-farians in dashikis, I have grown to love specific musics from all around the world. It began with ska, rocksteady and reggae. In late-sixties North-West London, the rolling rhythms and stac-cato beats of the Caribbean were the soundtrack of all our streets and the pulse of every playground. Watching Desmond Dekker gurning his way through 'Israelites' on *Top of the Pops* while skanking on the floral carpet of your council house in a Ben Sherman shirt two sizes too big was quite the education for a ten-year-old.

Reggae, particularly of the deep and sweet roots and culture variety, is still an abiding passion, the soundtrack of so many of my memories. I firmly believe the ubiquity of 'The Liquidator' and a double dose of 'Double Barrel' is the reason Londoners of all colours walk with a shoulder-rolling, rude-boy gait, those big throbbing basslines anchoring your feet to the street. It was also a springboard.

Once you've accepted the fact that magnificent music can come from other places, and especially if you've grown up in a roaring multicultural metropolis, where every Saturday night is a groovy global sound-clash, with reggae, rebetika and Irish rebel tunes competing to dominate the ether, then the barriers are down. I now love music from every corner of the globe.

My life-long hispanophilia led me first to flamenco, which is still one of the most intense but also most elusive live experiences, invariably involving frustrating but occasionally thrilling trawls through Andalucian back alleys deep in the still, steaming night, then on to tango and salsa and son. Travel for me now often has a partly musical motive. I seek out places with great music, and many sweltering adventures have been had in search of the swaying soul of the Latinate south. I've seen lachrymose cowboys sobbing into their mescal in mariachi bars and handsome bullfighters dancing Sevillanas. And unexpectedly, later in life I've eventually embraced a different kind of southern sound.

Despite deep teenage revulsion, I've even come to enjoy some country music. I still struggle with the shiny, overproduced cowboy-boots-and-Stetsons pop, which makes up much of current country. My neck is not red. But give me the plangent high-mountain wail of the Stanley Brothers, or their contemporary equivalent, Gillian Welch and David Rawlings, arguably the best live duo on the planet right now, who I would travel a very long way in a flatbed truck to see. Damn, I've even been known to play Jim Reeves records.

Gentleman Jim and Matt Monro, the singing bus driver, were the mellifluous sound of Sunday mornings in our house. Dad down the pub, elder brothers out playing football, just me and Mum in the kitchen, as she prepares lunch and listens to her small but precise record collection. In retrospect, my mother had pretty good taste. Apart from a couple of waxy Maxy Bygraves' worst and an execrable Des O'Connor album featuring a truly grating yet ingratiating little ditty called 'Dick-A-Dum-Dum' – which I still can't get out of my head half a century later – she mainly liked Ray Charles, Tom Jones, Mahalia Jackson and the peerless Tony Bennett. So of course I hated all of them.

Then I grew up. Then I met Tony Bennett, and he called me 'Sir', before stunning us all with an astonishing, unamplified 'I Left My Heart in San Francisco' at the Royal Albert Hall at the age of eighty-nine. I love a crooner, so I am now an obsessive Matt Monro fanatic, doffing my metaphorical hat as I cycle past the tenement block, where he was born in Finsbury, on a regular basis. What I am trying to say is, at this stage of life, I like most musics.

And I still actively like and consume music, still collect records, still get excited by new talent like Greentea Peng, Moses Boyd or Celeste, and consent to spend vast fortunes on a Lee Morgan live twelve-album box set on vinyl. I still pull on my glad rags and get excited about getting dressed up to go and see Nick Lowe, Nubya Garcia or Gregory Porter. I still go to gigs almost every week, sometimes two or three times a week, big ones at swanky venues, and little ones in windowless rooms near kebab shops. Like following QPR and wearing whistles and well-polished shoes, it is a big part of my own sense of what I do and who I am.

I am a music man, despite not being able to play a note and possessing a voice like a drunken sailor's sorry spar; I have made selecting tunes and interviewing musicians a big part of my working life. I even get paid for introducing acts on stage, so, to misquote Joni, I've seen gigs from both sides now. I know just how painfully accurate *Spinal Tap* is. In short, people associate me with music, so I often get asked that question: what's the best concert you've ever been to?

Sometimes I give in and say one definitive gig, even though I know next time it will be a different answer. But truth be told, pop pickers, having considered this conundrum over many years, it's a veritable top ten. Of course, this isn't set in stone, and different nights and bands will often suddenly re-enter my brain and remind me how brilliant they were. But all these concerts have consistently stayed with me. The list encompasses a variety of genres, in venues large and small. But it doesn't take too much perusal to see a pattern emerge, although these are in no particular order:

The Clash at the Rainbow, 1977
The Clash and Subway Sect and the Slits at the Coliseum,
    Harlesden, 1977
The Crusaders at the New Victoria, 1976
Dr Feelgood at the Hope & Anchor (or was it the Tally Ho?),
    1976
The Faces at Kilburn State, 1974
The Tom Robinson Band at the Marquee, 1977
Bruce Springsteen at the Hammersmith Odeon, 1975
Eddie and the Hot Rods at the Marquee, 1976
Tom Waits at the Dominion, 1985
Paul Weller at the Royal Festival Hall, 2018

With the exception of Tom Waits, who is the living artist I would pay most and travel furthest to see again, and Paul Weller with strings, a truly majestic, career-encompassing night just a few years ago – when I finally gave in and admitted that the mod man might just be a genius – every single one of those nights (and they were all nights, daytime music rarely does it for me) took place when I was between the ages of fifteen and eighteen. I was young. I was impressionable and those were the gigs which made a lasting impression. They were, in one way or another, life changing.

The one I missed might just have changed my life even more. Trying to remember back all those years is tough. After that

memorable debut with the Jackson 5, I cannot be sure what
came next. There was a bizarre musical interlude in our school
hall one afternoon in about 1973, when a band called Slack
Alice turned up to play for the massed ranks of painfully frustrated grammar-school boys. To this day I cannot fathom why
a hairy and hard-rocking outfit, fronted by a feline female
rhythm-and-blues belter in leather trousers and skimpy top,
were booked to arrive with all their gear at Orange Hill Grammar School for Boys in Burnt Oak.

Which teacher thought that was a good idea? Whoever it
was, I thank you. The band were pretty ordinary, in that
stodgy, seventies boogie style, but many a pimple was popped
during their musically forgettable but hormonally invigorat-
ing set. It was an education.

Seeing Slack Alice up close may have been an eye-opener,
but it wasn't quite the lunchtime treat some young Londoners
got in the seventies. Apparently Roxy Music played in schools,
as did Supertramp and Sweet. It was a thing. My sadly departed
mate George the Tailor from the Walworth Road regularly
regaled me with tales of the day Bob Marley played at his school
in Peckham.

In 1972 the nascent Wailer and his mate and mentor Johnny
Nash performed two forty-five-minute acoustic sets at Peckham Manor secondary modern, including 'Trenchtown Rock'
and 'I Can See Clearly Now', for an audience of South London
oiks in ill-fitting blazers. There are also reports of the two of
them appearing at a school in Neasden, where Marley was
living at the time, and where apparently they also had a kickabout in the playground.

I too had a game of football with Bob Marley, well sort of. I'd
seen him play what turned out tragically to be his last ever London
gig, a rather disappointing day at Crystal Palace Bowl in 1980,
where the music got lost on the wind and the audience seemed
more interested in getting stoned and diving into the lake than

really communing with the musicians. A while later I was invited by his press officer and close confidante Rob Partridge, a fellow QPR fan who I sat next to at Loftus Road and numerous away games for many seasons, to meet the great Jamaican global icon and join him in a little light kickabout in Battersea Park.

I turned up in a pair of plimsolls and cut-off jeans to find Bob and his band of Rasta mates in full kit, taking things extremely seriously, and after watching them for a few minutes, I developed a mysterious muscle strain which meant I had to sit on the sidelines and watch instead. Those Jamaican boys could really play, and Marley in particular, who was tiny and lithe, but magnetic to behold close-up, was a spectacularly good footballer, which I most definitely am not.

Sadly, of course, this was the last time I would ever see the Tuff Gong with his mane flying, as a short while later Robert Nesta Marley, musician, lover, poet and peacemaker, died of cancer, supposedly caused by a footballing injury. Rob Partridge, the greatest music PR who ever lived and one of the loveliest men, an educator who introduced me to Chet Baker, Damon Runyon and Nestor Makhno, also succumbed to cancer a few years later, and Tom Waits and Bono flew over for his funeral, at which a mariachi band played.

Rod Stewart also likes footie, of course, and I did once bump into him en route to a match. We met at Battersea helicopter pad; he was waiting with a couple of teammates to be whisked to a game at his gaff in Essex, where he has a full-sized pitch in the back garden, while I had just finished filming a piece about the Thames and had discovered that I suffer from chronic chopper sickness. I was as green as a goalie's jersey, so my excuse for not joining him in a jaunt out to the far east for footie was at least genuine.

My reason for not going to one of the most celebrated concerts of the century, the one that got away, also involved Rod Stewart.

The big question about why we like what we like, and con-
comitantly don't like what we don't like, is an extremely
complex one. Early influences, sibling or parental pressures,
cultural associations, class considerations and plain old personal taste all play a part. My dislike of the Beatles stems at least
in part from my elder brother's slating them for being a boy
band for screaming girls. My brothers were mods, into Georgie
Fame and Otis Redding, soul and ska. The Fab Four were not
considered cool in our house.

I've always been tribal in my affiliations, especially as a teenager, actively manning the barricades in the style wars. Which
badge you pin to your chest is vital, both in determining your
likes and dislikes. My dad was QPR, I am QPR, so it is
imprinted in my DNA to dislike Chelsea. My first true musical
love of my own choosing, as opposed to the soul and reggae
acts my brothers favoured, was Rod Stewart and the Faces.
And like all first loves, it burned fiercely: his poster on my wall,
tartan in my wardrobe.

So I had decided that if I really liked Rod, and indeed I did
really like Rod, that his nearest rival, in terms of playground
arguments about who is the best, was a certain David Bowie,
another charismatic London boy with noteworthy hair, so I
decided I wouldn't like Bowie. Aged thirteen I picked my side.
I even remember reading an article in which Mr Stewart said
that he didn't like platform shoes (although the stack-heeled
footwear he sports on the inner sleeve of *Gasoline Alley* is pretty
close), which I used as further ammunition against Bowie in his
knee-high platform boots.

So when my mate from the Watling Estate, Barry O'Keefe,
told me that he had a spare ticket to see David Bowie and the
Spiders From Mars at Hammersmith Odeon, and what's more,
I could give him the £2 for the ticket later when I got paid for
my milk round with Reg. I had a choice to make. I had the
opportunity to go to what has become legendary as Ziggy's

last gig, the most lauded and dramatic night in the whole Bowie story, perhaps the most celebrated single gig ever held in London town. And, because I was a Rod Stewart fan, I said no thank you.

I know people who were there that night, including Gary Kemp, the same age as me, who says it was genuinely transformative: eye-opening, earth-shattering, life-changing. He might not have been a musician were it not for that night with the Starman. And I said no. It might not have been the most wantonly stupid decision I've ever made – there are certainly plenty of competitors in that category – but it is perhaps the one I lament the most. Rare is the day I don't regret the greatest gig I never saw.

Somehow I managed to drag my sorry soul to see 999, Slaughter and the Dogs, Chelsea, the Boys, the Adverts, and the bloody Vibrators on numerous occasions, all of them bang average at best, while I actively spurned the opportunity to see some truly great acts. I was either invited to, or offered tickets for, and occasionally even had tickets but couldn't be arsed to turn up for: Fela Kuti in Brixton, Frank Sinatra at the Royal Albert Hall, Nirvana at the Astoria, Prince at the Camden Palace with the three-hour after-show show, Jeff Buckley after he had played live on my radio show. If you have the chance to see an artist you've always admired, take it. Every single one of the above is now dead.

I never got to see Marvin Gaye either. I did actually shell out a large sum of US dollars for a pair of tickets from a New York street-scalper to see the tortured soul man in person, only to discover as I tried to enter, that they were for the night before. Doh. Regrets, I have quite a few, but still, it is Ziggy's farewell that burns.

Because, of course, almost immediately after deciding not to go on that fateful night, I changed my opinion of Mr Jones. The Brixton/Bromley/Berlin boy has been the single most important musical artist in my life. He was always the prettiest star and the eternal embodiment of my beloved shape-shifting city and all the creative opportunities it proffers. Along with his glitter twin, Marc Bolan – the ace-face mod turned Artful Dodger of pop – Bowie taught a generation of us how to be whoever we wanted to be, and then become someone else just for fun. David Bowie, Ziggy Stardust, the Young American, the Thin White Duke was our life coach.

If you only have the recorded output of one pop artist, I would say pick David Bowie. That string of studio albums from *Ziggy* to *Heroes* is the best. *David Live*, though, is weak, and while I did get to see him live a couple of times, I have to admit that I was slightly underwhelmed by the experience. Maybe I wanted too much. Perhaps he could never live up to my exalted expectations. But also, the shows I saw were in big venues where he was too far away, lost in the production. I never quite got to feel the charisma, he never quite played the set I wanted to see. If only I'd been at the Hammersmith Odeon in 1973. *David Live*, I was never quite convinced, but David's life was the greatest inspiration.

Having turned down the chance of seeing Bowie at Hammersmith, I didn't make that mistake again a few months later. Mott the Hoople appeared at the same venue, buoyed by the huge success of their Bowie-penned and produced anthem 'All the Young Dudes'. I was probably one of the youngest dudes there on the night that a veritable rock'n'roll riot ensued when the curfew was called, and the fire curtain came down, but the band played on.

Fists flew, seats were ripped up, adrenalin was flowing and blood pumping; it was exhilarating, thrilling, scary. It was bloody fantastic, especially in the playground at school next day in the retelling. But it doesn't quite make it into the list of greatest gigs of all time because all those emotions and sensations were going to happen again a few years later, when I was old enough to really feel part of it. Mott the Hoople at Hammersmith was a premonition of punk to come.

PS Queen were the support act with Mott the Hoople that night, and I would almost definitely have seen them as I always got to gigs early in those days to get my money's worth. But I have absolutely no recollection of them whatsoever. Given that I can't stand their overblown operatic bombast, I'm quite proud of that.

Chapter 4

Dance Dance Dance

Do you go to gigs or do you go to clubs?

It seems like a fairly simple question, and of course at some stage of our youth most of us would have done both, but I believe it actually reveals, or at least once revealed, one of the great cultural and class divides in our country. Like state school or private, football or rugby, tabloid or broadsheet, cinema or theatre, council house or homeowner, smart or scruffy, it is a marker. Or it certainly was when and where I was growing up.

My elder brothers, although really into music – I still have their brilliant collection of 45s, many of them on import labels – rarely went to see bands play live. Georgie Fame at the Flamingo, maybe, or Geno Washington at the Ram Jam, but primarily they bought records. They pulled on their two-tone tonic strides and their Royals and stepped out to the Tottenham Royal, or to local parties, pubs and clubs, where they paraded and preened and posed, drank and danced, usually as part of a large group of local Burnt Oak boys and girls. It was communal and it was competitive: the sharpest threads, the neatest moves, the prettiest partner, the toughest crew. Music was played by DJs and selectors. They went to the dance.

And that was the same for most of the kids on the vast Watling
Estate in Burnt Oak, on the far-flung reaches of the Northern
line, where I grew up. Music was an ever-present soundtrack to
their lives, a rhythmic accompaniment to dressing up and going
out. And it was predominantly, almost exclusively, black music:
Tamla, soul and reggae, funky stuff made for movement and
mood, sweating or smooching, seeking action rather than sitting
and watching a performance.

There was no real concept of culture as something you, indi-
vidually, passively, consumed – it was communal and kinetic.
Very few homes had tomes and there were bookmakers, not
bookshops, on our high street. Theatre was a very distant, very
alien West End world. Going to the pictures was fun, but it was
also pretty hectic – you either went with a gang of mates,
bunked in and whooped and hollered and maybe tried your
kung fu moves in the aisles, or else went with a squeeze and
hopefully got a snog in the back row. What was the film about?
I have no idea.

Going every Saturday to support your chosen football team
was the real unifying cultural ritual of the boys on my estate,
most of them Arsenal, with a smattering of QPR and Chelsea.
They were diehards; dedicated and devoted, but a day at High-
bury or Loftus Road, and especially a jaunt on a decrepit
'special' train with all the wild boys to some far-flung northern
town, was far from a passive experience.

They were definitely not just spectators, but active partici-
pants in the days' events. These were the faces on the North
Bank and the Shed, part of a heaving, perpetually moving
mass, singing and shouting and swaying and shoving and
maybe rucking with the opposition mob. Going to football, as
I did in a pilgrimage back to the ancestral W12 homelands
every other week from about the age of ten, was a riot.

Another aspect of the almost sacred devotion to football is
that all the lads on the estate played the game as well as watched

it. And some of them played it very well indeed. They knew football. Every Sunday in our local marketplace there was a twenty-or-so-a-side match, which went on from first daylight to deep dusk. The cliché about sport and music being the way out for working-class kids was half true. I don't know a single professional musician who came from our neck of the woods, but the likes of Steve Perryman and Tony Currie progressed to the very top of the game, while many more were extremely able lower and non-league players, and a few decent pro boxers too. Most families could afford a pair of football boots or boxing gloves, and the local youth club, Watling Boys, provided free coaching to a very high standard, but a violin and lessons was a different matter indeed.

So it came as one among many seismic culture shocks when I leapt over one of those great invisible fault lines in the plate tectonics of British society and went to the grammar school. Here were lads with long hair and dirty jeans who played the piano, or the electric guitar, like their heroes in rock bands with ridiculous names – Van der Graaf Generator, anybody? They knew music and they analysed, compared, and criticised it. They also went to see it, live.

These were boys whose parents not only read books; some even wrote them. There were modest middle-class families with small libraries and classical collections, and flamboyant, theatre- and gallery-going families, who lived in large tumble-down houses full of old furniture and art, who wore clothes with holes in them. It seemed to me like a veritable bohemia.

I realised straight away that this was a ticket to a different town, my own personal way out. But I also adored the more tribal, visceral thrills shared with my mates on the estate. So for most of my formative years I had a split cultural personality. I also developed an adaptable accent to match. Grammar-school lad and council-estate kid. Clubs and gigs.

On weekends I was still the Burnt Oak boy, obsessed with

football and fashion, reggae and soul. The first record I bought
was a Jamaican ska 45, 'Mr Popcorn' by Laurel Aitken, from a
stall in Shepherd's Bush Market when I was ten. The first away
game I went to was Leyton Orient two years later, and I ran
amok round the far east with a bunch of ne'er-do-wells from
Ladbroke Grove. The first suit I bought was mohair.

But during the week it was my mates from the grammar
school who got tickets for the Jackson 5, the Faces and Mott
the Hoople, who lent me the first Roxy Music album, and
quoted Bob Dylan lyrics, who had M. C. Escher posters and
R. D. Laing books, who loved cricket and went to the cinema
to actually see films, some of them with subtitles. While my
tastes broadened, I still knew that Jimmy Cliff was far better
than Jimmy Page, and the Temptations and the Four Tops
wiped the floor with Jethro Tull and Uriah Heep. (Whether
the Temps are better than the Tops is still one of the great
musical debates.) But I also discovered that there was a big
world beyond the boundaries of the Watling Estate.

By the time I was fourteen, maybe just fifteen, Friday nights
meant going clubbing. We travelled en masse to the Bandwagon, a nightclub in the back room of a pub in Kingsbury, a
couple of miles and a couple of buses away. Mob-handed,
attired to the nines and sky high on hormones, the boys
and girls of the Oak would all gather to form an overdressed,
underage line in the car park outside. Standing on tiptoes and
puffing out our chests to appear older; anything to get past the
not-that-bothered bouncers and into sweaty heaven.

Once inside, the darkness captured and enraptured you,
draping your teenage frame in a superhero cloak of semi-
anonymity, while dragging you into its murky lair. The
half-light protected you while the sound assaulted you; deep,
primordial basslines, pumping, pushing, driving like an insistent sonic motor, with a piercing fusillade of horns punctuating
the throb. Over the top of this rhythmic battery came a chant,

repetitive and hypnotic, making your head nod and your knees nock, your stomach churn and your brain and body rotate. 'Bus Stop, Bus Stop', The Fatback Band, Brass Construction, Kool and the Gang, Earth, Wind & Fire, B. T. Express, the Ohio Players . . . FIIIIYER.

Walking into the Bandwagon in your dancing duds was like stepping into a boxing ring: intense and enticing, thrilling, frightening, pummelling, physical and visceral, it thumped you in the solar plexus and spun you round like a right hook to the temple. It was a perpetual-motion machine driven by vast reserves of high-grade North London teenage desire and imported American funk.

And then later, deep in the dangerous, glamorous night, near the end, when you had staked your place and dared to dance, stood your ground, held your own, made your mark, the selector would slow things down, change the charge and that girl you had glimpsed, had posed and danced for, might just become the girl you dance with. Warmth and breath and touch, loins near loins, skin near skin, eyes boring into eyes, the beat, the heat, the heartbeat. This was a chance, or maybe not, probably not, but just, possibly maybe. There was a lot at stake on a Friday night.

There would be other clubs; many, many, much cooler, better clubs, uptown joints with the best DJs and the best dancers, the nattiest dressers, the beautiful ones, there would be Crackers and the Wag. But still for me those Friday nights at the Bandwagon with the Burnt Oak boys, when I first got to crack the nocturnal code, are scorched into my memory. Then came Dr Feelgood.

Actually, Rachel came first. (Definitely no pun intended.) We might have met at the Bandwagon, I have no mental Polaroid of that precise moment, but I know she lived nearby but beyond the Watling. Her parents owned their home, which made her posh, and her favourite album was Marvin Gaye's

Let's Get It On, which made her irredeemably attractive. And she had an elder brother, and he plays a part in this story.

My club-going was a regular event, but my gig-going was still largely confined to occasional big shows by well-known bands in large, seated venues. Then a mate at school let it be known that his mum worked for the BBC and could get free tickets to the theatre in nearby Golders Green where they recorded a weekly show called *In Concert*. This mainly featured hairy heavy bands of the time playing a full live set. His hand was bitten off.

The difference with these shows was that we went to see acts we did not know, rather than ones we already knew we liked, which I realise now is one of the steps a big gig-goer must make. You take a chance. My companion for those recorded concerts was a brilliant but troubled Irish lad from school called Patrick, who became my buddy in rock.

We would sit for hours in his tiny bedroom listening to the latest album by the Stones, the Faces, Bowie or Roxy, poring over record sleeves, dissecting licks, analysing lyrics and arguing over Led Zeppelin; he loved them dearly, I thought they were unbearably leaden and deeply dreary. I hated heavy rock. Patrick hated funk and discos, wouldn't be seen dead at the Bandwagon. But we liked each other.

And together, courtesy of somebody's mum, we saw a stream of almost interchangeable, indistinguishable blues-rock bands in flared denim with long locks and even longer guitar solos. Wishbone Ash, Stackridge, Rory Gallagher, Blodwyn Pig, Curved Air, Bad Company . . . the list goes on and on and so did they. I'm not sure I can remember a single second of any of those shows, bar one by Thin Lizzy, who were also a hard-rocking guitar band with interminable solos, but one whose front man, long and sinuous and beautiful and black and Irish, had charm and charisma bursting out of his skintight jeans. He was a rock'n'roll front man I could dig, man.

I realised then that a shamanic figure of either sex up on stage is sexy, compelling, captivating. Charisma may be indefinable, but it is immediately recognisable. It's a currency worth more than bitcoin or gold. It is also a superpower, which very few possess, a power that can be switched on and turned up, to transmit to teenage boys sitting in the back row of an old theatre in Golders Green or on the terraces at Loftus Road. Stanley Bowles had it on the pitch and Phil Lynott had it on stage. Charisma has an effect upon us: narcotic, erotic, you name it, they've got it. The Faces were still the best band I had seen, Rod was still my main man, but Phil Lynott was some front man. He was a star.

Going to gigs was a different thrill, more cerebral and considered than going to clubs, but also with an entirely different focus. In a nightclub, the entertainment is provided by the crowd, by you and yours; you watch each other rather than a band, you are the star of your show, and the music is the soundtrack to your story, the dance floor your stage. That's why it matters so much what you wear, how you walk, talk, stand and move. It is Saturday-night fever every night.

There are very few star performers in the world of dance music because it isn't about them, and it isn't about live performance. It's music made for records. I did go and see one of those great seventies funk bands with some of the lads from Burnt Oak and the Bandwagon. For some reason we drove north out of London in a Cortina (probably) to a place called the California Ballroom in distant Dunstable, to watch Brass Construction, or maybe it was B. T. Express. I can't remember exactly because it wasn't exactly a gig – it was a show.

Dance music is functional; it is designed to make you dance, and whichever band it was in Dunstable, was essentially a show band, like my mum used to go and see at the Hammersmith Palais, when she met my dad dancing the jitterbug to Joe Loss and His Orchestra. Their job is to play the music just like it is on the record, and they did, and everybody boogied, and it was great and all that. But there was no Phil Lynott or Rod and Ronnie, this was essentially a disco with a live interlude.

The music of black America, soul and dance music in all its forms, has always been my abiding love. From first hearing 'When a Man Loves a Woman' and 'Fa-Fa-Fa-Fa-Fa (Sad Song)' on the *This Is Soul* compilation LP my brothers bought in 1968, I was immediately captivated. My brother Barry wore a black armband over his mohair whistle the day Otis died. Soulfulness is still the greatest quality music can possess, to my ears, and I have seen some great American soul acts along the way. But, often, far too often, they are not very good at all.

Cheesy, corny, showy yet perfunctory, running through the motions, pulling on the velvet suit and putting on the act. Take the money, sing a medley and run. What is soul music if you don't believe it comes from deep down in the soul? Why are so many of the US soul acts underwhelming on stage?

I understand that the classic generation of African American artists from the fifties onwards had to deal with the vile racism and segregation of Jim Crow, that they were ripped off and treated appallingly. I also know that many of them ended up playing on a kind of tawdry US, sub-Las Vegas cabaret circuit, where authenticity was not required, but spangly tuxedos, corny cover versions and shiny showbiz were. Chicken in a basket and cheese in abundance.

But it is still hard to take when you're excited to finally see the great Al Green, for example, and he turns up at the Royal Albert Hall and spends most of his time handing out roses 'to the laydees' and praising the Lord. This is the voice of 'Take Me to the River' and 'Call Me', starting songs, then stopping them a few bars in to mumble some more platitudes about beautiful ladies or the glory of God, before waving the microphone at the crowd so that the audience actually sing the song.

And doing that time and time again throughout his thankfully brief set.

The man has one of the greatest voices his God has ever bestowed – you could still hear that in the few moments he really let rip – yet he used it to rush his way through a hurried medley of his hits and back out into a limo. Who really thinks that medleys are a good idea? Why would Al Green do that?

And something very similar happened with Bobby Womack, Curtis Mayfield, various incarnations of the Drifters and the Four Tops and even the hardest-working man in showbiz, James Brown, whose late-career shows were quite hard work. That old J. B. magic had been reduced to a few grunts, a couple of spins and the old collapsing routine followed by the reviving cape. He spent more time on the floor than a Premier League footballer.

There's a big debate to be had about how showbiz pizzazz fits in with live music authenticity. Earth, Wind & Fire certainly put on a show, all bacofoil suits, glowing pyramids and spinning drummers, and it was great, if rather contrived, fun. But for far too many of the American soul acts, the biz seemed more important than the show and the show was pretty ropey.

Perhaps their cynicism was understandable, but a friend of mine promoted a performance here by one of the great US soul men, known for his poetry and piety, who proceeded to put a gun to my mate's head while demanding that he be paid up-front in cash or the gig would not go on. Then when the folding money materialised, he played a perfunctory forty-five minutes and fled.

Other great disappointments have come from artists I adored and adore still, despite the live let-downs. Nina Simone haranguing the crowd for twenty minutes because somebody dared to ask for a particular song, before throwing her shoe into the auditorium and storming off. Gil Scott-Heron, who is among the most inspirational men of our age, a sage and a griot

who could create moments of blinding insight, his rich baritone voice over the ancient African rhythm of the drum. I only
saw him once, but three times I didn't see him because he didn't
turn up, so ravaged by his addictions that he frequently failed
to show for shows. Or the great Gregory, the Cool Ruler, Mr
Isaacs, arguably the sweetest voice Jamaica has ever produced,
who could barely manage a note at the Jazz Café late in his life,
his pipes shot from time on the crack pipe, his performance
tragic, a sad and unedifying end to a once-beautiful man.

Contrast all those with Frankie Beverly and Maze, not so
well known to the general public, perhaps, but beloved by the
soul fraternity for putting on the best, most engaging, intensely
moving live performances imaginable. Watching them play
'We Are One' at Hammersmith Odeon was one of the most
rapturous experiences ever. Musically perfect, spiritually profound, life-affirming and soul-stirring. We really were one,
band and audience in unison, and I get goosebumps to this day.
True *ubuntu*.

I also get chills when I think about Dr Feelgood.

In 1975 I was still primarily a soul boy, going out with
Rachel who wore A-line skirts and cheesecloth shirts, bought
her clothes in Fiorucci, and liked her music on the All Platinum label, but her brother was a man of rock. It was Rachel's
brother who first uttered the term 'pub rock' to me. Things
were about to change.

Pubs were still places your mum and dad went to get away
from the kids for an hour or two, or your elder brothers gathered to get tanked-up before the footie. But Rachel's
brother – who shall remain nameless because I can't remember
his name – went to pubs to see bands play. He was a couple of
years older than us and a fanatical music fan of pretty much
every kind of music, and realising that I was a fellow traveller,
he invited me to go to gigs with him. The first show we went
to together wasn't at a boozer, but at the Rainbow, a

marvellous old art deco theatre turned concert venue in Finsbury Park. (It's now an evangelical church, which seems like a retrograde moral step if ever there was one.)

I'd bought a compilation LP called *The Warner Brothers Music Show* for fifty-nine pence, which featured a slew of West Coast American boogie bands, including the Doobie Brothers, who I liked because they were funky. They were touring with some of the other acts on that LP as a package show, with the Doobies topping the bill. We got tickets high up in the gods and arrived just in time to see the support act, called Little Feat, whose track 'Dixie Chicken' I knew from that compilation album.

I wish I could say I remember every number and note Lowell George's brilliant band played that day (I think it was a matinee), but I don't. I wish I could summon an image of the fat man in his white overalls caressing that slide guitar, but I can't. I wish I had known then what I know now – that Little Feat were one of the greatest, most funky and soulful bands of all time and that Lowell George was a doomed genius, who'd be dead before I saw the band again. But I didn't. I didn't really pay attention.

I do know that Rainbow gig, and the way Little Feat blew the Doobies off the stage, has become legendary and I was there, but only just. Truth be told, I'm going much more on hearsay than recall. It was a blur at the time, and it has become less vivid since. I only remember the crowd going batshit crazy. I saw Lowell George and can't really remember it. When it comes to musical memories of 1975, even the great Little Feat were about to be effectively erased by a bunch of psychotic rhythm-and-blues rascals from Canvey Island playing in a boozer.

Now this was early 1975. I was not yet sixteen, and not exactly manly, but there was never really an issue about access to licensed premises. Today we are rabidly puritanical about allowing teenagers under eighteen into anywhere where the demon drink is served, which has stunted the cultural growth of entire generations. I can't be the only parent who has helped their teenage kids forge ID so they could see a band or attend a dance. Music is usually performed in places where alcohol is served, so people in their formative years cannot now see music. Back then things were much easier. Provided you could see over the bar, you could usually get in and get served.

But it wasn't about drink. I didn't go to smelly old pubs, or sweaty old nightclubs come to that, to get pissed – I could barely afford a half. The intoxication came from the atmosphere and the music. Seeing Kilburn and the High Roads, Ian Dury's splendidly splenetic 'bunch of raspberries' roaring their way through 'Rough Kids', just up the road at the Bull & Gate in Kentish Town, was a mind-altering experience.

I realise now how much luck plays a part in all this. I was born at a good time, and I was lucky to have a musical mentor who didn't mind dragging a kid much younger than him along. I was also in a good place. It was a geographical blessing to be a music-mad youngster in North London in the mid-seventies.

Pub rock was a London thing, and more specifically a North London thing. There was a roster of big, dusty old Victorian drinking houses in a line north of the Marylebone Road, from Hammersmith to Hampstead. Many of them were originally Irish houses, which had back rooms or upstairs or downstairs rooms with a small stage, where showbands or folk bands had once played diddly tunes for the local Irish, or bearded jazzers in jumpers had serenaded a few trad fans.

The Red Cow, the Tally Ho, the Greyhound, the Brecknock, the Hope & Anchor, the Dublin Castle, the Torrington, the Bull & Gate . . . All of these were within half an hour or so of where we lived, so you could bunk the fare on the Tube with ten bob in your pocket, see a couple of bands and be back home before the last drunken ne'er-do-well had been turfed out of the public bar.

I went to less than half a dozen pub-rock gigs with my musical spirit guide before the relationship with his sister fizzled out, probably because I spent more time with him than with Rachel. Most of the bands I saw in the few months that teenage love affair lasted were good, hard-working, back-to-basics rhythm and blues or soul bands with a bit of country and a touch of vaudeville from Dury's mob. Pub rock wasn't a genre or a style, it was an attitude and a moment.

Kokomo were probably my favourites. They were a sprawling pub-rock version of the Average White Band — whose wonderful *AWB* White Album is still in my all-time best list — who managed to combine the sweet vocals and soaring harmonies I loved with an unpretentious, salt-of-the-earth, squash-on-the-tiny-stage, all-in-this-together vibe. I still think Kokomo's version of 'Angel' gives Aretha a run for her money.

Standing right up close to the stage, seeing the reds of their eyes, watching the bass player's fingers, feeling the vocalist's breath, meeting the guitarist's partner at the bar. It was the lack of pomp and pomposity of pub rock, the spit-and-sawdust veracity and in-your-face immediacy which was most affecting, markedly different from the distant us-and-them, stars-on-stage experience of the big gigs I'd been to.

I never got to see the Feelgoods with Rachel's brother but, emboldened by my experiences and intrigued by reports filtering through, I convinced a couple of the more game lads from school to accompany me on a mission to catch some maximum r'n'b. I hadn't actually heard them; back in those days you had to shell out for an album to hear a band, so had no real idea what to expect.

The atmosphere in that sweltering room that night was more akin to the build-up at a big match than a music concert. This was a partisan home crowd, tough-looking blokes chanting the band's name, building up an edge, fighting and shoving for space. It felt like you'd entered a particularly partizan boozer at an away game and might not come out in one piece. Then the band ambled on stage, four right dodgy-looking geezers from the Thames Delta, in iffy, ill-fitting suits, looking more like a firm who'd come to rob the pub rather than play music in it. They could have been villains or hod carriers, used-car salesman or bare-knuckle boxers. Could this really be the band everybody is talking about?

And then it began. Bang, like a blow to the gut, like a kick to the gonads, a full-on, instantaneous assault of brittle, bruising British blues, no intro, no messing, no quarter given. Sharp, staccato guitar, skintight bass and drums holding it down, and, on top, vocals delivered at full Essex pelt, barking like a bloke from Barking, with the persistent, rhythmic patter of a market trader in full flight. Boom. Boom. Boom. Boom.

Me and my mates were almost literally blown away; the whoosh of the band combined with the rush of the crowd was like a physical force lifting you up and off your feet. And it kept on coming, raining down on you, relentless, unrepentant, unrefined, like the oil that kept Canvey Island greasy. That swivel-eyed machine-gun guitarist, twitching and careering across the stage on rails, clashing with the dashing but dirty front man with stains on the strides of his once-white whistle, wailing like an estuarine banshee into his harmonica. It was rough yet precise, serious like GBH, spot on and pared down, music delivered without an ounce of flounce.

The sound these medical men made was simultaneously old fashioned to the point of being primeval, like something dredged up from the mud of the Thames, yet totally new, not like anything I'd seen or heard before. Not like a band was supposed to be. This was a new beginning, a shocking rock'n'roll rebirth with placenta all over the walls.

Dr Feelgood weren't punk – you certainly wouldn't have called them that to their faces – but punk would not have existed, could not have existed, without those four razor-sharp roustabouts from the arse-end of Essex. I interviewed both Patti Smith and Debbie Harry, the two greatest female icons and iconoclasts, the birth mothers of New York punk in later years, and they both told me that Dr Feelgood were the band that inspired them most. Patti Smith said that her epochal first album *Horses* had its famous monochrome cover because the Feelgoods had used a black-and-white cover for their debut album *Down by the Jetty*. She was a huge fan.

And within thirty seconds so was I. Besotted, but also befuddled – how could something so rough and raw, so wantonly unpolished, be so brilliant? It went against all the earnest *Old Grey Whistle Test* twaddle about musicianship and musicality, paying dues and polishing chops. Of course, I know now that the Feelgoods were actually brilliant at what they did, masterful minimalists, but it was also a lesson that the sum of the parts in live performance is what matters. The rush, the thrill, the look, the atmosphere, the feeling you're left with at the end.

I was left needing more, so took to seeing them every time I could. I also began following fellow Canvey Island adrenalin-and-amphetamine blues purveyors Eddie and the Hot Rods and the wondrously deranged Lew Lewis, the somersaulting, bank-robbing harmonica man, who seemed to play every week in a pub near me at one point. The hegemony of the no-holds-barred British blues bruisers was brief but intense. I remember one Hot Rods gig at the Marquee where the sweat ran down the walls and across the floor like a river and I had to wring my shirt out afterwards. 'Get out of Denver'.

As much as I loved going to clubs, still adored dance music, this was different gravy. But another deluge was coming to wash away everything in its wake. Punk was a year-zero tsunami and it changed everything precisely because it was the coming together of those two strands of British youth culture, the gig and the club.

Chapter 5

The Great Outdoors

Have you ever been hit on the head by a flying Party Seven?

If the answer to that question is yes, then I reckon there's a fair chance you saw Elton John at Wembley Stadium in 1975. Although there's also a possibility that you didn't see very much of Elton John at Wembley in 1975, perhaps because you were in triage for the head injury or more likely because you'd just had enough of *Captain Fantastic and the Brown Dirt Cowboy*.

Proximity to Wembley Stadium has been useful quite a few times in my life. We went there on a regular basis in the early seventies to buy snide suede budgie jackets with tulip lapels, platform shoes in coffee and cream or high-waisted trousers in lurid lime-green from the schmutter market, which took place in the old car park on a Sunday morning. You could always tell when there had been a game the day before because the lingering whiff of urine and hot dogs was overpowering.

Sadly, I wasn't there when QPR beat West Brom to lift the League Cup in 1967. My older brothers both went, but wouldn't take their snotty little seven-year-old sibling along, and my QPR-supporting dad had died a few months before. But I have been there every time (that's four times, including a

replay) my team have played there since. We even won once.
OOOH, Bobby Zamora.

I was present in 1971, aged twelve, to watch Johan Cruyff
and his wondrous Ajax team beat Panathinaikos 2–0 in the
European Cup final. My cousin Ian and I just rocked up and
bought tickets on the day. We were in the Panathinaikos end
with most of the large North London Greek Cypriot community and never have I heard such splendid wailing and lamenting
as when their team got thumped. I heard much worse things
when I went to a couple of England internationals in the 1980s,
when the xenophobia and racism from some sections of the
crowd were disgusting and I vowed never again. One of the
few promises I haven't found hard to keep.

Somehow I managed to avoid seeing Evel Knievel not quite
leap over thirteen London buses on his star-spangled motor-
cycle in May 1975, at one of the most bizarre events ever held
there. Almost the entire teenage population of the Watling
Estate, bar me, bunked into that one. But I was there with a
group of Orange Hill Grammar School chums just three weeks
later to watch Elton John. Sort of.

This wasn't the first rock concert ever held at the national
stadium; that honour went to Yes, whose preposterous *Tales
From Topographic Oceans* has become a byword for seventies
prog-rock excess and a major incitement to the punk-rock
revolution. But the gig with podgy Reg from Pinner on a
sweltering summer's afternoon in June 1975 is the one many
people of my generation remember, and it has become famous
for all sorts of reasons. Including flying beer cans.

I guess we need to talk a little about Sir Elton. He is of
course both the grande dame and the pantomime dame of
British light entertainment, a global superstar, a national treasure, a gay cultural icon and a Hertfordshire hero for saving
Watford FC.

He's a reformed alcoholic and coke fiend whose temper

tantrums were notorious. But he's now a doting father and loving husband, a tireless AIDS campaigner, a philanthropist, art collector, benefactor and survivor. He's a fully paid-up member of the rock'n'roll royal family. But he doesn't exactly ooze credibility.

Elton's career is a little like lizards and England cricket teams in that it has a very long tail. I'm sure he's written some decent songs since 1975, he's certainly sold bucket-loads of records, and by all accounts can still put on a jolly good show. But there was a time when he was proper.

The first half a dozen Elton John albums, up to and definitely including *Goodbye Yellow Brick Road*, were truly terrific records which would still grace any serious collection. In partnership with Bernie Taupin, he wrote and recorded songs like 'Mona Lisas and Mad Hatters', 'Country Comfort', 'Your Song', 'Border Song', 'Rocket Man' and 'Daniel': monuments of early-seventies country-tinged pop rock and proto-Americana.

In that era, Reg and Rod, two bitter friends and close rivals from back when they were both in Steampacket – albeit not at the same time – were trading blows like a pair of nimble middleweights at the top of their game, and although I personally always preferred Rod's slightly more soulful style, those Elton John records are some of the very best of their age. The combination of the two, with Roderick singing Elton and Bernie's 'Country Comfort', is a near-perfect neckerchief moment. Elton was bloody good.

So it is no surprise that when a gig was announced, headlined by the 'Rocket Man' man, with a stellar line-up of American acts including the Beach Boys, the Eagles and Rufus featuring Chaka Khan as support, and it was just up the road, we were eager to go. This was my first ever experience of an outdoor concert and I remember being super-excited. I also know now that I was permanently scarred by the events of the day. Not physically scarred by a flying Party Seven tin, but it came pretty close.

Our tickets cost £3.50. (Top tickets to see Bruce Springsteen in Hyde Park recently were £350.) That gave us access to the hallowed turf with a giant stage set up at one end, and there were 90,000 others encamped on the pitch and the terraces. A large percentage of those around us seemed to be American GIs or airmen from one of the bases in southern England, all buzzcuts and loud whoops, while there was also a sizeable contingent of extremely rowdy and near-naked beach- or bleach-blond Antipodeans.

They all seemed to be experts at this outdoor concert lark and at 11.30 in the morning, when the show started, they lugged in vast supplies of beer, spirits and food and set up elaborate base camps with coolers and tents and beds, and flags, including the stars and bars of the Confederacy, flying. They were all camped out and ready to go.

Of course, us local herberts had made no such preparations and had no provisions, so we had to queue up in interminable lines for everything from burgers to bogs. I spent most of the day wandering around going increasingly pink from the sun, (had factor 50 even been invented yet?) hungry, thirsty and in dire need of a pee, trying to find a decent vantage point, while Stackridge and Rufus and Joe Walsh came and went and made little impression.

It seemed to me that the music was something of a sideshow, a sonic diversion floating through the blistering air, which people would occasionally tune into in between the serious business of picnicking, getting paralytic or stoned, making out, climbing on each other's shoulders, and building pyramids out of large beer cans called Party Sevens. The bands were miles away, you couldn't really see them anyway, but worse, I didn't feel remotely connected to them. They were there to perform, and we were just distant spectators. It certainly wasn't the intense, all-in-this-together feeling we got from the Feel-goods in a public bar.

But that didn't seem to bother most people, who were clearly there for a big day out, fun in the sun with the music largely as an incidental accompaniment. They were having a raucous good time, and the more they drank, the more they whooped and the higher their precarious beer-can pyramids became, until somebody decided to start lobbing stuff to knock them down.

I don't know who cast the first can, but I do know that at some point it turned into a minor artillery war with largely but not exclusively empty vessels sailing through the air at head height. Bags of yellow liquid were also used as ammo in this sordid little skirmish. Most people seemed to consider it all jolly rock'n'roll japes, until I saw a girl take a can full on the noggin. Claret everywhere, Red Cross running through the crowd, while the Eagles played 'Take It Easy'. (OK, it could have been 'Desperado'.)

The Eagles had stepped up a gear, and the rednecks and GIs in the crowd gave it some good-old-boy rebel yelling. I think I preferred it when they were ignoring Stackridge. By the way, did you know that the Eagles recorded all those classic, laid-back, oh-so-American country-rock tracks in the deep South-West? SW13, that is. They were Taking It Easy at Olympic Studios in Barnes, a leafy London suburb stuck for-ever in 1956. Barnes, with its common and its pond and its cosy pubs and a level crossing that looks like Miss Marple is about to appear, is nine miles due south of Wembley Stadium and a very long way from Winslow, Arizona.

The Beach Boys, meanwhile, had recently recorded what I think is their greatest ever LP in glamorous Utrecht, and the resulting album, entitled *Holland,* is one of my all-time favour-ites. So I was determined to actually watch the Beach Boys, who were the last act on before Elton.

And I clearly wasn't alone. The atmosphere of the place seemed to shift and some sort of collective decision to concentrate upon the artists up on stage occurred. I suspect many of the Americans and Australians were there primarily to see the Beach Boys anyway, so the not-so-jolly japes ceased and the audience were finally galvanised by music. It was also clear, as classic sing-along hit followed classic sing-along hit, that the band were on great form and what's more, they had the perfect set to play for a stadium full of drunken, stoned, sunburnt people. At last we had good vibrations.

I realise now what the Beach Boys clearly knew then: that to capture the attention of a vast, distracted audience like that, you've got to go big and go popular. The Beach Boys songbook is full of massive, feelgood numbers, and while I might prefer the more subtle delights of 'Leaving This Town' or 'The Trader' (which they played), it was the huge hits from 'Wouldn't It Be Nice', to 'I Get Around' that really got the crowd going. You've got to give them fun, fun, fun. And they did, and everybody loved it. Me included.

And then came Elton. I do recall a rather well-received 'B-B-B Bennie and the Jets' early in the set, but it had been a very long hot day already, lots of concentration and energy had been expended on dodging missiles and singing along to surfer songs, and many people were more than a little battle weary; plenty were literally asleep. So Reg decided to play the entirety of his latest, not particularly catchy new album, which was so new nobody actually knew any of the songs.

My abiding memory of the afternoon, apart from the flying beer cans, the claret and the naked Australians, was of vast swathes of the audience traipsing unsteadily out of the stadium while Elton laboured away on *Captain Fantastic* to a few thousand of the faithful at the front. His big day out spoiled by a dubious decision to parade his new LP and also by the fact that the whole thing was just too big, too long, too far away. Well, certainly for me it was. I too joined the exodus and never ever got to see Elton John again. But more importantly, rarely have I been to a big outdoor concert again.

It wasn't entirely down to that less-than-wonderful Wembley experience all those years ago. I am just not temperamentally or sartorially suited to festivals. Not for me Glastonbury or Reading. (Well, it wouldn't be Reading anyway; heavy rock and tripping sixth formers have never been my thing, even when I was in the sixth form.) I went once to Womad to see my mates in a band called Working Week and got wound up by scores of idiot dancing hippies, head to toe in cultural appropriation and patchouli oil.

I was back at Wembley Stadium for Live Aid, perhaps the most globally famous concert of all time, and I didn't see it. I was briefly backstage with some friends, then left to watch it at home on television without realising that this was a historic event in the making. I gave little credence to a gig viewed by about 2 billion people, which probably says a lot about the state of my mind and the size of my ego at that moment.

Many years later, I just about saw Bob Dylan croaking his way through an indistinguishable series of songs, which may or may not have been 'Like A Rolling Stone', on a farm in Kent. It took me five hours and hundreds of pounds to get there after my car broke down en route, and I had to hitch-hike home at night with my thirteen-year-old son and his mate in tow after missing the last train. Some people like that sort of thing.

And most people seem to love the whole ritual of larking about in a field while music plays, as the festival experience has become one of the defining rituals of contemporary coming of age. I think it's partly down to the fact that young people are now effectively barred from licensed premises in cities. And as prices for live music have risen exponentially, so a once-a-year splurge, where you get loads of bands for your buck, perhaps makes sense.

It has become a necessary notch on the bedpost of life, a *de rigueur* act of cultural tourism. Going to Glasto is like losing your virginity or smoking your first joint; it is the equivalent of getting a tattoo, which allows the world to see how very alternative you are. But I don't know how much it is really about the music. I suspect people go to festivals not to actually see the acts, but to be able to say they have seen the acts. 'I've seen U2' – 'Yes, me too.'

When I see supposed legends like Kylie Minogue, Kenny Rogers or Dame Shirley Bassey up on that distant, blustery stage in front of a vast throng of indie kids, I really wonder why they are there. And that goes for both the artists and the fans. Were all those people enthusiastically swaying along on each other's shoulders to Rolf Harris playing 'Two Little Boys' at Glastonbury really such great fans of the wobble board and didgeridoo-wielding paedo?

The hegemony of festivals is also indicative of the way that live music has become dominated by big-ticket, bombastic, usually older acts. So if you want to see Red Hot Chili Peppers or the Foo Fighters, Coldplay, the Stones or the Who churn out their anthemic stadium schtick, that's where you go. Or maybe you want to be able to say you saw Stormzy or Dave but wouldn't exactly feel comfortable in a shebeen in Peckham.

Reggae should perhaps work well outdoors on a sunny day, all good vibes and gently swaying rhythms, but watching Bob Marley's music blowing listlessly in the wind in Crystal Palace Park, while the stoned-to-the-eyeballs, predominantly white audience frolicked and paddled in the pond, was no comparison to seeing his coruscating soul wailing away in the Rainbow with the nattiest dreads and the most righteous brothers and sisters in close attendance. All music sounds better bouncing off walls than blowing in the wind.

I was in Vicky Park for the Clash's famous Rock Against Racism gig in 1978, but it doesn't exactly go down as one of the best of the many times I saw Joe and the gang. It was a vitally important event politically, but the sound quality was terrible and the atmosphere more than edgy. Or so I'm told. This time it was me who was too inebriated to recall very much apart from the fact that the white jeans I was wearing in a failed bid to look a little like Paul Simonon were completely ruined. We'd started the day drinking in the LSE (London School of Economics) student bar and carried on, on the march en route to the rally in the far east, and ended up covered in crap in a squat in Hackney with my memory shot and my strides soiled.

I've often said that I don't like festivals primarily because I don't like mud, which is entirely true. Ever since getting a wallop from my mother for coming home caked head to toe in the stuff, aged about nine, after attempting to build a replica of Hadrian's Wall in our local park from the silt in the Silk Stream, a brook which ran through it, I've been wary of sticky dirt.

But it isn't just mud; I prefer my nature at a distance and my music close up. I was never one for the Boy Scouts, and the great outdoors is best kept that way. I'm an indoors soul who feels much more at home in a basement in Soho or a loft in SoHo than in a field out in the windy wilds. Especially when it comes to watching musicians. I'm also a dapper man who likes his wardrobe well pressed, his shoes polished and his music intense and intimate.

Given the choice between the pinpoint, pin-drop emotional precision of a plangent trumpet solo at Ronnie's or a head-shaking, ear-shredding rock-god guitar solo at Glasto, I know which one I'm going for. And I'm going for a double espresso and a sneaky amaretto afterwards in the Bar Italia followed by a black cab home to my well-made bed over a cider and a burnt vegan burger in a blustery tent which a fellow reveller is likely to piss over.

I am not personally cut out for roughing it. I would put camping down as one of the least enjoyable experiences known to mankind, rivalled only by skiing and folk dancing. All three of those occurred in my formative years during school trips. One to Austria, which may well have been the worst week of my life, where I spent the entire time frozen, sodden and bruised, queuing up and falling down, completely useless at something eight-year-old Austrians can do elegantly.

The other was a disastrous weekend under canvas, getting soaked to the bone and failing to impress the girl of my desires high in the Brecon Beacons on an A-level geography field trip. My Bryan Ferry-style attire from Laurence Corner, the famed army-surplus store, was completely inappropriate for Welsh weather, and I got soaked to the skin. I was also ill-dressed for a deeply embarrassing hoedown, which rounded off our great rural adventure, and where a dosey doe became a definitely don't.

I'm an urbanite, but it isn't just the quagmires and querulous crowds that put me off the festival experience. It's the whole nature of how music sounds when you're miles away, and what sort of music does sound good in a festival setting? The Beach Boys were terrific at Wembley because they naturally and sensibly played their greatest hits, which are great. But I want more than that, or maybe less than that: subtlety and style, élan and emotion, intimacy and authenticity, creativity and spontaneity. And I don't particularly want the swaying, braying, sing-along camaraderie with an army of the great unwashed.

If I want to belt my lungs out to some corny old tunes while hugging a drunken stranger, I'll go and watch QPR win an away game. At a gig I want to see and hear the musicians in great detail, ideally as close as possible. Ideally without some idiot bellowing in my lughole. Don't get me started on sing-alongs.

The closest I have come to a punch-up in my adult life came at a Ry Cooder concert a few years back in a very swish venue in Chelsea. It certainly wasn't a muddy festival, but the fellow in the seats directly behind me behaved like it was. He insisted on shouting every word of every song at the top of his voice straight into my ear. He then did the same with nasal twanging noises during Ry's slide solos.

He wouldn't accept my politely put argument that I had not paid a large sum to listen to a tuneless berk and that he ought to desist and let the maestro be heard just for a tune or two, and then became aggressive in asserting his right to murder some great songs. I literally had to leave to avoid getting into a fight I would probably have lost.

I guess I'm in danger of sounding like a grumpy old bloke here, but my aversion to all this stuff is not new and not just about the more sedate pleasures of seated venues and attentive but silent audiences. I've pogoed with the best of them, revelled in a riot to Sham 69 and danced a clumsy ceilidh to the Pogues and the Dubliners in a Kilburn dance hall on Paddy's night, and you don't get much more joyously rowdy than that. I just don't get the pleasure of standing next to a stoned and stinky stranger in harem pants and a keffiyeh in a queue for the chemical toilets while the Chemical Brothers rave on in a dance tent nearby, and Radiohead drone on on a distant main stage in another bloody county.

Each to their own is a very good ethos, and if an entire generation of (white middle-class) kids (and some of their embarrassing parents) want to sit on their arses in a field listening to Elbow, that's fine by me. Just don't expect me to join in. Having said all that, one of my most cherished musical memories is indeed of singing along (quietly) to some great musicians in the great outdoors.

Hamish Stuart, former guitarist and singer with the Average White Band, and one of the most honeyed voices this island has ever produced, has become a friend over the years. He has also become a publican, and for a few years he kept a charming house in a hamlet in Kent. It had a large beer garden at the back and every year he would invite a load of his musical buddies down to play in a little weekend-long hooley for a couple of hundred people.

He also invited me to DJ and MC and, like everybody else, I did it for beer and jollity, and it was jolly indeed. The likes of Paul Young and Mike Scott, Chris Difford and Terry Reid would turn up to sing a song or seven, everybody mingled together in the garden and a version of the Average White Band would always finish the night with a rousing 'Pick Up the Pieces'. Gentle, charming, civilised and thoroughly life-affirming, it was basically a groovy garden party, and I looked forward to it every summer.

Then one year I was behind the decks selecting a tune or two and a couple of middle-aged Scottish guys ambled over to say that they were going to play a little acoustic set and would I introduce them. I am ashamed to admit that I didn't recognise who they were and had to ask. 'I'm Benny and he's Graham,' was the answer delivered in a soft but strong Glaswegian accent.

Blimey, Benny Gallagher and Graham Lyle, the two arch-creators of neckerchief rock, along with the immortal (though sadly dead) Ronnie Lane, of course. That's Gallagher and Lyle from McGuinness Flint and Slim Chance, Gallagher and Lyle who played on 'The Poacher' and *Anymore for Anymore*, whose album *Breakaway* is one of the most sublime slices of melodic pop ever recorded. Gallagher and Lyle who've written for, played with and produced a veritable *Who's Who* of great musicians on great records.

These two were veterans of Ronnie Lane's legendary *Passing Show*, a wonderfully disastrous, madcap mishap of a tour, involving circus tents and gypsy caravans, broken-down buses and some of the most gorgeous melodies ever played, which I would have waded through rivers of mud to see. And here they were in a pub garden just about to pick up a pair of acoustic guitars and play with no fuss, no fanfare, just a couple of words from me to announce their presence.

I said a brief 'ladies and gentlemen' and they strummed and they sang and they charmed the setting sun. The Kentish sky turned a mellow mauve to suit their mellifluous sound as they smiled and laughed their way through sublime versions of 'When I'm Dead and Gone', 'Heart on My Sleeve', 'I Wanna Stay with You' and a 'Breakaway' so beguiling, so poignant and sweetly sentimental that I sobbed just a little into my beer as I softly sang along.

Maybe I do like festivals after all.

Chapter 6

The American Dream

Whatever happened to Bruce Springsteen?

In 1975 the hype was high, but then so was the hope. We'd missed out on tickets for the first show, but when they announced another performance a week later, we were straight on to the District Line and in line to see the new sensation. We only just made it, claiming some of the last seats in the very back row of the stalls. If we'd have been just a few minutes later, I would never have witnessed The Boss at his best. Perhaps the best of them all.

Springsteen was one of the artists who we talked about a lot with Patrick in his tiny bedroom. He had a copy of *The Wild, the Innocent & The E Street Shuffle* and I absolutely adored the deeply romantic, fedora-wearing, horn-blaring, loose, latinate funk of it all. I'd never yet been on a plane, but that record transported us to a mythical place of steamy tenements and creaky boardwalks, guys called Little Gun and señoritas named Rosalita. It was sexy and sad and absolutely made to break the brittle hearts of yearning grammar-school boys.

I had something of a long-distance and intensely naive love affair with New York at this time and for a long time afterward. I'd heard about the clubs, and I loved the clothes, the whole Latin hustle, high-waisted and elegantly wasted look. 'Walk on the Wild Side' and 'Harlem River Drive', New York Dolls, disco and funk.

I lapped up those gritty 'NYC falling down' movies that were all the vogue: *The Taking of Pelham 123*, *Serpico*, *Dog Day Afternoon*, *The Wanderers*, *Gloria*, films which celebrated the bankrupt city in all its tawdry, glamorous decay. Above all I loved John Cassavetes' films, with their seedy downtown Romeos, back-room wise guys and hard-bitten broads, and in my head, Springsteen was the soundtrack to thrilling, racy New York nights. (I know now that New Jersey is not New York, but I'd hardly been west of Chiswick at this point.) Then came *Born to Run*.

We pored over every detail of that record, adored the technicolour sound and the monochrome cover. We knew the name of every resident of Bruce's East Street, loved Danny Federici and Vini 'Mad Dog' Lopez best because they sounded like characters from a great gangster B-movie. I learned every lyric; 'Meeting Across the River' was my absolute favourite (and still is) – a Scorsese script in three minutes, sixteen seconds – and I was even prompted to write soppy Springsteen-inspired poetry.

The first words ever published with my name beneath them appeared in our school magazine and began with me stealing a phrase from one of my favourite tunes. (I did credit B. S., honest).

So we were more than a little hyped to see the band in person. But hype was a problem. His record company had come up with a silly slogan about London finally being ready for Bruce Springsteen, and a music-press backlash began even before he'd landed. Then when the reviews came out for the first show, they were pretty damning in their faint praise and gleefully fierce in their criticism; one reviewer even derided

Bruce for being too small. How dare this little Yank bloke get too big for his boots in the land of the Rolling Stones?

So perhaps there was a slight sense of trepidation mixed with the anticipation as the house lights dimmed and the E Street band started up, hidden on a stage still shrouded in darkness, as it was for most of the night. Out of the murk the slow, dramatic piano notes, the glistening, cinematic melody of 'Thunder Road' emerged, stark and lovely, followed by a plangent, pleading harmonica. The ride had begun.

And that emotionally draining, heart-soaring, life-affirming night is still draped in a thick blanket of mythology. Perhaps the band had sharpened up, maybe Bruce had really been nervous during that first performance, certainly they had something to prove. It could have been that the audience for the second London show was less cynical, more genuine fans invested in success, fewer critics and tastemakers. Or maybe the magic just decided to descend. For magic there was.

What's undeniable is that that second Hammersmith show has gone down in legend and up and up in estimation ever since. If you want to really wind up one of the legion of Springsteen devotees, tell them you were there. Tell them about 'Pretty Flamingo'.

My overriding memory of that show is of Springsteen as a shy but intensely charismatic figure, lurking in the shadows, a baggy beanie hat pulled low over his bearded face, his voice husky and raw, those wounded ballads delivered with a bruised sensitivity, soft and fragile, yet capable of soaring as the band flew through dynamic twists and turns. Masters of emotional manipulation, they had honed their skills in countless barroom shows and could twist an audience inside out. One moment hushed and dreamy, the next full-on hoodlum boom. From grave to grandiose in a heartbeat.

Clearly the intense pleasure felt by us out in the audience was infectious, and as the show progressed, so those waves of positivity started bouncing back and forth from the crowd to the band, now all smiles and swoops, Clarence Clemons blowing waves of joy as encore followed storming encore. The house was rocking. Then came 'Pretty Flamingo'.

I believe it was the first time Springsteen had ever played this particular cover, a tribute to the British beat-boom bands he'd grown up worshipping. It began with a sotto voce spoken-word introduction, a rambling yarn about growing up on the Jersey shore, watching the girls go by with Miami Steve. A lovely lilting organ riff almost imperceptibly joins in, edging us towards a tune, but which song is this? Slide guitar enters, taking everything slow and easy, a drumbeat joins in, soul-review style, and Bruce's storytelling becomes ever more musical until the point where he talks/sings about this one girl they used to see every day – 'the one they dubbed the Pretty Flamingo'.

The house did not erupt, it just softly slipped into ecstasy. Or at least that is how I remember it. And I would rather remember it than check. There is now a recording of that gig available, but I don't particularly want to sully my memory with the reality. Maybe it wasn't really that good, maybe the recording won't really capture the mesmerising intensity of it. Maybe Bruce Springsteen would never be like that again. That last one is not a maybe.

Whatever happened to *that* Bruce Springsteen?

A true American troubadour: a gentle, battered but always hopeful soul, an outsider capable of genuine lyrical sensitivity and rich musical diversity, a nuanced, romantic evocation of one particularly poetic, multicultural American dream. Listen to Springsteen's brilliant cameo on Lou Reed's bitterly cynical 'Street Hassle' to hear the last raspy gasp of that incarnation of Bruce.

How did this arch-romantic morph from that to a pumped-up, fist-pumping, check-shirt-wearing, white-bread, blue-collar,

'Born in the USA' behemoth? That particular song may be ironic, but it is also bombastic and straight ahead in a way the earlier, gentler incarnation of Bruce could never be.

That early Springsteen carried our hopes on his slender shoulders and our dreams in his bag of songs. But he turned his back on the lost and the lonely and seemed to consciously eschew the B-movie beauty and Latino swing of the man we saw that night at Hammersmith. Instead, he became The Boss, some sort of cartoon rock'n'roll superhero with tight jeans and bulging biceps. A friend who only knew the later, fully formed leviathan said, 'I've always thought of Springsteen as similar to Meat Loaf.' How sad is that?

I sulked more than a little when that big brash Boss Bruce took over, belting out brute, Rust Belt anthems. I had no great desire to go see him again in vast stadium shows; instead I reminisced about that night in Hammersmith, boasted about being there and it grew in tragic splendour with every retelling. 'I saw Bruce when he was still beautiful.'

But I did get a pair of tickets when he came to town with *We Shall Overcome: The Seeger Sessions*, an acoustic folkie tribute to those stirring songs of struggle and solidarity. And what's more, he was once more back at the Hammersmith Odeon. I was very self-conscious about revisiting that moment and I'm sure he was too, the symbolism of his return three decades later all too obvious, and he made a nervous joke about it during the show.

It was a lovely evening; a happy, carefree Springsteen, freed from the weight of *Born to Run* and 'Born in the USA', from idiots shouting his name in that annoying, elongated way they do. Up on stage he smiled, revelling in those timeless folksy tunes and the staunch message they carry. There's a direct rectitude in that old-time protest music which is hard to replicate in these more complex, cynical times, and he seemed to relish the emotional simplicity of his night's work.

I finally got to meet Springsteen fleetingly as part of a press event for the launch of his autobiography, shook his hand, heard his speaking voice, saw into his tired eyes. For me the book was a little disappointing; none of the elliptical genius and jagged poetry of Dylan's *Chronicles* or Patti Smith's fabulous and revelatory *Just Kids*. Instead in *Born to Run* he delivered a straight-ahead, note-by-note, gig-by-gig recounting of his long, determined and clinically calculated journey from A to B and way beyond. Bruce always wanted to be big.

I realised then that he is at heart a straight goer; a good man, but a numbers man. Springsteen plays the rock'n'roll percentages, he works out what works at any given stage of his life and then delivers it on stage. As a young man he donned the cloak of the poetic romantic, which only got him so far, so he became the everyman in plaid, then he became the fire-fighter's friend and the elder statesman friend of President Obama, the blue-collar guy at the White House. America's conscience.

He's clever and knowing and pretty damn good at what he does. And that's how he seemed in person too. Small, straight, slightly world-weary, deeply serious, a down-to-earth, decent guy doing a job.

Perhaps that other Springsteen, the one I first fell in love with on that night in Hammersmith never really existed. Perhaps it was me projecting my desires, my teenage aspirations and invocations onto his music, or maybe he grew up too. I'm glad I was there when we were both young.

I sat at the Hammy Odeon listening to mesmerising American folk music again a few years later in one of the more bizarre experiences of my gig-going life. This time it was the blessed pairing of Gillian Welch and Dave Rawlings, the arch-architects of a dreamy new bluegrass music, bohemian and knowing, hip and cool yet deeply authentic. They have played on my show a few times and could not be more charming or easy-going, huddled round a single microphone making deep-blue, high-mountain soul music.

Gillian is a hugely affecting singer, precise and yet powerfully human, with a style rooted in 1940s melancholia and a voice that reaches back into coal-black, bleak country darkness, and Dave is my favourite ever guitarist.

I have never had much time for overwrought electric guitar solos – Eric Clapton is not a god, he's an arse. But Dave Rawlings wrestling with that old 1935 Epiphone of his, all angular and atonal, rhythmic and lyric, is astonishing. The solo he coaxed out that night on 'Time (The Revelator)' is still lodged deep in the corner of my cerebellum where the very best stuff is stored. But then I saw him play it even better. I'll write about that later.

Gillian and Dave even played 'This Land Is Your Land', the same stirring Woody Guthrie anthem Springsteen had sung on that stage. But as we all sat in rapt wonder, loving that seditious old battle cry, the bloke directly in front of me sang along lustily and his wife clapped in time. They were David and Samantha Cameron, at that point inhabitants of Number 10 Downing Street as he was Conservative prime minister of this land.

It seemed politically incorrect for a Tory to be singing along to a famous Commie anthem written by a Wobbly. But it also felt truly surreal and a little unsettling to be watching a gig with the prime minister, like maybe seeing Margaret Thatcher pogoing at a Subway Sect gig. I fretted a lot about the fact that I now evidently like the same music and go to the same concerts as an old Etonian, Bullingdon boy Conservative prime minister. But then there were definitely a few public-school boys in bondage at punk gigs.

There were a few other contenders for great romantic American troubadour in the mid-seventies too. Tom Waits was one; the shambling, croaking, beaten poet of the West Coast, who was very close to early Bruce territory at times (whose is the better version of 'Jersey Girl'?), before their careers dramatically diverged. Tom deserves, and will indeed receive, a chapter all his own.

Patti Smith fitted that profile too, to this day one of the most consistently creative artists and cultural agent provocateurs of this or any age. I have a little Patti Smith shrine at home with all her books and photos, some Rimbaud, and some Mapplethorpe, such is my adoration, but *Horses* aside, to me she is a better writer than a recording artist.

She's a great performer, though, a warrior spirit guide, a rock'n'roll Boudicca whose presence casts a spell over any room with her shamanic evocations and piercing, incantatory yelp. An intimate, in the round, performance of her words and songs a few years ago at the Roundhouse was a memorable occasion.

Her silver-grey mane worn with bewitching pride; her politics proudly displayed alongside her heart on her sleeve. She is a model of how to grow old disgracefully and maintain the poetry in your soul and the fire in your belly. She can still do the pony like Bony Maronie. She is still proof that the America that can produce Donald Trump can also give us a goddess like Patti Smith.

But the American poet that time forgot, the one who ranked alongside Springsteen as his equal, in my mind, and never veered off that righteous, oh so wrong path is Willy DeVille. Largely overlooked now, always underrated, he was the very embodiment of the beautiful but damned rock'n'roll front man, the essence of that 1970s seedy, sexy Manhattan. Part uptown Shark, part downtown shaman, a flamenco-tinged Phil Lynott with equally bad habits, equally long legs but even better eyelashes. He had some tunes too.

'Spanish Stroll' might well be the single best single to have emerged from the musical maelstrom of 1977 on either side of the Atlantic. And the album it came from, *Cabretta*, is pretty damn good to this day. It is a crumbling Lower East Side, cold-water walk-up Carmen. It's the seventies filtered through the fifties, and it is timeless. I loved it immediately, yet somehow I never got to see his band, Mink DeVille when they came to London that year; there was just so much great music at the time that it was easy to miss one.

But when I finally made it to Manhattan a few years later, I sought him out. It might have been 1979 or 1980, 1981 maybe; it definitely wasn't CBGB's, but it was a similarly run-down, downtown, dimly lit, graffiti-smeared New York dive. It was perfect. He was perfect.

A glistening pompadour, Cuban heels, *West Side Story* strides and a frilly fronted shirt, his pencil moustache as razor sharp as his band, with their gothic doo-wop harmonies, Drifters-style backing vocals and Velvet Underground chord sequences. 'Venus of Avenue D', 'She's a Mixed-Up, Shook-Up Girl', a mariachi-style 'Hey Joe', a 'Spanish Stroll' to beguile a Chicana beauty, a show so steeped in a seductive, narcotic glamour that I still feel a little high thinking about it.

The crowd was pure New York, high-stepping low life: glamorous and vampiric, attractive and enticing, at least in the dark. These were the bad, sad and beautiful people who sing a siren song to young boys desperate to dance with the Midnight Cowboy. But do you really want to go there? Could you end up living there? Dying there?

Willy DeVille, a character invented by Willy Borsey Jr of Stamford, Connecticut, was the real thing; a stick-thin genius, a true recidivist romantic, living out his own blood-red voodoo incantations and heavy-lidded opium dreams, with a voice like Ben E. King on Quaaludes and an attitude like Lou Reed waiting for his man on Avenue C. A huge star in France, of course, where they love that Rimbaud stuff, but a beautiful failure everywhere else, destined to live in the perpetual half-light of the rock'n'roll periphery. And I loved him.

Willy DeVille was everything Bruce Springsteen wasn't. Willy's dead and Bruce lives on.

Chapter 7

The Long Hot Summer

It was a good summer to be seventeen. Back in '76 we could revel in long, lazy days of burning, burnishing sunshine, blue skies, followed by blue skies, followed by endless, balmy nights free from any guilt or fear. No climate-change concerns or apocalyptic guilt trips, just a bottle of Ambre Solaire in your bag, lemon juice on your barnet, and endless joy at the fact that we were living through the longest, hottest, most heavenly summer on record. And what records we had to go with it: 'Breezin'' by George Benson, 'Oh, Lori' by the Alessi Brothers and 'Lowdown' by Boz Scaggs.

It was a summer of soul, big boom boxes at the local lido and white socks in the disco, cologne and cocktails all round, but all that was about to vanish as the 52 bus ferried me to two life-changing live events within a few months of each other.

This was one of those pivotal points in the history of the streets and those who parade and perform upon them, a time of seismic cultural shifts and preposterous outfits, when the old sartorial/musical order got well and truly all shook up. By the end of that endless summer, I got my legs tied together and my

record collection in a right old state. John Coltrane changed
my life and the Clash changed my trousers.

At the start of 1976 I had a part time job in Soundrax, a
rather tasty record shop in Burnt Oak run by a super-suave
soulboy called Phil, with an encyclopaedic knowledge of CTI
albums, a wardrobe supplied by Woodhouse and Take 6, and a
gorgeous girlfriend who worked at Vidal Sassoon. He was the
master, I was his wedge-head apprentice: big floppy fringe,
bowling shirt, pink peg trousers, plastic sandals sold to me by
Don Letts in Acme Attractions on the King's Road and, most
proudly, a copy of 'Always There' by Ronnie Laws on the Blue
Note label, bought on import from Contempo on Hanway
Street under my arm.

By now I had a burgeoning stack of vinyl and a trouser tribe
to call my own. Despite the Springsteen and the Feelgoods and
the fact that I went to lots of rock gigs with my school chums,
I had pinned my pastel colours to the jazz-funk mast. This was
the true working-class, multicultural London music and fashion scene. An overlooked, underground world of brilliant
teenage dressers, amazing dancers and great DJs playing ferocious tunes.

Crackers in Soho was the club to be at; gay or straight, male
or female, white or black, none of that much mattered, especially at the now legendary Friday lunchtime session. That
involved bunking off school, donning your finest finery and
watching the hottest hoofers in London town spin and shuffle,
freeze and hustle as they tried to cut and wound each other on
the tiny, terrifying dance floor. Crackers took no prisoners.

It was there in the dark Soho recesses that I first heard Lonnie
Liston Smith's epochal 'Expansions', with that chiming tri-
angle intro, the looping, circular bassline and the mesmeric
freeform keyboard run; it was at that moment, on a dance
floor, that I first heard jazz and it stopped me in my tracks.

Dexter Wansel, Freddie Hubbard, Donald Byrd, Roy Ayers,

Ronnie Foster, George Benson . . . I remember being almost physically knocked back by this music, confused and intrigued. It was complex and difficult, but always with a driving funk beat, and here were kids from Tottenham and Brixton dancing to it like teenage dervishes in Fiorucci. I didn't really understand jazz, but I knew I loved it and I wanted to hear more and to learn more.

Phil was well up on this jazz thing and I remember one day he took me to one side and said with a certain solemnity, and maybe even a slight sneer, 'Robert, if you think you like jazz take this home and give it a listen.' I was being tested. It was *Coltrane* by the John Coltrane quartet on the Impulse label, the one with the blurry blue cover and the lustrous 'Soul Eyes'. That's a lovely ballad, but it also has some truly challenging modal playing, deep and disorientating, compelling and confusing, lush and sometimes unlovely. The moment I put it on, Coltrane made my world leap and shudder. Who knew music could do that?

My love affair with jazz was really cemented by that one wonderful record. I remember my mum shouting at me to turn it down or even better, off, which was always a good sign. Of course, I turned it up. I didn't understand what John Coltrane and his three majestic spiritual accomplices were doing on that LP, but I somehow knew that I had to find out.

This was music in a different tongue, one which sounded daunting and scary, but which suggested that it held the key to great joy or sadness, maybe even wisdom, or all of those in one note. Most of the music I loved up to that point had come from the African diaspora: soul, funk, Tamla, ska and reggae, but this was music that was darker than black, full of knowledge, rich and profound, reaching back across continents and ages but also looking far forward; modern, abstract, futuristic.

I remember Phil being surprised and perhaps even impressed when I said I loved the Coltrane album, and I did and I do, still

have that copy to this day. Don't think I ever paid for it.
Though I've certainly paid my jazz dues since. I've bought
thousands of jazz records, read scores of books, been to hundreds of gigs, and the first one was in that steamy summer of
'76 in a venue in Victoria, which you can get straight to from
Burnt Oak by taking the number 52.

I boarded the bus that evening with just one other guy, one
of the slightly older, very natty black dudes from the estate,
who made me feel exalted just to be in his company. Despite
the fact that the band we were going to see was the Crusaders,
one of the premier American jazz-funk acts of the time, there
were no other takers for the tickets I procured. It was that old
club/gig divide, and most of the jazz-funk contingent from
Burnt Oak didn't really understand why we would pay £3 and
go all that way to see a band when you couldn't even dance and
weren't likely to pull.

The venue that evening – the New Victoria Theatre – was
strictly seated and very sophisticated, my first uptown, dressed-
up, West End night out. Most of the audience were older and
certainly cooler, the cream of London's swish soul crowd, a
dressed-to-the-nines, multiracial crew sashaying into the plush
theatre. I felt both a little out of place and out of my league.
This was grown up.

The Crusaders were the A-Team of fusion, blending their
impeccable jazz muso credentials with funk, soul and even
rock elements, all combined in a slick but still authentic sound.
This was way before they had a massive crossover disco hit
with 'Street Life', and they were definitely still on a jazz cru-
sade, still a band for the cognoscenti.

From the very first note, this was a different live experience. I
don't recall any sort of introduction or interaction with the audience. No attempt to whip anything up, get people going – this
was not rollicking rock'n'roll. The group walked on to polite
applause, stationed themselves by their instruments and prepared

to play. The buzz was intense but internalised, the crowd excited but hushed, still, expectant, here to listen, concentrating and waiting for something to happen. And it happened.

Joe Sample on keyboards, Wilton Felder on sax, Stix Hooper on drums, Wayne Henderson on trombone, Robert 'Pops' Popwell on bass and Larry Carlton on guitar. These were masters, seasoned music men and prime exponents of their craft. And as those first, crisp, sonorous notes emerged from each of them, and the crowd responded with a kind of exhalation of anticipation, I knew that I had a new love.

This wasn't a show. There was no front man, no visual focus and there were no songs as such – strictly instrumental. It was entertainment of another kind. The audience would often recognise a favourite number from one of their many LPs, before watching it veer off into flights of unpredictable virtuosity, shifting and morphing as it ebbed and flowed. Nothing sounded like it did on record; those were just musical springboards, sketches compared to these fully fleshed live explorations. It was music of the moment. Jazz is always aware of its past, but fully immersed in the present and creating the future as it goes along.

Nobody jumped around or put on an act; it was pared down and untheatrical, rigorous and involving. The men up on stage looked at each other rather than at us, studying every move, anticipating the changes, watching the fingers, sensing the patterns. Feeling it. These brilliant fellows, all stature and élan, were august artists painting collectively with sound. Sometimes they smiled.

Abstract, angular, textures and colours, washes and daubs, long, spun-out phrases employing repetition and repetition, mesmerising and enveloping. It was mood music, emotional, expressive yet mysterious, non-linear, unpredictable, but with a great spiralling groove and an insistent internal logic, which revealed itself slowly as each piece unfolded, grew and expanded. Each tune an odyssey.

It required a lot from the audience. You had to listen simultaneously to each individual instrument, but also to the collective whole; the ensemble as they meshed together, then separated and took solos, flew free without a safety net, drove it to the very edge, then stepped back into the tapestry of sound they were weaving together. You had to really listen, use your ears like never before, as sometimes it would be pinpoint precise; a couple of exquisite blue notes placed just so from Joe Sample's piano, or a forlorn wail of Wilton Felder's horn, while others would almost knock you back with the muscular oomph of their collective creativity.

This wasn't quite the sumptuous cacophony of Coltrane, but nor was it pop music. Rhythmically, the Crusaders held it tight and pulsing, hypnotic, funky, but they used the funk and the groove as a starting point, the bassline as a base camp for long musical explorations and extrapolations. They were making it up as they went along.

I began to understand what jazz was, what improvisation is: a mercurial act of alchemy. Taking the raw ingredients of a tune and then heating them up, cooling them down, dragging the melody out like molten metal, adding notes and tones, twisting and contorting the very atoms of the piece. The Crusaders performed this rich, sensuous magik, this ancient/modern voodoo incantation live in front of us, up there, out there. I was completely spellbound, captured and enraptured. In thrall to jazz.

Having spent so many hours of my life watching great jazz musicians improvise since, I still cannot quite explain how they do it. It is a form of conjuring and a tightrope act combined. There's telepathy, certainly, empathy is essential, years of training, mastery of the instrument, but then the ability to let go, to race away into the unknown. Trust is the essence of jazz. Freedom and trust.

1976 was also the year of the greatest QPR team ever: Phil

Parkes, Gerry Francis, Dave Thomas, Stanley Bowles et al, and I watched that wondrous side week in, week out, tearing other teams apart with their fluid, unpredictable football. The genius of a mazy Stanley Bowles dribble or a diagonal Gerry Francis through-ball, the team rotating positions, constant motion, befuddling opponents. Total football they called it. They played jazz.

It strikes me now that going to see jazz music is less like going to a choreographed concert, where what happens is pre-ordained, and much more like watching sport, where the end is always unknown. It is spontaneous and improvised, simultaneously a group endeavour, a team game, but also highly individualistic. The band act like a football team, creating constantly shifting shapes; the back line is the defence, a platform for attack, a solid launchpad for the soloist to go off on a mazy run down the musical wing.

Live sport, particularly football, which does not have set plays or patterns, is in constant flux, an ever-changing kaleidoscope, unpredictable and full of tension. And so is jazz. When a soloist begins to improvise, you never know how it will be resolved, and nor do they, which means you are on the edge of your seat. It is visceral and vital – you can hear them thinking, human creativity in real time, before your very ears.

I'm not saying I thought any of this, that night watching the Crusaders as a seventeen-year-old jazz ingénue. But I do remember realising that what I had witnessed was a level beyond in virtuosity and creativity, that there was beauty to behold in this stuff. But there was also something very special in the relationship between performers and audience. That despite the lack of obvious interaction there was a real connection, a commitment, and a communion between the two, which was unique. Spiritual, maybe.

I remember thinking that I was going to study this music, learn everything I could. Once you get pulled into the miasma of this most intriguing art form, you have to explore, to examine, both forwards and backwards, finding the links, understanding the lineage; Parker to Monk to Miles, to Coltrane to Coleman to Albert Ayler. No one ever went further than sweet, troubled Albert Ayler floating in the river.

You join the dots and fill in the gaps between bebop and hard bop, cool to soul, to funk, to modal, to spiritual, to free. You buy your seventeenth Lee Morgan LP, and you learn the stories; all of them sad, all of them beautiful. It's been a lifetime of study, a master's in jazzology and a Ph.D. in those suave, tough, too often tragic pioneers. Jazz is the greatest contribution of the collective genius of the African American experience. And it has to be seen live.

To this day, jazz is also what I listen to at home, usually the further out the better. My wife calls it 'nervous breakdown music' and I understand why. If you haven't learned the language, the grammar and syntax of jazz, you don't get the meaning, can't hear the musicality, so it is largely a solitary pleasure, but it is perhaps my greatest pleasure. And all that started in that sweltering summer of 1976, listening to Lonnie Liston Smith on a dance floor, John Coltrane in a council house and watching the Crusaders after a ride on the 52 bus.

The fabulous 52, the transport of my youth, also takes you to Ladbroke Grove. I have known that journey all my life; it was our route to the ancestors every Saturday. The Elms's were Westies, driven out when the Westway was driven through those tangled old streets, but pulled back by family and footie, so every week we made the cross-town schlep to W10 and W12 by bus. But that day in August 1976 I was heading west for a very different reason. This was going to be my first taste of Carnival.

It may well be hindsight, but I would say now that something was in the air, that you could feel it coming like a distant tempest on the horizon. That long hot summer had boiled

away for week after sweltering week and there was an under-
current bubbling beneath the surface. I'd started to spot some
oddly attired characters at the clubs; Bowie freaks with dyed
gunmetal-blue or postbox-red hair and PVC pegs. There were
girls and boys in Thin White Duke suits and mascara, pierced
and pouting, shimmying away artfully to 'Golden Years' at
Crackers or the Global Village. All the tribes were out posing
on the street, provoking and pushing boundaries with their
dress, especially down the King's Road, which was the main
parade ground and catwalk.

I vividly remember being on the Tube and a group of kids
got on, half a dozen of them, perhaps a year or two older than
myself, and they looked like nothing on this earth. They looked
amazing. Girls with peephole bras and suspenders, boys in bin
bags and safety pins, all of them with extraordinary hair and
make-up and a fabulous fuck-you attitude, as the entire carriage
stared open-mouthed at these exotic, provocative creatures,
heading God knows where. I just wanted to know what tribe
they were. Wanted to be with them.

I'm sure now that they were the Bromley contingent, the
vanguard of the movement of the moment, which was about
to blow everything else out of the water. I'm not sure anybody
had coined the term 'punk' at this stage, and it hadn't yet solidi-
fied around a raucous style of anarchic rock music. This was a
fashion scene, to be seen in the most cutting-edge funk clubs
and boutiques, a sartorial revolution. But it was also a change
in the weather: things were starting to get stormy.

And my first experience of the maelstrom to come was
when we alighted from the 52 bus and headed for the sound
systems under the Westway in August 1976. I was with a couple
of mates from Orange Hill, nice grammar-school boys, and
none of us had any real idea what we were going to Carnival
for, except perhaps to try and smoke dope, eat some jerk
and dance clumsily to some reggae. We hadn't expected to be

confronted by an armed phalanx of police in full riot gear pre-
venting us from going anywhere. Under heavy manners.

This was the SPG, the Special Patrol Group, the hated unit
of the Met who later became notorious as the shock troops of
Thatcher's torrid, torn Britain. And here they were in 1976, in
a line across the Grove with batons drawn, barring our way. We
could hear music blasting away in the near distance, and in my
mind it was Junior Murvin's sweet and deadly 'Police and
Thieves'. These police officers looked at us as if we were dirt.
When we tried to get past them, one said directly to me: 'Why
do you want to go in there with all the fucking n*****s?'

Chant down Babylon.

We did get into Carnival because I lied and said we were
going to my nan's house and gave an address, which was within
the exclusion zone. I don't know if they believed me, don't
suppose they cared; they were waiting for the action to begin.
But I think I knew even then that the casual, callous racism of
that copper was part of a major faultline appearing. You'd
better decide which side you're on.

Carnival back then was still very much a local affair, and
very much a Caribbean one. This was pre-gentrification and
Notting Hill was still a front line. Wandering those streets,
watching the parade, I was nervous, even though I knew the
terrain, as the tension was palpable. We were on the edge of an
eruption, but the soundtrack was great.

I'd grown up with the sparkling pop reggae of Trojan
Records, but once ensconced in the jam around the giant bass
bins of a sound system, tucked under the monstrous motor-
way, yards from the house my dad was born in, it was apparent
that this was different gravy. I and I, dreader than dread.
Although no band played, this was live performance of the
highest order.

I'd never been to a reggae club – the soul and reggae scenes
were very different and separate back then; the reggae crowd

was predominantly black and pretty hardcore. 'Soulboy' was a term of abuse used by Jamaican reggae heads for what they saw as the 'effete' black kids whose rank apostasy made them defect to smooth American soul music. Here beneath the Westway, surrounded by riot police, the basslines pumping straight to your solar plexus, was strictly roots.

The selector and his crew were the centre of the action, theatrically flipping sides, pulsing the bass, driving the rhythm, picking up the dance, but the crowd skanking and hollering, jumping up and jamming down were the fulcrum of the entertainment. Then a toaster stepped forward to take the mike. Talking triple time with trickery and rhyme, goading and teasing, chatting slack and chanting righteous, rocking the streets of my ancestral homeland over those elemental roots-rock rhythms. This was London town, my town in a rub-a-dub style.

Amid the bobbing tams and the trilbys, the Rastas and the rude boys, and the many ordinary black families going about their culture, there was a scattering of those spiky, punky people. Leather biker jackets and fetish wear, brothel creepers and drainpipes, eyeliner and bin liners welcome here. They had chosen to be here on the rebel side of the line. They were there for the clash to come.

The energy that day was pulsing, but it grew dark and as the skies grew dimmer, so those riot police moved in and it all kicked off. Sticksmen were certainly active, dipping in amongst the crowds, but my impression was that the forces of the old order had come that day to prove a point to the defiant ones who dared to claim these streets as their own. Heavy-duty discipline.

And it was a spectacle and it was furious, biblical, burning and looting, and it was terrible and bloody terrifying. Exciting too, missiles raining down and fights going off in all directions. And the Rastamen, they held their ground, and the policemen, they swung their batons. Dirty Babylon. And the Clash, they took their photos. Don Letts from Acme Attractions in the war zone of the Grove on the back cover of their first LP. The punky reggae party had started.

I scarpered, scared and thrilled, but also determined to be part of whatever this was. I went and bought a Marlon Brando-style *Wild One* biker jacket from Lewis Leathers, a copy of 'Police and Thieves' from Rough Trade and waited for the weather to break.

Chapter 8

Oh Bondage! Up Yours!

Punk was a pyrotechnic display which lit up London town. It was a moment as much as a movement, a crackling, all-consuming conflagration which burned bright and fierce, lighting the way for a generation of young musicians, artists, writers and designers, and propelling spectacular stars into the firmament. But it also laid waste to all around it in a fury of scorched earth, year-zero zealotry. Then it was done, over, a brief but brilliant immolation, though its embers smoulder still. Punk was a great gig.

What was the first punk performance I ever saw? There was a band called Bazooka Joe, featuring a young Stuart Goddard (Adam Ant). They were art-school, 1950s revival r'n'r thrash merchants, who attracted a certain cool North London crowd. The gang who became Madness were Bazooka Joe fans and the Sex Pistols supported them on their first-ever outing. After a show at Hampstead Town Hall in 1975, we all got chased up the hill by irate Teddy boys for the very first (and certainly not the last) time. But Bazooka Joe were harbingers, at most.

I'm discounting Eddie and the Hot Rods, fantastically frantic as they were, for basically being old-time, oil-slick rhythm and blues on speed. I wouldn't even dare include the Feelgoods for fear of Brilleaux's ghost. The Hammersmith Gorillas had great facial hair but not much else. I saw the Stranglers early on, but never really got on with their moody baroque and roll and their phalanx of Finchley boys providing muscle at the side of the stage. I saw the Vibrators, who went to my school, but they were old rubbish with their flares taken in, more hack-neyed than acned.

There was a memorably blistering gig by the Tom Robin-son Band at the Marquee, one of so many jam-packed, instant-weight-loss evenings at that great old Wardour Street dive. But this was the only one where the entire room sang 'Sing if You're Glad to be Gay' at the tops of their voices. It's only really in retrospect that I realise how genuinely liberating that was. This was only ten years after homosexual sex was partially legalised, and 'queer' and 'poof' were still common-place insults, 'gay bashing' an all-too-common occurrence. And for me, a straight council-estate kid, more used to shout-ing obscenities on the football terraces, to be hollering about the joys of same-sex love with my arm around my mate in a room full of sweaty blokes, was a big threshold to cross. It was powerful, it was important, but it wasn't punk.

I was told to go and see the Sex Pistols by Steve Marshall, who I'd been to infant school with. He had shaved eyebrows, was wearing a dress and Dr Martens, and said something along the lines of 'they're terrible, but they're brilliant'. At that point I was still primarily a jazz-funk fellow, and the idea of a stage full of blokes who couldn't play their instruments was a stage too far, so I missed out on one of the seminal events, and it was over a year before I finally saw the Pistols in the suppurating flesh.

Those who did go to early Pistols gigs talk of a seismic shudder going through the room, as everybody realised the world was about to change. They played to the hippest crowd in town, and there was a shocked quietude in the room, not the wildly pogoing abandon of later gigs, as people appraised what this meant for them personally. You had to decide whether or not to climb on board the train.

Truth be told, I was something of a reluctant convert. There was a kind of phony punk war period, when I looked the part: biker jacket, winkle-pickers, drainpipes, mohair jumper from Acme, records by Patti Smith and Patti Palladin, but hadn't really crossed the line, and could still be found at funk clubs. But then so could so many of the 1976 scene makers.

The audience for those early punk gigs was tiny, a coterie of a couple of hundred kids at most, many of whom went on to form bands. Some of the early punks, mainly the male musos, were committed rockers who adored the MC5 and the Stooges, but many more were Bowie and Roxy fashionistas and funka-teers, art students and shop assistants, hairdressers just waiting for the next wave. When it became a tsunami, we all had to hide our Marvin Gaye albums.

I can tell you (courtesy of the internet) precisely when I went to my first punk club: 17 January 1977, the Damned at the Roxy (I presume named after Bryan's band), which a few months before had been Chaguaramas, a gay dance club in deserted Covent Garden. Later on, at the Vortex in Soho I was pogoing away on precisely the self-same sticky dance floor that had been Crackers, the spiritual home of the London funk scene. Punk was culturally squatting in the remains of the past.

Punk is always seen as the great fracture, yet it was as much about continuity as change. Most of the early punks had been faces in other scenes, whether it was Bowie, rock or funk; it was the coming together of those two hitherto separate worlds of club and gig, DJs and bands. And of course the DJ at the Roxy, Don Letts, was more famous than many of the bands. Many of the people in the spiky vanguard, the early safety-pin adopters, had rarely been to see live music before, but once unleashed, punk had this ineluctable pull.

Standing in line outside the Roxy, for the first time as a seventeen-year-old, was one of those moments which has never left me. You had to look right; punk was every bit as sartorially rigorous as the most elitist jazz-funk crowd, and once inside there was a super-cool DJ playing tough import tunes, and a series of impossibly trendy cliques were posing and preening and waiting to pogo agogo. It was like the Scene or the Flamingo had been a decade before. Suddenly we were in the swinging seventies.

Unlike at dowdy rock gigs – where the hippies sat on the floor and a certain stoned, 'entertain me' ennui was the default cool setting – there was a searing sulphate edge in the air, an intense, almost insane energy. The crowd were as exciting and entertaining as the performers – a performance all to themselves. It was aggressive but not threatening, exclusive but not excluding. 'You can do it' was the prime message of punk. When you arrived at the Roxy, you knew you had arrived.

The Damned were very good that night in a hammy Hammer Horror gothic style. 'New Rose' is a splendid record, and they could really play. But born-again Screaming Lord Sutch acolytes were never going to be my thing. There was a large dollop of music-hall theatricality about some punk bands; Johnny Rotten, with a villain's sneer and a knotted hankie on his head, was as much Max Wall as he was Iggy Pop.

I don't think punk was ever really, and certainly not primarily, about the music. It was an attitude and an aptitude, a desire to shake things up and shape what comes next. What was brilliant that night, so fucking unbelievably brilliant that I became a complete convert, an instant red guard of the cultural revolution, was the feeling of being at the epicentre of a righteous whirlwind.

The seventies is either portrayed as a grim and grotty era of strikes and power cuts or else as space hoppers and Choppers and glam-disco excess. And of course neither of those clichés are particularly accurate. Dreary post-war Britain was all around us, but those long hot summers were big fun if you were young. Money was never really an issue because nobody had any, the sexual liberation of the sixties had finally reached the masses, the still-decaying, bombsite city was a wonderful playground, and the prying gaze and constant pressure of the internet was way in the future. We were free.

But the backdrop to this anarchic spirit was a malignant torpor shrouding the land, a severe post-sixties hangover. Random and tribal violence were unshockingly commonplace – you'd see some kind of punch-up at almost every event and almost every night was alright for fighting. Many was the time I was attacked for wearing the wrong colour scarf or trousers, and I got battered for the crime of having a silly haircut. Being young was perilous, yet growing up did not look like a great option.

The old, stale, stultifying, still-fighting-the-war culture of little England was all-pervasive. Backward-looking, class-ridden, corporate, insular, hierarchical, censorious, racist, homophobic. Pubs closed early, TV started late and not much happened in between. And punk was about to challenge and maybe even change all that. It was the future, as opposed to 'no future'; it was the searing light revealing just how dark it was out there. And I wanted to be part of that.

After that first night at the Roxy, on the otherwise empty platform at Covent Garden, I met some guys from West London who'd also been at the gig, and we struck up a bond because they were wearing bondage. It was a badge of honour and an instant community. They are still friends to this day.

All youth culture is based on the idea of being an outsider but being inside your tribe, simultaneously standing out and fitting in. And moving through the streets of dreary, run-down,

randomly violent London town dressed like that took some
considerable chutzpah. There were no half measures. I'd definitely decided what side I was on. And along with a small group
of mates from school, we set about going to as many punk gigs
as possible. Over the next year or so we saw: the Subway Sect
(who I loved), Eater, Slaughter & the Dogs, The Damned, 999,
Siouxsie and the Banshees, Generation X, the Sex Pistols,
Chelsea, the Boomtown Rats, the Buzzcocks, the Only Ones,
the Rezillos, Adam and the Ants, the Jam, the Cortinas, X-Ray
Spex, the Stranglers, the Boys, the Slits, ATV, Sham 69, the
Lurkers, Penetration, the Adverts, Elvis Costello and the
Attractions, Ian Dury and the Blockheads, Wreckless Eric . . .
And that was just the British bands. Add in Patti Smith, Cherry
Vanilla, Blondie, Television, Talking Heads, Richard Hell and
the Voidoids (who I loved), the Ramones, the Saints, Johnny
Thunders and the Heartbreakers, Wayne County, Suicide,
Pere Ubu.

And we saw many of those multiple times. Oh, and of
course the Clash. We'll come to the Clash in a moment.

I don't really understand now how we could afford any of this.
We were still schoolkids in early 1977, then I was a student at the
LSE, living off a grant at my mum's council house and going out
to see bands three or four times a week all across town. Nights at
the Nashville, the Roxy, the Hope & Anchor, the Moonlight, the
Vortex, the Music Machine, the Marquee, the 100 Club.

It was cheap; getting into a gig cost about the same as getting there on public transport, except, like almost everybody,
we bunked the fares on public transport. Maybe we had one
drink, probably not, sometimes we shared our little packet of
speedy blue pills. The rush was being there, and we were everywhere. Including Harlesden.

There are certain events in most lives where you can look
back and say things might be different if I had not have been
there. One of those was the Coliseum, a crumbling old fleapit

picture house in Harlesden. It was the Clash's first performance of 1977 and my first chance to see the band everybody was talking about, writing about, arguing about.

Like all great epochs of British pop culture, there was a schism. In the sixties you'd been for the Beatles or the Stones, in the eighties Spandau or Duran, the nineties Blur or Oasis. In 1977 you picked the Pistols or the Clash. And without having seen either, I had opted for the latter. It was the striking Jack the Dripper visuals, the earnest Notting Hill Carnival politics, the Westway romanticising, the 'London's Burning' ferocity, the 'Police and Thieves' bassline. The Clash came on like the Opus Dei of punk. By comparison, the Sex Pistols' vaudeville nihilism seemed slightly cartoonish. I was always more Television than Ramones.

And arriving at this decaying old picture palace, which usually showed kung fu and porn films, in a run-down, distinctly ungentrified part of Irish/West Indian North-West London – publicised via xeroxed flyers and attended by the upper echelons of the punk fraternity – was the first time I felt like an insider. In with the in crowd in my Seditionaries strides.

Those lads we'd met on Covent Garden station were there, as were a Welsh contingent I'd palled up with on the King's Road, then we saw the guys from the Subway Sect, who we'd already seen play live a couple of times, and they recognised us and said hello. A girl called Little Debbie, one of the chosen ones who worked at Malcolm and Vivienne's shop, nodded to me. I was now seventeen going on immortal.

Of all the gigs in all the world and all that. If I want to try and summon up what it felt like to be a teenager in all my excitable, invincible, insufferable arrogance and ignorance, I close my eyes and travel back to that night in Harlesden amid the fraying velour and the baying crowd crammed together, waiting for the Clash to come on stage.

We'd already had our senses assaulted. First by the Slits in their first-ever gig. They were monumentally terrible, tuneless, shameless, chaotic beyond comprehension and yet absolutely compelling. These were riot girls way before their time: sexy and feral, completely unhinged, totally unconstrained and almost unlistenable. I would never see the fairer sex the same way again. After all the macho bullshit of so much swaggering crotch rock, the Slits were a provocation and an education that lasted just under twenty minutes but stayed with me for a lifetime. Go girls, go.

Then came the Subway Sect. Graham Smith, my arty mate from school, who was with me that night, had silk-screened some T-shirts with the legend 'Everyone is a Prostitute', the opening line of a Subway Sect song, and we proudly wore them as we made our way to the front of the stage to see the band we'd already adopted as our own.

Their schtick was a kind of monotone, droning anti-rock'n'roll, closest perhaps to the art rock of the CBGB's bands like the Talking Heads, but without their slick chops. Led by the laconic but potent Vic Godard, they were downbeat and clever and kind of cool in a distant, detached fashion, brilliantly dressed like a thrift shop, West London version of the Nouvelle Vague. Some of the more splenetic punks disliked them, so we loved them dearly. And to me they remain one of the best, least valued bands of that era.

Next up were the Buzzcocks, who were already veterans of the scene, the first of the great Manchester bands. Their debut record *Spiral Scratch*, with the anthemic 'Boredom', vied with 'Anarchy in the UK' to be the best of the early UK punk rock releases. But although their bouncy hundred-smiles-an-hour set went down well, after the aural assault and artful anarchy of the first two acts it was too tuneful, too playful, and too close to pop music for my liking. I was already a deeply devout punk absolutist. Besides, the sulphate had kicked in and I was anxiously waiting for the Clash to come.

It's that freeze-frame moment again. The four of them up on stage, but inches away, a three-pronged attack, each one looking just so, looking just and righteous, revved up and ready to go to war. The audience high on anticipation, pumped and primed, the air so thick you could choke on it. Then a shout from Strummer, a split second before the barrage is unleashed, and instantly that little part of London is indeed burning, the Coliseum is on fire.

It's hard to avoid militaristic metaphors with the Clash. They were a tight fighting unit. The look: short hair, fatigues, boots, the sound, the snare-drum rolls and double-time beats, the chants and machine-gun runs, Jones marching on the spot, Simonon swinging his bass like a rifle butt, Strummer punching the air, rallying the troops. It's not parade-ground polish and precision, but swift, sharp guerrilla tactics. They were a ragged rebel battalion, an all-conquering salvation army come to save us from all the crap. Or so it seemed when I was seventeen.

From that first explosive second onwards this was shellshocking, gut-wrenching, perpetual motion, pin-you-up-against-the-wall punk rock. It was a blur then, it is a distant blur now, like nothing I'd seen or heard or felt before or since. Bodies were being launched around the room like shrapnel, ricocheting off each other. It was mad and merry, but serious like nothing I'd ever witnessed before. It felt for that night like our very lives depended on this. There was charisma from the stage, chaos from the crowd, energy and exaltation from all quarters.

Yet it wasn't just an adrenalin-rush attack. With those loping basslines and chopping guitar chords and Joe's pleading, plangent vocals, hoarse and raw, cajoling and commanding, this was a kind of roots music, soul music, maybe, with intense intent. Strummer had a messianic quality, a veracity and profundity, which could be felt even when the lyrics were inaudible. There was something of the preacher or la Pasionaria; a 'they shall not pass' fervour from deep down in the gutter and high upon the mountain top.

Seeing that band on that blistering Harlesden night was as close as I ever got to a revelation. The Clash became my new creed, going to see them our new calling. The White Riot tour was about to begin.

I have followed Queens Park Rangers around the country and even very occasionally the continent, since about the age of thirteen or fourteen. Any football fan who goes to away games will tell you that is where the true craic lies. Rendezvous early at Euston or St Pancras, beer bottles clanking in a carrier bag, hope still abiding in your heart; whatever the result, an adventure awaits. Arriving in a distant town with your little crew, scouting the lie of the land before plotting up with the rest of your team's travelling fans in a pub, crowded, rowdy and raucous, then heading en masse to the ground singing your rousing songs.

There's an intensity and a camaraderie, a peacocks-on-parade, look-at-us bravado, which is unreconstructed, unruly and occasionally unedifying but always fantastic fun. The fact that it is only the hardcore fans who travel is part of the thrill, a backs-to-the-wall, us-against-them, all-in-this-together brotherhood of true believers. Or like-minded fools.

To this day, I love away games like a small kid, get excited the night before. And following the Clash around southern England on the White Riot Tour that summer of 1977 was like a series of great away games where we always won. Kicking off in Guildford was good, but I seem to remember we had grief getting home and some kind of milk train was involved. We hitch hiked up the M1 to St Albans, getting a lift almost all the way from a pair of female followers of the Bahá'í religion, who spent the entire time trying to convert us, but we'd already found our faith. Brighton was a brilliant punk beano by the seaside, but the most remarkable one was a performance on the pier at Hastings.

One of the last shows on the tour; we had by this stage formed a significant group of London fans who would all meet up to travel together to the gig. Also, by this point in time, there had been something of a sartorial adjustment and the London boys, especially that crew from the West, had got rid of the now-clichéd punk accoutrements and instead adopted some old-time ton-up rocking gear. Drape coats, drooping, oily quiffs, biker jackets and caps, motorbike boots, creepers, old Levi's with chains. Paul Simonon was, as ever, our style influencer, and we looked just dandy as we poured out of Hastings station mob-handed, mid-afternoon.

This was the time when punks versus Teddy boys, and their rather theatrical tear-ups up and down the King's Road, was a big tabloid story and the prime moral panic of the day. There was a small group of fresh-faced, local, spiky-haired, still safety-pinned punks standing staring at us as we made our way up the road, which provoked a little gently mocking jollity from the hard-bitten London boys and girls. Then suddenly, sirens blaring, the rozzers arrived in about half a dozen cars and vans, leaping out like a cheap seaside episode of *The Sweeney* and pinning the thirty or so Londoners up against a wall.

The local coppers had been reliably informed that we were a hardened gang of cockney Teddy boys and rockers who had travelled down from the Big Smoke with the intention of confronting the Hastings punks, storming the pier and quite possibly smashing up the Clash gig. We were marched off to the local cop shop giggling hysterically while trying to persuade these yokel Old Bill that, despite appearances, we were really punks and Clash fans, honest guv.

Somehow, after a while we managed to convince the constables that we were not Teddy boys after all. I seem to remember it involved singing Clash songs at the tops of our voices. Rather reluctantly, they eventually let us go but insisted that we must head straight to the theatre and that we should have a full police escort all the way. We arrived at the pier, flanked by the boys in blue, to a huge round of applause from the crowd waiting outside the gig.

The Clash were on top form, but all I really recall was berating some of those seaside safety-pin kids for spitting and throwing cans at the support act; Richard Hell and the Voidoids. I adored their angular, jagged NY sound, with Bob Quine's jazzy, atonal guitar. It was art rock. I also knew Richard Hell was perhaps the man most responsible for the whole *Blank Generation* aesthetic and got enraged by the locals' learned-by-rote punky shenanigans. Respect is always due.

The other gig we went to on that tour was the crescendo in the middle, the home game where it all kicked off and the Clash came of age.

The Rainbow in Finsbury Park is probably my favourite ever venue. Smack bang in a suitably grotty part of town, with the long-gone George Robey, a proper rough-house pub opposite, it was the perfect size for a big gig. Grand, with that splendid art deco foyer for hanging out and people-watching, but with a nicely faded touch of old-time opulence. Or at least it was until it tragically became a born-again, happy-clappy Brazilian evangelical church, which has always struck me as sacrilege. Every time I go past, I get flashbacks to the night of the big tear-up, the high point of the whole punk caper.

It was only a couple of months after that Harlesden show, but in that time the Clash's debut album had been released to justifiably great acclaim, and the clamour to see them meant that they could easily fill the Rainbow. Also, in that time I had gone from ingénue to in-crowd, we were on first-name terms with Joe, Paul and Mick (though I don't suppose they knew my name) and I remember looking down my nose rather at all the new Johnny-come-lately Clash kids in town. It's amazing how quickly you can become a complete twat.

I also frowned upon the Jam, who opened the show. We'd seen them before at the Nashville, I think, and I was less than impressed by their skinny Bri-Nylon mod suits, their two-bob bowling shoes and their reheated maximum r'n'b. They weren't proper punk, and as I was now a teenage Torquemada, it took me a long time to forgive their heresy. But the first record I ever played on my radio show in 1994 was 'In the City', and the best gig I have been to this century was Weller with strings at the Royal Festival Hall.

The Clash at the Rainbow was recently voted the best-ever London gig of any century by *Time Out* and it's hard to argue against that. Though for me personally it's the sheer shock and roar of that first Harlesden show which most sticks in my memory. As Sade once sang, 'It's never as good as the first time.' But there's no denying that the Rainbow show was pretty explosive.

It's been dubbed 'the riot at the Rainbow', but in fact it was just a collective correction, moving the furniture a little, like my family did when we had a shindig in the house. Whoever decided to keep the stalls seats in place for this gig made a big mistake, so, egged on by Strummer, the crowd decided, quite calmly, actually, to dismantle them. They were passing chair parts overhead until a huge pile of rubble lined the side of the auditorium and where once had been stalls was now a pogo pit. Rip it up and let's dance.

Technically the band were way beyond where they had been just a few weeks before; more polished, more precise, bigger, grander, but just as powerful, the complete punk package and the absolute epitome of primal, prime-time rebel rock'n'roll. It felt genuinely like some sort of revolution was underway; we were storming the barricades of the old staid order and the Clash provided the battle hymns.

Of course, in retrospect this sounds a bit silly, it's only rock'n'roll and all that. Ripping up the seats at the Rainbow was

little more seditious than my rocking uncles tearing up the Shepherd's Bush Odeon two decades earlier to Bill Haley's 'Rock
Around the Clock'. But to this day, I genuinely believe there was
a profound revolution taking place, if only in our heads.

I was enlightened, enraged, invigorated and irrevocably
changed by punk, and just possibly the entire nation was
changed by punk. That conformist, corporate, classist, censorious England was purged by the fire. A radical, anarchic,
autonomous idea emerged, which was 'you can do it'. I think
of it as the three-chord trick.

The core message of punk, famously emblazoned on the
cover of *Sniffin' Glue* was 'Learn three chords and you can start
a band'. But equally, despite being an oik from a council estate,
or a student in a squat, you can be a filmmaker, a graphic
designer or a music promoter; you can start a magazine, a
clothes shop, a nightclub, a record label . . . There was a creative and even entrepreneurial zeal, which pre-dated Thatcher
and changed the face of this country. By singing 'No Future',
the Pistols proved you could create one.

But whereas the grim Grantham Reaper was a neo-con,
conning us into believing that individual success, defined by
how much money could be made – the Darwinian dog fight of
capitalism – was what mattered, punk was communal, coopera-
tive, tribal, cultural, its adherents driven by the desire to do
something, make something together, not just to make money.
Where Thatcher was retrogressive, culturally conservative,
punk challenged the homophobic, racist, sexist shit that we
had grown up thinking was normal, and for many of us
changed it for ever.

I learned so much in the year of punk; it was a crash course
and a trial by fire, and I decided there and then that my own
future would somehow revolve around this stuff I loved. I had
seen a light shining on a path.

I also saw the Clash again a few times, but the thrill had

diminished after that relatively ropey second album. I remember one gig at the Music Machine in Camden, and another at Hammersmith Palais, where my mum and dad had first met. I was in Vicky Park for the Rock Against Racism event, but as I've said, I can't remember much of that. As punk rock became more commercialised, more clichéd – too many nights watching third-rate ranters in smelly pubs, too many fights with too many skinhead dickheads shouting 'Oi!' and cartoon Mohicans begging from tourists on the King's Road – my always-short attention span turned elsewhere. I thought my Clash fan days were done.

But four years later I was in New York. I was now the supremely arrogant boy reporter and international hosiery correspondent for *The Face* magazine. I bumped into Mick Jones at a downtown club, and he invited us – myself and Chris Sullivan, one of that Welsh vanguard contingent from the King's Road in 1976 – to come and see the band play at a glitzy uptown discotheque and casino called Bond's. I didn't expect much; I thought of the Clash as a spent force.

Blasé I may have been; my musical thing by this stage was No Wave, not new wave: James White and ESG, Kid Creole and Liquid Liquid. I was also undoubtedly wasted. New York in 1981 was awash with chemicals and much of it was a blur. And yet, despite all that, despite the doubts and the drugs, the moment the band began – 'London Calling' replacing 'London's Burning' as the storming set opener – the roof was lifted off that glittering room and joy was manifest.

I was pinned back and taken right back by the sheer force generated by that now-formidable foursome from my old manor. But it was so much more than just raw power: they had become a glorious, multi-dimensional, multicultural marvel. Undoubtedly the greatest rock'n'roll band in the world at that moment in time. Just maybe the greatest of all time. It's amazing what can happen when you're not watching.

Funky rhythms, broken hip-hop beats, booming reggae basslines, Spanish lyrics, soulful r'n'b harmonies, even the hint of Levantine spice. The Clash were rocking the casbah and storming Manhattan. It was the Westway calling to the world, the Golborne Road conquering Gotham City. And New York went wild. For seventeen nights the Clash filled Bond's, their fans stopped the traffic, desperate to get the hottest ticket for the coolest show, shaking the Big Apple to its core. I was so proud of my boys.

And I am immensely proud to say that I got to know them all a little over the years. Mick – always a true son of the Grove – I see regularly at football. He sits behind me in the South Africa Road stand at QPR, visibly fretting. (Glen Matlock from the Pistols is also just a few rows away; we are *the* punk club.) Mick even turns up at away games, where I usually bump into him in a crowded urinal at half time. He's a quiet man but a solid one; never forgotten his roots.

Paul Simonon is every inch the cool man about town, still the best-looking, best-dressed bloke in any room. He's also a fellow Hispanophile and I've spent time with him in Spain talking bulls and bollocks, bought his paintings, admired his hats. He has a winning gap-toothed smile and an easy, bohemian charm.

Joe was different. I met him many times socially, had close mutual friends, but would never say I really got to know him, perhaps because I was always a little in awe, always still the tongue-tied fan at the front. But also, Joe had this aura about him which I found difficult to penetrate; that famous bullshit detector sometimes made him guarded, but also made me – a prime bullshitter – nervous. But whenever I did meet Strummer, I was aware of just how important he was in so many lives, including my own. Then one morning in 2002, just before heading off to present my daily radio show, I got a call from my producer and he just said, 'Joe's dead.'

That day was one of the most extraordinary and moving ever, rivalled only by the day David Bowie died, in an outpouring of love and loss, grief and gratitude. I cried like a baby and so did my city, his city. We loved that man, and it became apparent that Joe Strummer, the angry, folky squatter, the gentle, poetic minstrel, the Che Guevara of punk, and the great band he led, had shaped the opinions and the feelings, enlivened the lives of so many of my contemporaries, to a degree that we did not realise until suddenly he was gone. A part of so many of us died that day. It was London mourning.

Chapter 9

Other Punk Stories

I finally got to see the Sex Pistols at their last ever London appearance. It was just before Christmas 1977, at Brunel University, way out west in Uxbridge, and I resorted to hitch-hiking again, getting a lift from a guy in a jalopy all the way up the Uxbridge Road from Shepherd's Bush roundabout. It turned out he too was heading to the show because he was a photographer for *Sounds*, one of the big three music papers of the time.

I was an avid devourer of all the music press, a huge fan of the Kents, Parsons and Burchills, Giovanni Dadomos and Vivien Goldmans, but still thought of them as a caste apart. I remember telling my mum I wanted to be a writer, and she replied, 'Oh Robert, they have people who do that,' and the implication was that those people didn't come from the Watling Estate. But here was a scruffy bloke in a beat-up car, not that much older than myself, a Brentford fan, if I recall correctly, who although a snapper rather than a scribe, was a regular contributor to one of the big inkies. That got me thinking. It was the three-chord trick.

I remember grilling him about what being a freelance

contributor entailed as we sat in traffic somewhere near North-olt, and the germ of an idea was planted – I can do that. It was a proper schlep and quite why the most famous/notorious band in the land were playing at a student hall in the back of beyond, I'm not sure, but when we got there, I met up with a large group of mates who had gathered from all corners of town, of which approximately half of us had tickets. Anarchy ensued, which I guess is exactly what Malcolm McLaren wanted, as gates were stormed, punches thrown, glass doors smashed, and tabloid headlines created.

The room was heaving and seething, a merciless squash and a squeeze from a crowd with a berserk desire to see this thing before it combusted and vanished. It was the most hysterical atmosphere before a gig I have ever known; we knew this was one you'd be telling the grandkids about. Somehow I think we also knew that this could well be our last chance to see the great rock'n'roll chimera.

With the band playing in front of an old white sheet with 'The Sex Pistols' clumsily scrawled across it in spray paint, in case we didn't know who we'd come to see, the gig was both intensely exciting but also bizarrely down-at-heel and do-it-yourself. Compared to the Clash at the Rainbow, which had a grand, triumphal feel, this was still a grubby little local affair, with an almost comically British, *Carry on Punking* atmosphere about the whole thing: part manufactured Mary Whitehouse outrage, part situationist spectacle, part music-hall routine.

Cook and Jones all geezerish Shepherd's Bush street-urchin swagger and thumping power. Sid Vicious, lithe and studiously surly, stripped to the waist to show his scars like a punk Coriolanus, and of course Lydon, a snarling provocateur with a knotted hankie on his head, snot hanging from his hooter – an Archway Road Richard III – hunched over the microphone and prowling about sneeringly while the barrage behind him poured forth. Nobody could do disdain like Johnny Rotten. Malcolm stood on the side of the stage like Fagin's heir.

Magnificent, ridiculous, brutal yet somehow fragile, this was not built to last. As the whole thing exploded, in a febrile cacophony of terrible sound quality, brilliant theatrics, and a couple of cataclysmic tunes, you just knew you were at a seismic, era-altering event. The Sex Pistols were high-concept art rock born of a King's Road fashion boutique, the mid-seventies zeitgeist incarnate in bondage. The music was one-dimensional yet incredibly potent, the atmosphere intense, close to insane, the effect genuinely transformative.

The Pistols – who only really made one album and played a mere handful of gigs – shocked the drowsy old UK out of its torpor: electroconvulsive therapy for an entire nation. A generation who had bought into punk would not put up with the stolid status quo. (Or the mindless boogie of Status Quo.) I could argue that it was the liberating iconoclasm of the Sex Pistols, more than the merciless free-market ideology of Margaret Thatcher, which resuscitated the 1970s sick man of Europe. This was the real big bang. Punk made Britain great again.

On an individual level, I came away from that gig determined to do something, to be part of this party. What I did of course was go to more and more gigs. Just by buying into punk, a personal rubicon had been crossed and simply being there was a statement of intent.

In retrospect, and even at the time, actually, many of the bands were pretty ropey, a slew of second-rate chancers and copyists. Some were good. Generation X had the advantage of Billy Idol's cheekbones – he was truly beautiful to behold, as was Siouxsie Sioux from the Banshees, who we saw scores of times, though they were always a little too goth for my spartan taste. X-Ray Spex were barmy and intriguing, and Ian Dury and the Blockheads and the whole Stiff Records caper provided some much-needed fun, theatricality and musicality.

But the likes of the Lurkers and the Members, 999, Chelsea and all that second wave of new-wave nonsense were lumpen and stodgy. Tripe in tight trousers.

But we went because that's what punks did. I could no longer go to funk or jazz clubs because it didn't fit the tribal profile, though many's the time I went home with punk rock ringing in my ears and secretly played Curtis Mayfield or Bob James records to soothe my amphetamine-addled brain. Reggae was of course allowed, and I had become an instant authority on roots and culture, snapping up import seven-inches on one of Joe Gibbs's labels from Dub Vendor for some musical light and shade. Then one day I went into Rough Trade on the Grove to see what was new, and Geoff Travis, who ran the place, convinced me not to buy the new single by the UK Subs or whoever, but to take a beautiful, deep import soul tune by Al Green instead. I literally smuggled it home inside my biker's jacket.

For about eighteen months my life was consumed and defined by my musical and sartorial affiliations. I only fancied girls who looked like they could be in the Slits, and only had mates who could name all the members of the Heartbreakers. Keeping the punk flame was part of the deal, and woe betide any bands who did not fit. The Jam were one example – too mod, too suburban, so they were given short shrift. I thought the Police were a preposterous and pretentious cod-reggae pop group made up of old hippies, and I wasn't wrong.

One night at the Camden Palace we all laughed out loud and jeered theatrically at a support band from Ireland called the Boomtown Rats. With their lanky would-be Mick Jagger lead singer and their keyboardist prancing about in stripy pyjamas (who has bloody keyboards in a punk band?), they were playing hokey pop rock at the wrong speed, and we told them so. Some twerp even leapt up on stage and tried to push Geldof off. Sorry, Sir Bob.

The apogee of my personal punk gatekeeping came one night at the Vortex, waiting for the Banshees to appear yet again. There was a kerfuffle in the crowd as a small retinue of middle-aged blokes pushed their way through the spiky morass, barging people out of the way while a photographer took pictures. Suddenly the epicentre of this mêlée, a short, stocky, dark-haired bloke with a huge maniacal grin gave me a little shove, so I told not him not to be a twat.

'Do you know who I am, dear boy?' he asked with an inebriated slur. I was of course completely aware that this was none other than the arch rock'n'roll agent provocateur Keith Moon, thunderous drummer of the Who, darling of the tabloids, doyen of the drunken, roistering classes. I had been a Who fan, loved *Quadrophenia*, but this was 1977, the past was over, 'no more heroes', the Beatles, Elvis and the Rolling Stones meant nothing to me and besides, he was behaving like an oaf for the camera. 'Yes, I do – you're an old fart from some dinosaur rock band,' was my reply in keeping with strict punk orthodoxy. 'I'll burn your hair off,' he said, while producing a lighter from his pocket. 'I'll knock your block off,' said I, or words to that effect.

For a second I really thought I was going to have to indulge in fisticuffs with a rock'n'roll legend and very probably lose, until he suddenly threw his arms around me in a big bear hug and offered to buy me a double brandy. Impressed by my fortitude in standing up to him, suddenly we were best mates, and I spent the rest of the night dictating a teenage punk manifesto to Keith Moon and his journalist mate, who was with him.

That Thursday my picture was on the front page of the *Melody Maker* and the story of Keith Moon's night with the punks a double-page spread. I loved it, loved the fleeting fame it gave me at the LSE, but also loved the idea of being part of the narrative; more than just a fan – a face; though it was all marred by the fact that the writer, who was as pissed as Mr Moon, got my name wrong. I could do better than that, I thought.

Keith Moon, who had seemed like an impossibly old man to me at that point, was in fact just thirty-two, while I was eighteen. He was, tragically, less than a year away from death and I was a year or so from starting my career as a music writer. And the two were definitely connected. Without punk and its myriad adventures and eye-opening encounters, I have no idea how my life would have gone. It pulled back the curtain and invited you to join in. For all the purported nihilism, it was utterly positive in its energy. But that energy was running out; the fireworks display was coming to a messy end.

The latter stages of the punk hegemony were marred for me by an increasingly violent atmosphere at gigs. I remember countless shows where the factional tensions spilt over and a kind of mob misrule prevailed; a surfeit of fighting on the dance floor. This was not the theatrical nihilism and situationism of those early art-house shows, but a nasty, often politically motivated terror.

The noisy new kids on the block were a bunch of bawling and brawling, lowest-common-denominator herberts from distant Hersham called Sham 69. After the bravura élan of the Sex Pistols and the roots-rebel authenticity of the Clash, that was quite a comedown. They were part of a scene which came to be called 'Oi!', a bastardisation of the original skinhead movement of a decade before, and an ugly offshoot of punk, which reduced it to cropped hair, big boots and terrace chants. But nevertheless, we went to see Sham at Acklam Hall, a venue built into the undercroft of the holy Westway, just yards from the house my father was born in.

The politics of punk veered from the theatrical anarchism of the Pistols to the romanticised solidarity of the Clash, but a new, grim, far-right presence began making itself felt. This

was a time when the National Front were a real, viciously violent force on the streets and terraces, and trying to translate
that support to the ballot box. I'd seen Chelsea's large NF fac-
tion sieg heiling their way up Loftus Road enough times, been
on Anti-Nazi League demos, and knew precisely which side I
was on. My lefty, trades-unionist dad had fought Mosley's
mob on these very streets where Sham 69 were about to play.

Although Sham were not themselves Nazis, they had picked
up a bunch of skinhead fans who were full of learned-by-rote
racist bile, all bleached jeans, naked torsos and stiff-arm salutes.
And when I saw a phalanx of these silly suburban stormtroop-
ers arriving at the venue deep in the multicultural heartland of
Ladbroke Grove, I knew it wouldn't end well. Though in
retrospect, I think it went OK.

Jimmy Pursey, who fronted Sham, had an undeniable charisma and a certain exuberant barrow-boy charm, but the band
were way below basic, which was the very essence of their
appeal for the knucklehead Nazis, who were making their
presence increasingly felt in the hall. There was often an aggressive atmosphere at punk gigs; usually I felt much safer there
than out on the streets, where looking different was still a
provocation, but this was getting nasty. Little skirmishes were
erupting all over the venue when suddenly an exit door burst
open and a group of local rude boys and Rastas, and their com-
rades from the local estates, who had obviously heard they had
Nazis in the neighbourhood, came pouring in.

I would say all hell was unleashed, but in truth I thought
this was divine intervention. The skinheads, who instantly lost
their swagger and their bottle, were battered from pillar to
post, running screaming from the hall, while the band banged
on about going down the pub. My last joyous sight of the night
was of a load of topless, terrified race warriors legging it igno-
miniously up Ladbroke Grove, back to whence they came.

'Punk's Not Dead' became a slogan among those who grew

their Mohicans for money and went to Crass concerts for fun. But for me it was definitely moribund. All the glamour and the glory had gone, to be replaced by an increasingly grubby sense of self-wallowing. Begging for drug money from tourists was never the message of punk, which was the very essence of Oscar Wilde's dictum about being in the gutter but looking up at the stars. The original punks aimed as high as the sky.

The next wave of bands championed by the music press – mainly from the North Country – were part of an icy ill wind heralding a depressing, post-punk hangover. The Gang of Four, Joy Division, Wire, Cabaret Voltaire . . . I saw them all and couldn't understand, couldn't stand their drab style, their introspective, self-flagellating, pseudo-intellectualism and dreary pessimism. I can't be doing with dour. I really thought that for me at least the whole caper might be over before I'd even left my teens.

So I grew my hair into an exaggerated asymmetric wedge, pulled on some shoulder pads and brought out the Roxy and Bowie records again; this boy kept swinging. I even sneaked to a couple of soul and jazz gigs, including a memorable night almost nostalgically watching War performing 'Me and Baby Brother' and 'Low Rider' at the Hammy Odeon.

Another event in this otherwise fallow time of 1978 was a performance by an avant-garde art collective called Throbbing Gristle, who released one intriguing electronic record called 'United', and played the oddest, artiest gig I'd ever witnessed or ever would witness. They were suspended in a cage above the Architectural Association near Tottenham Court Road and could only be viewed by looking into mirrors arrayed around the courtyard below. Baffling, pretentious, preposterous, but intriguing and challenging and fun. They were never going to become U2.

Then another arty, synthesiser-driven band: the Human League, hailing from Sheffield, but devoid of the usual grim post-punk trappings, more glam than glum, put out a brilliant single called 'Being Boiled'. It was arch and sharp, brittle and angular, yet definitely danceable and beguilingly upbeat, a bit early Roxy Music, a bit Euro-disco, and what's more, the lead singer had the same silly haircut as me, only even more so. There was something in the hair.

With hindsight, there were two live concerts that heralded the coming of the next scene to take over my life. I'd seen Bryan Ferry playing his first ever solo show at the Royal Albert Hall in 1974, the first time I ever visited that most august arena. Ferry is an awkward performer, too tall to be graceful, too self-conscious to be natural. But the overall effect of the night was powerful, and indeed prescient, because he had great hair, and the crowd had perfect footwear and make-up. It was the audience who made it memorable, the audience who heralded what was to come.

Similarly, David Bowie played at Earl's Court in 1978 in his Thin White Duke persona, all billowing white shirt and jaunty sailor's hat. Of course, the Dame was wonderful, though personally I found the gig a touch underwhelming. I never took to watching music in aircraft hangars and after the blood-pumping, spittle-flecked immediacy and intimacy of say, the Clash at their most ferocious, it was all a little stagey and safe, but once again the audience were a revelation.

Huddled together among the masses were small groups of faces, many of them familiar from early punk gigs or even pre-punk funk clubs, and they were looking just fabulous, darling. Simultaneously futuristic and nostalgic in diamanté and hair dye, slapped up and suited and booted in Vivienne Westwood and Antony Price, army surplus, Sam Brown belts and forage caps, art-school creations and thrift-store adaptations. It was a tribal gathering and a movement in the making. A short while later, when that electronic Sheffield band popped up at the Marquee, they were there too in all their finery. Me included.

I think that the Human League were the last group I ever saw at that smelly, sweaty, grotty basement in Soho, which might have been the greatest venue of them all. A pint with the rockers in the Ship opposite, get in that unruly line to file down to the black hole of Wardour Street and enter a cramped, dark and dangerous world of heat and noise and passion. Being boiled indeed.

My overriding memory of that night was the heat, which was beyond tropical, beyond endurable. It was so sweaty and ram-packed in that tiny box that when Bowie and Iggy Pop turned up later, they couldn't get in, which just ramped up the buzz even more. Somehow everybody knew this Human League show was pivotal. Punk was over and something else was taking over.

The band were beautifully aloof, Phil Oakey hiding behind his fringe, all of them behind synthesisers, filling the room with modern sounds. My overriding memory was of watching two beautiful young boys somehow make enough space in that rammed room to dance together in a slow, exaggerated jive that could have come from Weimar Berlin or Hollywood's Golden Age. That and thinking that I should not have the same haircut as a bloke from Sheffield.

But I also thought that something was coming together, something strikingly new and yet seemingly old, something electronic and yet romantic. Punk was definitely dead and the 1980s were starting a year or so early.

Chapter 10

All Mirrors Are Redundant

The stage looks different from the other side.

The live performance which most profoundly changed my life came on a Saturday morning in a grotty rehearsal room on the Holloway Road with about a dozen people present. I'd been invited, along with a small group of the wilfully over-dressed denizens of the Blitz Club, to see a new band formed by Gary Kemp, who was the most prominent of a group of boys from the Angel, Islington, who were regulars in that now famous Covent Garden den of iniquity, vanity and raging creativity.

I'd been introduced to Gary one Tuesday night at Billy's, the Meard Street forerunner of the Blitz, where Steve Strange first held court and DJ Rusty Egan premiered his electronic, Teutonic style, and we'd become fast friends. The man doing the introducing was Steve Dagger, who was studying with me at the LSE; he'd gone to Owen's Grammar School with Gary and his gang, and fancied himself as a potential pop Svengali. So when he said, during a comparative political structures lecture, that Gary – who I knew played guitar a bit – had formed a band and he, Steve, was managing them, it was no great surprise. When he said they were playing on Saturday morning it came as a shock.

As a student I was only used to seeing mornings from the dark side, and the thought of watching a band at a time when I'd usually be in bed was bizarre. But I dragged myself over there and joined up with such staunchly nocturnal stalwarts as Steve and Rusty, Chris Sullivan, Melissa Caplan, Christos Tolera, photographer Graham Smith and a few other prominent Blitz faces. We'd unknowingly been gathered together by Steve Dagger to give our verdict on whether or not this group could be some sort of spearhead for our burgeoning scene. Gary has since described it as the most important show they ever played.

It didn't feel particularly portentous, standing in this dismal, dank room, in a warren of murky, black-painted rehearsal studios in a condemned building on the always grimy Holloway Road. London back in late 1979 was far from glamorous. This was the now notorious winter of our discontent: strikes, power cuts, picket lines, rubble piled high, dead bodies rotting in the mortuaries, and it smelt like a few had decomposed in Halligan's rehearsal rooms where this as-yet-nameless new band were about to perform to a few tired nightclubbers in silly trousers.

To cut a long story short, 'To Cut a Long Story Short' was the first number, and the moment I heard that staccato synthesiser intro, I was intrigued. The sound was bang on the money for that moment – electronic, insistent, dark but danceable – then a few bars later, Tony, who I knew less well than the other band members, started to sing, and that enormous, barrel-chested, almost operatic holler emerged. Blimey.

My first response was one of relief. I'd dreaded having to lie to my mate and tell him his band were good when they weren't, but thankfully they were. And they looked terrific too, swathed in all sorts of dressing-up-box finery but still smart Islington soul boys at heart. And what's more, they were handsome chaps, especially Gary's little brother Martin, who was just eighteen and just about everybody fancied. Never underestimate the lure of physical attraction.

I could look them all in the eye in the pub afterwards and say that it was mightily impressive. I knew nothing about their backstory as a would-be power pop band called the Gentry, but I knew they needed a suitably pretentious and meaningless moniker, so suggested Spandau Ballet, which Chris Sullivan and I had seen scrawled on a toilet wall in Berlin. Dagger loved it, Gary agreed, so Spandau Ballet were born.

The reason that particular performance was so important for me personally is that it led directly to my first appearance on stage and then on TV and, most pertinently, to my first published article, a live review in the NME. Spandau's first proper gig was at the Blitz itself. Crammed onto the tiny stage, they were an instant hit with the collected cognoscenti, and were immediately offered a recording contract by Chris Blackwell from Island Records, who was in attendance. But they held out for a while longer and held a few more carefully contrived, increasingly febrile, invite-only shows in unusual venues. And that's where I came in and came on.

I'm not sure who suggested that I should get up on stage and introduce the band by reciting poetry, though it was probably me. I came up with a splendidly pompous little prose poem that went like this:

'From half-spoken shadows emerges a canvas. A kiss of light breaks to reveal a moment when all mirrors are redundant. Listen to the portrait of the dance of perfection. Ladies and gentlemen . . . the Spandau Ballet.'

Typing this now, of course I cringe a little at its teenage earnestness and pretension, but then I was a teenager at the time. I am actually rather proud of nineteen-year-old me having the bottle to get up on stage, remember my preposterous lines and deliver them with sufficient brio to silence a room full of the hippest, most cynical faces in London. Let the show begin.

The first time was at Mayhem Studios, an aptly named Dickensian warehouse in Battersea owned by Toyah Willcox, where Chris Sullivan and I put on a party at which Spandau played. It might just have been the first ever warehouse party in London and it descended into complete chaos due to some liberally applied acid. The police arrived halfway through the set to see a scene reminiscent of Dante's *Inferno* in drag, and ended up dragging out a noisily hallucinating man wearing a papal legate outfit and motorbike boots while the band played on.

That confirmed to me that I did not want to be a promoter, nor really a performer, though I rather enjoyed my brief moment in the limelight. The stage feels and looks very different when you're on it. It's extremely unglamorous and rather dangerous. There's a veritable assault course of wires and gaffer tape, instruments and obstacles, the spotlights are blindingly bright, so you can't see properly, the crowd is a noisy blur, the pressure is on, and time seems to play tricks. Did that take thirty seconds or was it three minutes? I would not want to spend my life and earn my living up there – it's too intense, too magnified, too theatrical for me. But for the duration of an introduction, it was fun.

So I did it again, only this time it was being filmed for a Janet Street-Porter ITV show called *Twentieth Century Box*, which also documented me getting ready for the night, buying clothes, getting my hair done and genuinely being a poser and a peacock before doing my party piece on stage. Shot in arty black and white, it is a brilliant portrait of the time, embarrassing to watch but also wonderful. We were young working-class kids armed with the powerful arrogance of ignorance. We didn't know you couldn't do this stuff. So we did it anyway.

What I did next was entirely down to Steve Dagger. After Spandau's third or fourth show, Steve said, in his typically matter-of-fact manner, 'Right, you're going to write a review of our next gig. We'll become a famous band and you'll become a music writer.' And we did and they did and I did.

I penned my first review at Steve's mum and dad's council flat in Holborn. It was written longhand in biro on lined notepaper. We then walked together to the *NME*'s office in Carnaby Street to save the bus fare. By this stage I was beginning to doubt the wisdom of all this – surely they wouldn't just print my schoolboy scrawl – but Steve insisted it would work as he pushed me up the stairs to the office.

Once inside I asked for the live editor (I think Gary Crowley was the receptionist at the time) and was pointed in the direction of a chap not that much older than myself. I thought, *He's going to throw me out of here, so I might as well go for it.* I wandered over to his desk, caught his attention, then launched into a little improvised tirade along the lines of: 'Your paper's shit, there's this whole scene going on at this club called the Blitz led by a band called Spandau Ballet, they're going to be enormous and you're so out of touch you know nothing about it.' I slammed my bit of shabby notepaper down and waited to be dismissed.

But instead, he actually read it, and asked if we had any pictures. I said we did, because my mate Graham Smith had taken some, and he said they would run it next week. Simple as that. I walked back downstairs in an amazed daze and told Steve Dagger what had happened. He just said, 'I told you.' And we walked back to the LSE.

I got a cheque for £15 for that review, but more importantly, I got a foot in the door and a glimpse of a potential future. I don't know who that live editor was, but I can only thank him for being so open to a stroppy young herbert with a ridiculous haircut. Suddenly, despite my mum's words, I was a professional writer. I was 'people who do that'. And it was all down to a love of live music.

Within a matter of months Spandau were on *Top of the Pops*, I was at *The Face* magazine, chronicling this new decade called the eighties, and half of the kids from the Blitz – Boy George and Steve Strange, Chris Sullivan, Andy Polaris, Siobhan Fahey, Marilyn et al – were forming bands or forging solo careers, while many others became designers, dancers or DJs, photographers, artists or writers. Well over half of the original hardcore Blitz Kids went on to become extremely successful, even world famous in their chosen fields.

People have often asked what it felt like when suddenly everybody around me started getting famous, and to be honest it all seemed pretty normal, perhaps even inevitable. The Blitz was our equivalent of the Cavern in Liverpool, or the 2i's in Soho for earlier generations. It was a hothouse of egos and talents, a Petri dish of ideas, with big padded shoulders to climb on. Youth culture is like fungi: it flourishes in dank, dark places and once the seed had been planted, we thrived. We'd been taught by punk that we could do it, so we did.

Spandau were a terrific live band at this stage, still punky, rough around the edges and funky enough to come out with something like 'Chant Number One'. The big, bloated hair and power ballads were to come later, but at the start they were a proper cutting-edge club band. And the gig they played on a battleship on the Thames is still one of the most extraordinary I've ever witnessed.

I didn't get to see the notorious Sex Pistols riverboat performance, but I did enjoy *Rum Sodomy & the Lash* aboard a Thames cruiser when the Pogues played a promo gig for their debut album. I have no tolerance for any form of waterborne transport, especially when mixed with copious amounts of alcohol, and I remember spewing over the side somewhere near Tower Bridge while the band played unsteadily on. Thankfully HMS *Belfast* doesn't go anywhere at all.

Dagger booked the gig by telling the people who ran the

ship that it was a private party with a quintet playing. All of which was essentially true, but also complete bollocks, as this turned out to be one of those nights. The ship, an old Second World War cruiser, was like something from the set of David Lynch's film *Eraserhead*: low ceilings, pipework everywhere, gauges, cogs and wheels, tiny, convoluted corridors, steep metal ladders between floors. The band were set up to play below decks in what had been the officers' mess, with a tiny stage just tall enough for Tony Hadley to stand up on. And a right mess it was about to become.

Word was well and truly out that Spandau Ballet were the band to see, so all the faces and big figures on the London club scene were present: a glamorous, hilarious cavalcade of dandies and poseurs, New Romantics and old queens flouncing across the gangplank to board the ship. There were cowboys and gangsters, Cossacks, rabbis and nuns, Marie Antoinette, Yuri Gagarin, and Little Lord Fauntleroy. A group of ticketless scoundrels dressed as pirates somehow procured a rowing boat and attempted to scale the ship from the river. Philip Sallon, the most extravagant of London's glitterati, arrived in a wedding dress festooned with fairy lights and proceeded to plug himself in on deck.

Because of the stipulations of the licence (and because this was supposed to be a sedate private party), food was served, but this buccaneering and deeply hedonistic crowd had little desire to eat cheese, ham and trifle, so a food fight started, making the whole place even more perilous. The staff, mainly old salts, were mortified by the shenanigans, and one complained to Dagger, 'I've just seen two blokes dressed as sailors rogering each other in the toilets.' It can't have been the first time.

It was mad and magnificent, completely surreal, and hugely successful, the crescendo of Spandau's campaign to secure a major deal. All the record labels were present; they had to be impressed by the buzz and by the band, who probably never

played better. Intense, cocksure, cool yet still sweaty; the perfect package. They knew they had cracked it and there was a
triumphal abandon about them on board that boat. It was the
last time I recited my intro and almost the last time in London
that I really felt part of the set-up. They were bound for big
things, and I was happy to watch them sail off into the sunset
of global success.

Spandau were good, but they weren't the best live outfit to
come out of the Blitz. Nor were Ultravox, or Visage or Culture Club or Bananarama, or even S'Express or Wham! or
Sade, who had all been, to some degree, Blitz bands. Blue
Rondo à la Turk, a now near-forgotten bunch of zoot-suit-
wearing, wild-dancing, Latino funk merchants were one of the
most coruscating and joyous live acts I have ever witnessed
anywhere in the world.

After the brouhaha around Spandau, who eventually signed
in a record-breaking deal with Chrysalis Records, almost anybody with a Blitz membership card and a lairy outfit could
secure a recording contract and a major advance if they wanted
one. I knew I never wanted to be a musician – I couldn't sing
or play an instrument – but that didn't stop my chums Chris
Sullivan and Christos Tolera, two of the most prominent characters from that scene, from deciding to start Blue Rondo.

The two Chrises may not have been musicians, but they had
impeccable taste in clothes and music, and they were both fine
visual artists and charismatic personalities. Chris was a Welsh
ex-soul dancer, dandy, punk provocateur and promoter, while
Christos, who was a Greek Londoner in the same year at school
as Martin Kemp, was arguably the best-dressed kid in this or
any town. Around them they gathered a disparate and often
desperate bunch of South Americans and Northern Soul aficionados, with varying degrees of stylistic and musical ability,
and an array of mental health issues, and set about forming a
band.

I'd been in New York with Chris when we watched the wonderful Dr Buzzard's Original Savannah Band play their farewell gig together. We'd got to know the genuinely august August Darnell just as he was morphing into Kid Creole. The whole zoot-suit forties swing thing was happening, and Chris wanted to create something similar, but much tougher, forged, as ever, through the filter of the punk-rock DIY ethos. Like John Lurie did with jazz and the Lounge Lizards, only more abandoned and danceable.

One of the guys that Chris recruited was Mark Reilly, an old mate from the soul scene who could play guitar and do the splits. (Mark went on to become Matt Bianco.) Another was Moses Mount Bassie, who was just learning to play sax but dressed incredibly and was one of the best movers I've ever seen. A couple of bona fide Brazilian musicians on drums and bass, and a deeply unpredictable but loveable percussionist in a full-length robe finished off the not-quite-magnificent seven.

I remember watching them in early rehearsals and to say they were loose is like describing Margaret Thatcher at the time as a little uptight. The songs Chris and Mark Reilly had written were extended jazz funk jams with a Latin edge, closest perhaps to War, if half of the members of War couldn't play properly. Chris wrote lots of clever lyrics and then proceeded to chant them almost in tune over the top while clanging a cowbell and dancing like a dervish. Christos couldn't sing at all, couldn't much dance, but you couldn't take your eyes off him. They looked wonderful and sounded terrible but brilliant. Just like the Pistols, but with congas.

I gave Blue Rondo great coverage at *The Face*, who lapped them up because they looked so fantastic, and besides, they were true faces on the scene and word was out. Signed almost immediately to Virgin Records by Richard Branson personally, who schlepped down to Bournemouth to see them in a secret gig during the traditional bank-holiday shenanigans, he fell instantly in love with them, and I can well understand why. By this stage they had tightened up enough to put a show together, and what a show it was.

Details of all and any Blue Rondo gigs are hard to come by. The internet doesn't consider them worthy of recording, and they were so wilfully hedonistic and wayward that nobody involved, including their long-suffering and sensible manager, my best mate from the LSE Graham Ball, can really remember much. I saw them almost every time they played in the UK but cannot tell you what venues or cities they were in. I had no real role to play in the proceedings; I just wanted to watch them do their thing because it was so much fun.

Cinematic in their sartorial styling, authentic in their taste, passionate in their self-belief, dynamic and kinetic in their performance, the band's shows were a blistering rhythmic blur of banging and blowing, chanting and dancing, with spontaneous leaps from the stage to perform improvised moves, twirling facial hair, whirling limbs, big smiles and a couple of catchy sing-along numbers along the way. The crowds – perhaps the best-dressed audiences I've ever seen – lapped it up, loving the spontaneity and ferocious commitment, the clamour, and the craic. Blue Rondo gigs were like the wildest weddings you've ever been to.

The fact that most of them weren't great musicians or singers was perhaps one of the reasons they were so wonderful live. It meant they maintained that punk rigour, never falling back into slick muso coasting, as so many soul, funk and dance bands do. But it was almost impossible to capture that energy and abandon, or that wayward charm and charisma in the studio, which requires a different set of skills. They had a couple of almost-hits, but nowhere near enough to sustain a career, and after a while it disintegrated.

But if you asked me which band from the 1980s I enjoyed watching most, I'd say Blue Rondo à la Turk every time. 'Klactoveesedstein.'

Chapter 11

First Impressions

Before moving forward to the next next big thing, I want to muse a little on first impressions. Thankfully for all concerned, the first impression of the band who would become Spandau Ballet was a positive one. But then I believe you can usually tell if a group or performer is any good within a note or two. One memorable example of that came one night at the Nashville.

I think it was Split Enz, a New Zealand band in gimmicky black-and-white harlequin suits, who morphed later into Crowded House, who were top of the bill. Or maybe it was the Doctors of Madness, or Deaf School. For once, the internet doesn't seem to know, and I can't be sure because whoever was headlining that night in early 1977 at the Nashville Rooms, a big old dusty pub-rock boozer in West Kensington, paled completely into insignificance compared to the unexpected support act.

Sometimes you just know straight away that they have got *it*, whatever *it* is. In this instance, that instant *it* was a collection of dazzling, bittersweet songs, a strangely compelling nasal voice, a pair of glasses like Buddy Holly and a name brazenly nicked from the annals of rock'n'roll royalty. With just a guitar for accompaniment, this speccy, geeky chap began strumming and singing in his tortured, strangulated style, and the whole room was immediately transfixed. Elvis was in the house.

I know now that Elvis Costello, née Declan MacManus, had a musical life long before that night at the Nashville: he'd been in pub rock bands playing the London circuit, probably even this particular pub. But this was his first ever appearance as a solo artist with a regal name and he did something memorable, something almost impossible. London audiences are notoriously hard to impress, particularly for support acts, who have to battle against the buzz of the bar and the lure of a pint or a piss. I've seen countless poor sods singing dispiritingly into a vacuum, which sucks all life out of them as punters turn their backs and turn up their conversations, ignored and ignoble. But not Elvis.

There was something instantly compelling about this bloke, who stared through his bins as thick as jam jars with an air of disdain. Somehow he stood in an aggressive fashion, all angular and awkward, which was just right for the punky tenor of the times. Then he launched straight into one of those snarling yet tender tunes which made up that brilliant debut album *My Aim is True*. And the whole pub stopped in its tracks, silent, intrigued, then ensnared. He had us straight away. All hail the new King.

I have never forgotten that first deeply impressive impression, can still see him standing there, all attitude and ambition. He was arrogant, certainly, a proper 'fuck you, I know I'm brilliant' look, even though he looked like a geography teacher with piles, fidgeting and wincing. Splay-footed and horn-rimmed, he was an unlikely rock'n'roll star, but a star he knew he was. And so did we.

Perhaps that confidence came from the songs themselves, brilliantly crafted vignettes, which hooked you on first hearing. 'Alison' was an instant stand-out, a standard which still sends shivers to this day, just as it did on that revelatory night over forty years ago. But it wasn't just the songs – it was the whole package, the entity now known as Elvis Costello, which came to life on that tiny stage. It was remarkable, memorable, but it wasn't unique.

I've seen this now maybe four or five times: a new, unheralded, largely unknown artist makes such a massive immediate impression, they jolt you with their talent, so that you just know they are going to be very big indeed. Timing is a big part of it. Sometimes, as with, say, Amy Winehouse, they are completely raw, totally fresh and yet a blinding flash of fully formed brilliance. Others, like Elvis himself, or more recently Gregory Porter, are overnight sensations after years of labouring away, because finally it has all fallen into place. Their time has come.

The first time I really became aware of this was when an Icelandic indie band called the Sugarcubes played a live session in our old BBC Radio London studios in Marylebone. They were alright in a whacky, Icelandic fashion, but one member of the band, a tiny, elfin creature with ill-matched clothes, her hair in bunches and energy in abundance, stood out as something extraordinary. She was kooky and wonky and sexy and, even in the few minutes we spent together, joyously life-affirming. She leapt about and smiled and talked with this charming, sibilant accent and just about everybody present had an instant crush on her. And then the band disappeared.

But Björk didn't. Next time she was in my studio, she was a star; her debut album *Debut* had made the world aware that all that force-of-nature charm came allied to significant talent as a songwriter and singer. The world was now smitten with this otherworldly creature, and I swooned again in her presence. But I did not see her live for many, many years. Then my own young daughter discovered Björk and asked me to take her to see her at the Royal Albert Hall. I didn't really know what to expect or whether that miniaturised, seemingly very intimate appeal would translate to such a large venue. Maybe Björk magic only works close-up.

From our seats at the back of that giant hall she was about six inches high on that daunting stage, wearing a wonderful all-white creation and backed by a chamber orchestra. No elaborate set, no props – no need. She strolled about, spoke softly, smiled broadly and within seconds she had enchanted that entire room. The concert floated by in a heady waft of wonderfulness; I can barely remember a tune, but will never forget the way this mythical siren kept us entranced, almost hypnotised, dizzy, and giggling. It was a form of sorcery. Shall we call it charisma?

It is that inexplicable quality, which is a coming together of personality, presence and performance, a combination of traits and skills which are both indefinable yet instantly recognisable. Like the blind man and the elephant, you might not be able to describe it, but you know when it's there in the room. And a good tune or two helps too.

What makes a great front man or woman is a complex question.

Amy Winehouse was in my radio studio on Marylebone High Street when I first saw her and saw she had it. I'd heard about her before I heard her, though. Her father Mitch was a regular at Porchester Baths in Bayswater at a time when I went there for a steam and a *schvitz* every Wednesday afternoon. A cab driver and a dapper man with his clothes on, he was part of a group of loud and lairy London characters, predominantly but not exclusively Jewish, who would sit around draped in just loincloths and argue and joke in the relaxing area. And once they discovered that I am a radio presenter, they would playfully harangue me to let them appear on my show. But not Mitch.

Despite the fact that we now know he thinks he can croon a

bit, and he's not exactly a retiring man, it was his daughter he would urge me to showcase. 'She can really sing – she's gonna be big,' he would say. A little later he got me a demo of a couple of tracks from her first LP, *Frank*, and I was impressed enough to do as he said and get her on my show, for her first ever radio appearance. I knew already that her blend of classic jazz and contemporary street smarts was good, that she could indeed sing, but I had no idea yet how remarkable she was in real life, live.

This very young girl, pretty, savvy and brash, came into the studio, full of bluff bravado, a classic teenage mix of gauche braggadocio and awkward temerity, with a ripe contemporary London accent and vocabulary, and a knowing yet guileless grin. She was simultaneously shy and shameless, tiny and vulnerable. I had no idea what she was going to sound like once we opened the mikes; I just remember hoping she didn't swear. And then the red broadcast light went on and she did what Amy did, and it was just unimaginable.

I don't recall what she sang, and nobody thought to save it for posterity, but I do vividly remember thinking that this stroppy little cab driver's daughter from Southgate had somehow imbibed or intravenously mainlined Dinah and Ella and Billie and maybe even a little Anita O'Day and yet sounded like no one but herself, like no one else. She sounded like my beautiful multicultural city, full of reggae and hip-hop and soul, ancient and modern, sassy and joyous as she slurred and slid the words, dipping behind the beat, then chasing it back up, closing her eyes and tilting her head. At one point she did this little shake and shimmy thing, like very little girls do at weddings, which was endearing beyond imagining. And then she was done.

I was speechless but she was full of chatter, just matter of fact, not overly impressed by what she had just delivered, because she knew she was that good. I believe Amy was deeply insecure about everything except her singing. She was open and unfiltered and emotionally naked to a point which became both compelling and disturbing. The same sometimes painful, sometimes playful, but always astonishing honesty which made her songwriting so potent was there in her performance. She was real.

Many artists are a clever contrivance; Declan MacManus took a long time to settle on Elvis Costello, thereby finding his métier and never looking back. Bowie went through numerous incarnations before becoming Ziggy and conquering the world, Marc Bolan was the comeback chameleon, only making it after endless attempts. But Amy was just always herself, perhaps unbearably herself. I saw her a couple of times in concert and all that little-girl charm and supernatural talent and nous was evident in spades. A once-in-a-lifetime talent.

But increasingly what was also apparent was the fact that she was suffering for her art and our pleasure, haunted by her own voracious demons, and hounded by a merciless gutter press who would not let her be. I also saw her occasionally on the Camden Town streets we both called home, looking increasingly threadbare and careworn, her beehive sagging, and she would always smile and say hello. Then one morning, out of the blue a package arrived at my house with a platinum disc for *Back to Black* with my name on it and a thank-you note from Amy. Made me proud.

Another morning a few years later I had just got off a plane at Seville airport with my family, heading for our summer holiday in Andalucia. We were queuing up for the car hire when my wife switched her phone on (I refused to have one at this stage) and a message flashed up on the screen. It just said 'Amy's dead'. Made me hollow.

The phenomenon of the 'phenom', the preternaturally talented kid who comes blazing out of nowhere is well known in sport. The whole world knew just how good Lionel Messi was going to be long before he reached La Liga. From the age of eleven he was revered and raved about. Raheem Sterling was sold for millions of pounds to Liverpool by my beloved QPR before he had ever appeared in our first team. He was fifteen. Word was out.

But you don't always need inside info – you can just see it on the pitch. In a couple of little local examples, we were watching QPR away at MK Dons in an FA Cup game a few years ago when my own teenage son Alfie immediately spotted – literally within one or two touches – that the lowly Dons had a formidable new talent called Dele Alli. (Albeit a talent which has not exactly fulfilled his promise.) A couple of seasons later, a young South London lad named Eberechi Eze made his debut for Rangers and within seconds we had turned to each other and nodded, smiling broadly; we knew – anybody in the ground who knows football knew. He had it.

In sport it is immediately evident in the way these special ones hold themselves – their stance, their demeanour and their gait, their aura, maybe. Watching one of the real thoroughbreds – Maradona, or Viv Richards (and I've seen both) – you are made aware that there is an aristocracy of posture, an ethereal grandeur allied with a lightness of being which means that despite their physical attributes they float above. To almost quote the Beatles, there's something in the way they move, an effortlessness, an ease; the very good ones glide. In cycle racing the French use the term *souplesse* to describe the ability to look beautiful on a bicycle, to dance on the pedals like Jacques Anquetil.

Alfie and I were both lucky enough to be at Lords to see Jimmy Anderson make his England Test debut. I looked it up to discover he took 5 for 73 against Zimbabwe in 2003, none of which I had remembered. But the sight of his first delivery, the way he ran towards the wickets, his action, his arm, has been seared onto my retina. He had it. He had time in his domain.

Mastery of time, making the world slow down or speed up as required, is the true sorcery of the rare ones. It is speed of thought, or maybe beyond thought, which buys them that extra, invaluable moment of grace. And there is something similar in music.

Wynton Marsalis was Lionel Messi. To continue this sporting analogy, it is fair to say that Art Blakey's Messengers were indeed the Barcelona FC of jazz. Blakey, the diminutive doyen of hard-bop drummers, ran his band like a jazz boot camp, recruiting the hottest young players of each generation, taking them up on the bandstand and out on the road and honing their talents in the forge of live improvisation until they shone.

Sax men Hank Mobley, Wayne Shorter and Jackie McLean had all been Messengers early in their stellar careers. But it was trumpet players in particular who graduated from Blakey's hard-bop academy with flying honours; Donald Byrd, Kenny Dorham, Lee Morgan. This was the Eton of swing, but because Blakey was such a stickler for presentation, they had much better uniforms.

He wears a whistle and he plays a trumpet. Wynton Marsalis was just nineteen when I saw him make his debut at Ronnie Scott's, as the much-heralded new horn prodigy in Art Blakey's Jazz Messengers and he wore his suit very well indeed. The house was heaving and crackling with anticipation, because word was well and truly out that this new kid from New Orleans was the next in line. Jazz is a lineage, a baton passed, and to see the next Bird or Miles or Trane early in their career is something every jazz nut wants to do and to brag about having done.

There was also a kind of culture war going on (there usually is in jazz) which pitched fusion – which had been dominant ever since Miles went electric – against a kind of neo-retro return to bop, and the music's acoustic, swinging roots. And by opting to play with Blakey – then nearing the end of his long career as the high priest of hard bop – and to wear a tailored suit with a shirt and tie in a perfect Windsor knot, young Mr Marsalis had very clearly chosen his side.

As part of the ensemble, Wynton took his place at the side of the stage and joined in with the horn parts, all eyes and ears waiting for the moment when he stepped forward to take his first solo. Having said it's all about how they move, with Wynton it was his extraordinary ability to stand stock still which really made him stand out. When he wasn't playing, he was statuesque, his horn by his side, his composure impressive, his demeanour immaculate, immovable. Then when the time came, he stepped forward with extraordinary authority, almost solemnity, he raised his golden horn up to his lips and blew us all away.

Every great trumpet player has his own distinctive tone; Louis Armstrong is avian, flighty and reedy, Miles is lunar, haughty and aloof, Chet gossamer-thin yet sad and soft, Lee Morgan sharp, crisp and shining bright. This teenager with a still-cherubic chubby face, in just a few notes in a basement in Frith Street established his sound, which was full and rich, august, patrician, polished, pure almost beyond endurance. Like ringing a bell. And it chimed and it chimed.

I own almost every record Wynton Marsalis has made since that extraordinary debut and I almost never play any of them. He is the most technically gifted and prodigiously talented player of his or any generation, as accomplished at classical as he is at jazz; he knows it all and he can do it all. And therein lies the problem. He makes records which are precise and learned and, to me at least, slightly dull; accomplished but academic, like he's teaching us a lesson. I interviewed Wynton once and he was funny and rude and enjoyably scurrilous, but he never lets that come through. He was also fiercely clever, a quality he doesn't try to hide.

During a spat between Wynton and Chet Baker, who was

the exact opposite of Mr Marsalis – untrained, unrehearsed, sloppy, intuitive – Chet famously said, 'If I could play like Wynton Marsalis . . . I wouldn't.' Which is a great line, but I can only imagine Chet hadn't seen Wynton Marsalis live at Ronnie's. Because more than two decades after that amazing debut I was sitting once again in my favourite seat in front of the bar waiting for the suave son of New Orleans to blow his horn. Only this time with a certain trepidation.

Would we get the arid, demagogic Wynton, or the swinging quicksilver kid I first saw two decades before? I'd been at the Barbican for one of his big-band, Ellingtonian affairs, which was mighty impressive, in an Open University way, but I didn't even stay for the encore. Again, it felt more like a presentation than a flesh-and-blood jazz gig. He's almost too good; no tension. But a quartet in a club is different, that's when you see the whites of their eyes and feel the fire of the breath; that's my kind of jazz.

And Mr Marsalis, stockier now, but still wearing fine suits, walked casually on stage, introduced the band in his soft, sing-along Louisiana accent, then went straight into a solo so clear and rich, so tonally complete that it summoned Buddy Bolden from the grave. You could hear it clean across the river. They probably heard it in the Bar Italia. He had lost none of that power and that beauty, but now had an added subtlety, sadness, the richness of experience and the musicality of a life lived. In a darkened room, in a classic claustrophobic basement, with just a couple of hundred aficionados present, he played with fire and ice, could change the temperature of the room with a phrase. All the pain and all the joy, all that jazz.

I saw Joss Stone at Ronnie's when she was just a teenager. Her London debut was an afternoon showcase presenting this West Country lass with a voice like Aretha to the assembled, deeply cynical ranks of the music press. I invited her on my show straight away, but can't claim too much insight for that, as the entire room was queuing up to sing the praises of her amazing, out-of-body singing voice.

I don't always get it right, of course, particularly when it comes to bands. I saw both Duran Duran and Depeche Mode very early on in their trajectories and dismissed them both as no-hopers. I saw Depeche, a band I've grown to admire enormously, in a tiny club by a bus stop in a dreary parade of shops in Rayleigh in Essex called Crocs, because it had baby crocodiles in a pond. (This was the 1980s.) And decided they were shit.

It wasn't the presence of reptiles which put me off, but my own prejudices. This place was so far away from town, it all looked so suburban, so not Spandau Ballet or the Blitz. It was their dodgy haircuts and their hokey local fans and their distant postcode I was really dismissing rather than their music, because basically I was a complete snob. The same was true of the Duranies – Birmingham only produces heavy rock bands, I thought – as I waved them away imperiously. I was just as dismissive of an unknown Irish mob my press officer mate Rob Partridge from Island Records took me to see.

I think it was in a pub somewhere in West London, or perhaps a club in the West End; it was certainly before they had made much headway over here. I just saw a bang-average overblown rock band from Dublin in dark clothes, trying to sound American and epic and ending up like a Simple Minds tribute band. A bit like the Boomtown Rats without the lanky bloke. And that's what I said. Thankfully Rob took no notice of my jaundiced opinion, signed them to the record label he loved, and watched them become just about the biggest band on earth. Bono was there at his funeral.

I would quite like Gregory Porter to sing at my funeral. He started out singing in church, where his mother was the minister, so he's drenched in gospel, but the man can sing anything, anywhere. I've watched with great satisfaction as he has gone from my first glimpse at the Pizza Express in Dean Street, a tiny windowless room below the Soho restaurant, to selling out numerous nights at the Royal Albert Hall. I've watched him close-up in my radio studio on half a dozen occasions, backed only by a beaten-up old upright piano, and once a capella, standing next to him in a record store. He can sing in any room and fill it with his voice and his immense, intense humanity.

I'd first heard of Gregory from a fellow jazz fan who'd seen him in a tiny supper club up in Harlem and come back raving about this big guy with an even bigger voice. He was already in his forties, a proper grown up, yet only just starting to break through. Not that many people here knew about him, so his first ever British appearance, in that subterranean pizza parlour, wasn't exactly rammed. But the moment the man emerged on stage, the room filled up with him.

Gregory is a physically large man, not fat, but big in all dimensions, a fine and clearly fit figure of a fellow, who is imposing to behold. But it is more than that; he is more than that. He has a gigantic presence.

I've only met a tiny handful of people whose very being, their aura, completely dominates a space like Gregory. One was C. L. R. James, Trinidadian writer, historian, activist, Marxist, cricket critic and the cleverest person I have ever encountered. I interviewed him on Railton Road in Brixton in the late eighties when he was in his late eighties, white-haired, frail and pipe-cleaner thin, yet so shining bright, with such luminous laser eyes, impeccable manners and terrifying intellectual precision.

Just walking into the room in which he sat was like entering a force field. Stuart Hall, himself a man of considerable charisma, was with him, and even he seemed to recede in stature, to cede to the presence of such a giant. C. L. R. had such towering authority, the accumulated heft of a remarkable life lived, that he was charming, terrifying, captivating and completely overwhelming, even before he had said a word. It wasn't his voice, which was high and thin, it was his essence, which was mountainous.

The same could be said in a very different aspect about Richie Havens. He walked into my radio studio kaftan flapping, bangles jangling, soft eyes smiling benignly, and it was as if some beatific spirit, a kindly sprite had descended upon W1, spreading a waft of wellbeing in his wake. I usually have little time for old hippies and didn't expect much of Mr Havens because he was both of those. He was also the gentlest, most sweetly sublime soul I have ever been in the presence of. I don't deal in Dalai Lamas, but he was a wholly holy man, a teacher, a rabbi, a guru, a warm blanket in a cold world. I'm sure he played a live number for my show, though I don't recall it, but I will never forget his effect upon the room.

The word 'numinous' is usually applied to structures or spaces: cathedrals for example, or ancient dolmens, which have a tangible, spiritual air. But it can apply to people too. Simply by walking into it, Richie Havens turned my radio studio into a temple, so infectiously numinous was this lovely man. Cat Stevens, now known as Yusuf Islam, also has a similarly enchanting softness, an infectious gentility, which radiates from him. Gregory is different. Gregory is a big bear hug of a man.

From the moment he walked onto that tiny subterranean stage in Soho on his first night in town, everybody present felt as if we were being wrapped up and kept warm by his mere proximity. And then he opened his mouth and that broad baritone voice poured forth. Somewhere between Paul Robeson and Bill Withers, like molten mahogany, rich and rounded, enveloping and uplifting, capable of rising to righteous anger, but always underpinned with a reassuring note of decency, humanity and, above all, humility. It took Gregory a long time to get where he is going, and he has remained incredibly humble, which is a big part of what makes him special. It wasn't just me – everyone in that room knew.

And I am proud to say that I got to know Gregory well, to talk with him and walk with him, and every single second in his company reaffirmed that first life-affirming impression. Here was a man who made the world better by his being, and who made people love him. His maturity and experience have made him round at the edges, in balance, measured; he knows what failure feels like; you believe he's lived it, a man not a boy. But why did it take so long for him to become a star?

Perhaps like Elvis Costello and David Bowie and Marc Bolan and so many others who had to reinvent themselves, he had to wait to find his moment, to find himself. Perhaps he had to wait to find his hat. Elvis needed his name; Gregory needed his balaclava. I've never asked Gregory about his distinctive headgear. He had it on that first night I saw him and every time I've seen him since; it is an integral part of his persona and to question that always felt intrusive.

Now it is his talisman and his trademark, maybe even his gimmick, like Alvin Stardust's gloves with the rings on top. But I believe that he originally wore it to cover some marks or scars on his neck, some scars which maybe made him too self-aware to perform. I have always assumed that in order to overcome his self-consciousness, to have the kind of confidence you need to stand up on stage in front of a room full of strangers and invite them into your aura, that hat was the thing. Gregory Porter, the man who made his life with a hat.

Chapter 12

The Show Must Go On

I struggle with theatre.

As kids we went to the cinema regularly, the whole family, arriving halfway through whatever was on at the local Odeon, then sitting through the next showing until my dad said, 'This is where we came in,' at which point we'd all get up and traipse out. My most memorable memory of my socialist father was the two of us watching *Spartacus* together, and him, a soft old hard-left trades unionist with tears in his eyes, explaining that Kirk Douglas dying on the cross, dimple aquiver, was a metaphor for the treatment of the working classes. I thought my dad was Spartacus.

I went to Saturday-morning pictures with all the local herberts leaping up and down and hollering in the aisles, throwing sherbet dabs in the air, so that it snowed on screen. I went with schoolmates to cowboy films and *Carry On*s, and much later to arty movies in strange languages, and with girls to wherever we could get a seat in the back row. I went to Paris just to see *A Clockwork Orange*, but I never went to the theatre.

I tell a lie – one trip to the Palladium for a pantomime starring Cliff Richard, taken by my Aunt Glad when my dad died,

about which I recall nothing but the considerable consolation
of a pineapple Mivvi at half time. Theatre was not part of our
culture; it was something other people did, including the
school play, which I assiduously avoided being involved in for
fear of being made to wear tights or a toga. I can stand on stage
and be me, no problem, but the idea of acting is sheer hell. And
watching it might be even worse.

The first time I ever went to a theatrical event of my own
volition was when I was seventeen and attempting to impress a
flaxen-haired flower-power girl in the lower sixth form who
smelt of patchouli and the potential for free love. I bought us
tickets for a show called *Future Shock* at the Roundhouse, which
had been recommended by one of the hairy boys at school as
just the thing to wow a hippy chick. This was dubbed 'rock
theatre', so I figured if I didn't like the theatre I'd probably like
the rock. How wrong can you be?

I have no idea what it was about, and I'm not sure the cast
did either. It involved loads of emaciated, long-haired actors in
various states of undress incanting and wailing, emoting and
projecting, and occasionally singing overwritten songs in a
strange, unnatural fashion while a terrible prog rock band
noodled away behind them. It was as insufferable as it was
impenetrable, and it became deeply embarrassing when a male
member of the cast with his male member on display walked
through the aisles and decided to deliver his lines directly to
my date, who proved to be less liberated than I had imagined.
The shock was very much in the present. Welcome to the
theatre.

Despite that traumatic teenage experience, I have tried to
enjoy theatre, God and Larry know I've tried. I've been to serious, insightful plays with long pauses and silly comic plays
with one-liners; I've tried the classics and I've tried cutting-
edge, the West End, the fringe, the Globe and the National.
Occasionally I've even quite enjoyed some of it, bits of it,

though the best bit is invariably the gin and tonic with your name on it sitting in the bar at half time. (Alright – I know it's supposed to be called the interval.)

The fact that theatre is deemed to be important, cultured, elevated and yet I don't get it shames me, so I keep going, keep hoping, keep trying. But try as I may, I cannot get over the knowledge that they are acting, that it is all just make-believe, dress-up and pretend. I know those thespians will be in the pub afterwards bitching about the director or fretting about the time of the last bus to Muswell Hill. I know that bit of painted plasterboard is not really a Roman city or a nightclub. No matter how lavish or stylish, how clever or cultured, it all looks like amateur dramatics to me.

Suspension of disbelief is impossible, no matter how brilliant the writing of Pinter, or the acting of Rylance – though sometimes both can be so brilliant that I can enjoy them for what they are without ever believing any of it. Suspension of disbelief is impossible if I can see the side of the stage. And plays are always too long. Always. I once sat through six interminable hours of some baffling Italian nonsense called *My Brilliant Friend* at the National Theatre, praying to Gods I don't believe in that the end was nigh. (It wasn't.) But even in normal-length plays there will be periods spent staring at the ceiling, studying the cornicing, hoping that soliloquy or that scene is the last. Unless of course it's a musical. Because if it is a musical, chances are I will already have left.

I cannot quite answer why I am so allergic to thespians singing. But it is something to do with truth: I know they don't mean it. There is a direct relationship between truth and beauty in song, I have to believe that they believe it, that the emotions, the sentiments are genuine. Actors are acting when they sing; it is a show, a performance; the great singers make you believe in the veracity, the authenticity of the song.

Stand-up comedy is another area of performance that I'm

not comfortable with. I am all too often embarrassed by comedians, by the inherent desperation to get a laugh, by the studied cruelty in the banter and the heckling, by picking on some poor soul in the audience, by the whole process of paying somebody to make you laugh. Isn't that what friends and family are for? Tommy Cooper and Morecambe and Wise were funny on the telly, *Only Fools and Horses* was a work of genius, but I cannot stomach ten seconds of Ricky Gervais's rampant misanthropy and some posh bloke in a suit acting the oaf.

I like watching dance, flamenco and tango in particular. I love some cinematic musicals: *Singin' in the Rain*, *Guys and Dolls*, *West Side Story*. I adore *Oliver!*, *Mary Poppins* and *My Fair Lady* on screen, so went to see all three on stage and could not stand a second of their shallow, showy theatricality and stilted stage-school projecting. The minute an actor, any actor, starts to sing in that over-precise, far too practised, far too polished, annunciating clearly while pretending to sound soulful style they all seem to employ, I break out in the screaming abdabs. Please stop, please – this is murder.

How anybody can sit through an ABBA jukebox musical, or a Queen one, I have no idea but, actually, it might be even worse when they are songs that you love which are being mullered up on stage. *Girl From the North Country*, a musical featuring some of Dylan's finest, was well written and acted, but the moment the cast started to belt them out, I wanted to run up the aisle and protest at such blasphemy. No matter how shot and rotten Bob's voice is these days, it is a million times better than that.

Show tunes are, of course, the worst, especially when sung by anybody who has been to RADA, the Guildhall, or even done tap lessons in a local hall. It is especially unbearable if accompanied by projecting: exaggerated facial gestures, arms reaching out, eyes pleading, or a touch of hoofing. Please make it stop.

It is the artifice, the artlessness, the hammy jazz hands, the infuriating, alienating, inauthentic, trite over-the-top-ness of it all. It's not the songs as such; Chet Baker singing Lerner and Loewe is about as heartbreakingly beautiful as it gets. In the end it comes down to whether you believe the singer means the song, and the minute an actor sings, I know they are acting the song, putting on a show. I am allergic to showbiz. Saturday-night TV makes me break out in hives.

So how come I think Tom Waits might be the greatest showman on earth? How come I would pay more money and travel greater distances to see Tom Waits – who is the most theatrical of live artists – than any other performer alive? I guess because he's Tom Waits.

I have been lucky enough to have witnessed the Tom Waits experience every time he's appeared in London, except the first time, when he headlined at Ronnie Scott's to rather indifferent reviews in the mid-seventies. I would love to have seen him just at a piano on a tiny stage, but I assume that actually he is best seen in all his big-production pomp, with his stage sets, his props and his lighting. Give the man an umbrella and he will bewitch you with it.

The first of those shows was 12 May 1979 at the London Palladium, and like all of them, it is imprinted directly onto my mind, never to be forgotten. I was already a huge fan of his dishevelled bar-room balladeer persona, those heartsick, heartfelt, skewwhiff jazz and blues tunes with the cinematic lyrics and those wondrous rhymes – I knew pretty much every word of every song from every album, but I didn't know that he would put on such a choreographed and theatrical performance. I guess he is from Tinseltown.

Edward Hopper sets and Francis Ford Coppola lighting rigs would normally send me scurrying for the exit, but Waits's persona, which is clearly a complete work of artifice anyway, just fits so wonderfully standing on a stage beneath a burning neon sign and a crooked lamp stand, his snap-brim trilby tilted just so as he delivers the tragic tale of Burma-Shave. He's a good actor in movies, especially if Jim Jarmusch is involved, and an even better actor on stage because he only ever plays one part.

He has a phenomenal command of dynamics; most of the set delivered *sotto voce*, keeping you listening as intently as possible, in an audience hushed and leaning forward. But then that great gravel growl will emerge, and the room reverberates with its roaring power. Like the old cliché says, it is an emotional rollercoaster ride, but one in a broken-down old fairground somewhere near Coney Island where the carneys all sport liquorice tattoos.

Tom's schtick is emotionally manipulative, no doubt contrived and controlling, but so beguiling and engaging because it is ultimately believable. If you are there, you have already bought into Tom Waits's world, the self-mythologising ragged-trousered troubadour. And he never lets it slip, never once steps out of character; he plays the lead part so well because being Tom Waits is his life's work.

The brolly came into play when 'Small Change' got rained on, and so did Tom, in a cascade of blue lights and blazing trumpets at the end of the set. Or was that at the Dominion Theatre a few years later, when Romeo was bleeding, dying live on stage and signs of Tom Waits Mark II were already emerging?

There is a great schism in the career of Tom Waits, a fault line which emerged when he married Kathleen Brennan, joined Island Records, and released *Swordfishtrombones*. Which is when I flew to LA to interview him. Before that album he was essentially a wayward jazz balladeer; afterwards he dived deeper into deranged vaudeville territory, employing that wailing-in-a-bone-yard-through-a-megaphone voice. He growls and groans over angular, avant-garde rhythms and choppy staccato beats, percussive, dissonant and disturbing. Personally, I think everything up to and including *Rain Dogs* is a masterpiece and everything afterwards is rather hard work, at least on record. Live, though, he is still magnificent.

His last London show at Hammersmith was one of the hottest tickets of all time and one of the coolest shows ever. Walking there through the massed ranks of scalpers and pleading fans offering ridiculous sums, I kept touching my breast pocket to confirm that my tickets were still there. I was not going to miss this one.

The atmosphere before the show was as tense and nervously expectant as any I've ever known. There is a saying in Spanish: '*Corrida de expectación, corrida de decepción*', meaning the most anticipated bullfights are the most disappointing. But not this one. From the moment Mr Waits shambled on from stage left he was shambolically majestic, and the crowd were ecstatic.

The stage set was a breaker's yard strewn with bizarre detritus, which Tom prowled around, growling menacingly, stripped-back and barking mad. He stood in the middle of it, hunched and humble, intense and quite possibly insane he brooked no dissent and took no prisoners. The set was discord ant and urgent, dark and pungent. He was funny and ribald and strident and tough. It was way out there, and the audience went with him all the way.

This was grunge and grime Tom Waits style, yet he was still capable of great tenderness. He sang 'Christmas Card from a Hooker in Minneapolis', which is officially the saddest song of all time – no husband and no trombone. I've heard that song a hundred times, but this time he made my knees buckle.

And he finished the show with 'Time', one of the prettiest, most poetic ballads ever written about the ticking of the clock, his voice soft and sweet and melancholy. Pathos kept firmly in check, romance smouldering, time stopped yet slipping away. The last line of that last number tells us that Tom will only return when the fiddler is paid. Only he never did return – not yet, anyway. It was his last London show and I would travel very long distances to see Tom Waits again.

I once travelled to LA. It was when he first signed to Island and my mercurial mate Rob Partridge became his press officer. By this stage I was a lead writer for *The Face*, so Rob suggested I should take a trip to the City of Angels to interview Tom about his radical new fish and brass album. The only problem was I couldn't drive at the time, which is something of an impediment in LA, so Rob suggested that my then girlfriend should also go as my chauffeur.

This was in the days when record-company budgets were splendidly elastic, so Island Records paid for us both to fly to LA and stay for a week in the famed Chateau Marmont. He gave me Tom's phone number and told me to call him when I got there to arrange a meet. Even then this seemed like a rather laid-back arrangement, but then Rob was a very cool guy.

So Sade and I checked into our swanky suite, rather different from the squat we called home in a disused fire station in Tottenham, and I used the hotel phone to call Mr Waits. He didn't answer but instead I got an answerphone message which began with a burst of congas, followed by that uniquely whiskey-soaked voice saying, 'Hi, this is Tom – I'm at the beach.' And that was it. I left a message saying we were in town for the interview and to contact me at the Chateau. Then heard nothing.

The next day I repeated the exercise: same response; third day, no news. By now I was fretting rather, when eventually I got a missive via the hotel saying we had to meet Mr Waits the next day at 4 p.m. at the Traveller's Rest Café, at an address somewhere in south-east LA. They then told us this was just about the most dangerous barrio in the entire city and whatever we did, to please not stick around after dark.

So it was with more than a little trepidation that Sade and I took a map and tried to navigate our way to our rendezvous.

About five freeways later, we eventually arrived at a grubby Honduran diner, its net curtains thick with grease, in a run-down, low-lying residential neighbourhood straight out of South Central casting. I doubt that Tom actually lived there, but choosing this as the venue for our interview was a theatrical masterstroke. We were immediately in Tom Waits territory.

We'd arrived early, so we went inside and ordered some chilli and rice and waited for the man to arrive. Finally, fashionably prompt, he shuffled in, intentionally looking twice his biological age and at least twice as hip as any man on earth. Sade, not wanting to play gooseberry during our interview, said she would go and sit outside in the car, leaving Tom and I to talk into my old cassette recorder.

An old black-and-white TV was playing baseball noisily in the corner and Mr Waits speaks in a low, gruff whisper, his diction buried beneath the gravel, so I asked him if we could request that they turn the TV down. 'That would not be a very good idea,' was his wise reply, so instead he suggested we continue the interview outside in his car.

So we sat in his beaten-up old maroon Volvo and talked, or rather I asked a few questions and Tom Waits spun wondrous tales, while I listened spellbound to his largely apocryphal answers. It was one of the greatest series of soliloquys I've ever witnessed, totally in character, completely captivating and almost totally made up.

For example, when I asked him about his wife, he told me: 'She's an aerialist with the Circus Vargas. We met at a funeral; we were sheltering beneath the same umbrella. The guy choked on a wishbone.' He described *Swordfishtrombones* as 'music with scales'. When I enquired as to whether he had made much money in his career he said, 'Man, I'm so broke, I can't even pay attention.'

I didn't mind for a moment that he was not going to give me any insights into the man behind the mythology; I was just thrilled to be privy to such a spellbinding private performance from a clearly very private person. When I asked whether he had ever been under pressure to make his music more commercial, he said, 'Of course, but I would rather fail on my own terms than succeed on someone else's.' Maybe that is why he puts on such great shows.

So captivated was I by his company that time flew by and dusk started to descend over the barrio. We were parked outside a mariachi bar called Los Quangos; the music started up while lowriders rolled up and down the street and the characters of the night began to emerge.

Sade was parked in our hire car directly in front of us and I could see she had fallen asleep on the back seat. Moments later, I saw a group of four or five guys, bandanas round their heads, tattoos on their faces, gang colours prominently displayed, walking menacingly towards the car with my girlfriend inside and the sudden memory of what they had said in the hotel hit me. My mouth went dry; my heart almost stopped.

This group of men saw the sleeping beauty in the back seat and stopped to peer in, circling the car with my girlfriend inside, which left me in something of a dilemma and my girlfriend in possible danger. What am I supposed to do in this situation? So I asked Tom. Without missing a beat, he said in his usual faint drawl, 'Man, you pray the doors are locked.'

The men with the colours just smiled at Sade, who woke up with a start, and then walked on into the club.

Being part of the Tom Waits show for a while made me understand why his is the only kind of theatricality I seem to enjoy. Tom, like Bob Dylan and Joe Strummer, David Bowie and Marc Bolan, is a master of self-invention, an act so complete and all-pervading it becomes real; they are playing a part so thoroughly that it becomes who they are. And they are giants.

Chapter 13

Diamond Life

I watched a performer being formed. How Sade became a singer and then a star and eventually a terrific live artist was a unique insight into the process of learning and mastering stagecraft. It was also an object lesson in how to shape a hugely successful career in music without too much collateral damage along the way.

First off, it is important to say that Sade is a brilliant human being. I chose that word carefully because she is and always was lustrous; she shone. It wasn't just her looks, though we should never underestimate the power of beauty; we love looking at beautiful people and she was always that. But her luminescence was more than skin deep; she had a grace and a poise, but also a steely strength and an unshakable balance, an emotional heft, which made her magnetic, even when she was an impoverished student. She was also good at stuff – almost any stuff – which added to her unimpeachable taste, meant she could have turned her hand to whatever she chose. How she settled on music and then set about getting good at it is an interesting story.

I seem to remember her telling me that she had joined in rehearsals with some old schoolmates in a band a few times back in Essex as a teenager, but having studied fashion at St Martins, alongside so many of the bright young Blitz things, that looked like her chosen path. But fashion design is a tough call and although Sade is a tough woman, it looked like the world of fashion, with its couture houses and luxury brands, would entail too many compromises for her.

She modelled for money, but only rag-trade sizing stuff, nothing glamorous, because she hated that sort of glamour, disliked the showy side of the fashion world, and wasn't comfortable with the cut-throat economics of it, was never a businesswoman. She was destined to be a success at something but didn't want to lower her standards to achieve it. Equally though if she committed to something, she would give it her all. Maybe music would work.

We went together to a Grace Jones gig in a club in Berlin and I could see her intently studying the artist who was probably closest to her own sense of herself: a strong, independent woman of colour, uncompromising and unflinching. Only Sade was subtler, more subdued by nature than Grace Jones with her flamboyant theatricality. Then when we watched just about everybody around us start to gain some traction in the music industry, I think that showed her a potential path, prompted her to think that if George O'Dowd could decide he was a singer, or Marilyn, or Steve Strange or Chris Sullivan, or George Michael or the Bananarama girls, then why not her?

Another person who had a similar thought process was a North London friend of mine (and firm friend to this day) called Lee Barrett. He was very much part of the Blitz scene (that's his bottom in my Levi's on the front of The Face 'Hard Times' cover) and he had decided that band management was his forte. He'd got a group together called Arriva, based around the songwriting talents of his mate Ray St John, and they went for a more poppy version of the then terribly trendy Latin funk sound of Blue Rondo.

It was en route to a Blue Rondo gig in Cardiff that Sade's musical career effectively began. Lee was driving a van full of mates of the band from London and had insisted that Sade and I should sit in the front. Somewhere round about Reading he suddenly asked the question he had clearly been planning all along, as he said to her, 'Can you sing?' Without missing a beat, she said, 'Yes.' That was it.

Lee asked her to come and join his band in rehearsals as a backing singer, though I suspect her striking looks and London connections were of paramount importance in his mind. I asked Sade why she thought she could sing and she basically said, 'Well, can't be hard, can it?' That was it. Except of course it wasn't. Not quite.

At first, she couldn't really sing that well, at least not in a conventional backing-singer, belt-'em-out sense,. But she very quickly assessed her limitations and began working within those to develop a style of her own. She also immediately realised that she needed songs which suited her voice and persona, so she started choosing them and writing them.

Despite the fact that she had no formal musical training and could not play an instrument, she knew good music, she had excellent taste, growing up loving Marvin and Maze, Donny Hathaway and Curtis Mayfield, lovers' rock and Blue Note jazz, and so just assumed, rightly in fact, that for her at least, songwriting would come naturally. 'It can't be hard, can it?'

She started by modifying and enhancing a song already in the Arriva set called 'Smooth Operator'. This became her number, and she would step forward and take the lead on that one song. And it only took that one song. It was apparent almost immediately to anybody with eyes and ears who was the star of the show. But not yet to Sade. Or maybe Sade wasn't yet ready to be a star.

Arriva, now called Pride, morphed into a more soul/jazz sound reflecting the growing influence of the girl at the back, but also of a couple of fine young musicians from Hull, Stuart Matthewman and Paul Denman, whom Lee had also recruited and who became Sade's right-hand boys. They set about writing new songs for the set together and playing loads of live gigs to showcase them. Therein was a small problem. Sade hates showing off.

Anything grandiose or self-aggrandising, overblown or showy is absolutely antithetical to her nature. A perfectionist and a minimalist, for whom a millimetre is a mile, the vicissitudes and unpredictability of live performance, the exaggeration and projection did not come naturally. So it was with something approaching amazement, mingled with intense pride for my friend, that I watched her, studied her from the side of the stage, show after show, as she diligently distilled what suited her, what worked for her, developing small gestures, smiles and movements, comments and characteristics; a repertoire of subtle Sade signals which could communicate with an audience, while retaining her integrity and dignity on stage.

For some, this restraint was seen as an icy persona, perhaps even a glacial pose, which made me laugh heartily because Sade is one of the least icy people ever. Sade isn't cool – she is warm and occasionally fiery, fiercely friendly, funny and kind, mischievous and single-minded, but congenitally understated, embarrassed by anything over the top, and she had to find a way to make that work on stage. She is not Freddie Mercury. But by the time she got to Live Aid she could share a stage with him and hold her own.

She is, though, very loyal and rather stubborn, so Pride – a quality she has always valued – went on longer than they probably should have done, too proud to acknowledge the inevitable. She felt emotionally committed to the band, a sprawling eight-piece, they played in all the right places: the Wag Club, Ronnie's, the Dirtbox; they did a set on a flatbed truck outside the Beat Route on Greek Street at 3 a.m. to impress the crowds emerging on a Friday night/Saturday morning.

Pride got low down and dirty, and they were pretty damn good in an all-action soul-review way, but it was when the girl with the hooped earrings stepped forward, stood still and sung 'Cry Me a River' (or 'fry me a liver', as she would occasionally interject) that the audience went quiet and really concentrated. In a buckskin jacket and jeans or a second-hand dress, the girl with the almond eyes and the steely gaze had it, but then it was back to big-band funk and boogie with the rest of the band.

Then it was back to a squat in a disused fire station with the bath in the kitchen and an outside toilet on the balcony. Life was pretty tough, money too tight, but Sade's resolve and her confidence in her ability never wavered. That was when she wrote 'When Am I Going to Make a Living'. The answer, of course, was when they finally gave in and acknowledged what was obvious to most: that she had outgrown Pride and Sade was the star.

Pride eventually just got worn out and worn down and slowly slipped away, leaving Sade and her boys, augmented now by keyboards player Andrew Hale, and a handful of excellent new songs, like 'Your Love is King', 'Hang on to Your Love' and 'Sally', co-written with Stuart Matthewman. Her image, striking and stark, a beautiful, strong, assuredly independent young woman, was everywhere. Their first gig under her moniker was at Heaven and such was the clamour that hundreds were turned away. But could she cut it live?

Sade had worked hard on that distinctive contralto voice of hers; clear yet textured, honest, open, plangent, potent, but controlled; almost vibrato-less, no melisma, completely free of the ululating and cheap musical gymnastics that so many Saturday-night TV wannabees employ, yet capable of conveying genuine emotion. It is a unique sound because it is absolutely her voice – no artifice, no coaching, no auto-tuning, no doubt it's Sade. Part Ibadan, part Clacton, wholly authentic.

And when the first smoky, spoken notes of 'Smooth Operator' rang out and the audience responded, you just knew. I knew from that night on that she wouldn't be in a squat too much longer. She would soon make a very good living indeed.

But Sade still didn't always look completely at home up on stage as the primary focus of a show. It was now all on her admittedly broad shoulders and occasionally that showed; she could look awkward, unsure if this was really for her. To this day that is the reason Sade is a band not just a girl; she needs her unit, her tight-knit family around her to flourish, especially up there under the glare of the lights and the gaze of the crowd.

But she persevered and developed a whole load of less-is-more techniques, which enabled her to maintain grace under pressure, including a backless dress, a composed stance, a compelling stillness broken only by the occasional coquettish two-step, a wiggle and a killer grin. It's amazing what you can accomplish with a shimmy and a smile. The record companies now saw what they'd all been missing, and she and the band signed to CBS. The rest, as they are wont to say, is history.

On the day of her *Top of the Pops* debut, showcasing her first single 'Your Love is King' in 1984, the outside toilet in that squat was out of action, so while there was a long limousine waiting in the scruffy Tottenham street to ferry her to the BBC studios, she had to pee in a bucket. She literally did not have a pot to piss in. By the time she came home that evening, poverty was behind her.

Diamond Life was an immediate international hit and was the biggest-selling debut album ever by a female British artist. It was instantly massive, especially in the States, and so was the attention it brought, especially here with our prying tabloids. Sade is far from shy, but she is uncomfortable with the excesses of celebrity: it is too obvious and tacky for her. Sade and

Madonna emerged from a similar milieu in New York and London at roughly the same time (Sade first met Madonna when she was a dancer in Danceteria and was at the Camden Palace for her London debut). But their response to fame has been diametrically opposite. Madonna craves the limelight; Sade likes the shade.

Writing and recording methodically, slowly, late at night, with her boys around her, away from the public gaze, is what Sade loves most. But that is not easy when you are a sudden global pop sensation, and the feral British press are hounding your every move and concocting preposterous stories about you. One time a paparazzi photographer fell out of a tree opposite her apartment and injured himself, so she made him and the police who arrived to nick him a cup of tea. She wasn't so much upset by scurrilous tabloid stories – she's strong as hell – but she was embarrassed by them, by the whole gaudy fame game.

So she played it cool, made elegant videos, had huge hits, made fortunes, moved around a bit: Madrid and Jamaica, then settled on the English countryside, where she kept horses, and kept friends and band members close. In a music business which is notoriously manipulative, especially of female artists, she pulls every string, makes every choice. She's not remotely a recluse, she's just comfortable at home and comes out whenever she feels ready. On her terms, in her time.

And every time Sade makes an album it is instantly, internationally successful. Songs of love and family, caring, involving, subtly political, sometimes soothing, sometimes soaring, the proverbial quiet storm. And they sell big bucketloads, particularly in America, where she is seen as a mammoth star, especially among the African American musical community, where the likes of Kanye West, Drake and Beyoncé worship this poised and centred woman of colour as a virtual deity.

Here in Britain she is sometimes dismissed as some sort of

superficial coffee-table crooner, all lip gloss and *longueurs*. She's too stable and sane for our overly dramatic tastes. Sade was far too subtle for the white, middle-class rock bores who prefered noisy boys or screeching indie chicks, too tasteful for the trashy pop scene. She refuses to play the star card, parade her scars, reveal her flesh, or sell her soul, she doesn't do public suffering or emoting, won't play the media game, doesn't do interviews, social media or TV shows, and so seems remote, aloof. Actually, she's just herself.

If you want to know more about Sade, it's in the songs; she is a fabulous storyteller, heartfelt and direct and in America they really listen. And when she plays live there, as she does with every album, every few years, they go absolutely wild.

A Sade show in the US is like a major community event, and the audience reflects that. She always said that she wanted to appeal to all age groups and all demographics, and she does; grandmas and their grandkids and every generation in-between are there. It is an uptown, upscale event, the big gig, uniting the often-segregated racial communities of US cities, though it has to be said the black audience really turn out for this girl. They see her as one of their own and her shows become a focus for pride, posing and parading, dressed to the nines, flash and fine, excited but reverential, crackling with anticipation, waiting for a visit from the British queen.

I hadn't seen Sade for a while – I mean we literally hadn't been in a room together – before she invited me to see her in New York. We'd kept in touch, cards and calls, but it was the first time in far too long since I'd met up with her and the band, who had all been firm friends. Backstage beforehand it was so gratifying to see that nothing had changed, they were still the same jokey, tight-knit group, while Sade was still fussing over them, very much the matriarch of the band, and still very much the warm, open friend of old.

But maybe something had changed; there was a collective

ease, a calm professionalism, despite the fact that this was a big gig in a tough town, a feeling that they really knew what they were doing. I left them to their final preparations and went to take my seat outside, feeling a mix of anticipation and gratification. She was right, we were right all along.

The crowd for Sade shows in England tend to be a little stiff, think they have to be cool, waiting to be impressed. Here was totally different; this might be Manhattan, but there was no pretence at anything other than extreme excitement, and as showtime got closer, so the collective glee at her imminent arrival swelled and rose. Then as the house lights dimmed, so the roar emerged.

I am inevitably taken back to that girl in a high ponytail in a lowly squat assuming she could sing, assuming she could write, then diligently, elegantly, often stubbornly making it happen. Watching her all those times, fighting her inhibitions, challenging her limits, growing and learning, becoming this Sade.

Her band, the same boys she gathered together all those years ago, always appear first, reminding us all that Sade is indeed a band and a brilliant one at that, tight and funky. Paul Denman's bass worn high on his chest sets the tone – this is music for the soul and the solar plexus – and an insistent, earthy rhythm fills the room. Then she slides onto the stage, barefoot, elegantly but simply attired, small and lithe and smiling, and the tsunami of sound envelops the arena, a welcome so warm and embracing that I catch my breath and feel intensely proud of my friend, nervous but proud.

I needn't be nervous; she knows how to do it now. Sade has developed a show; choreographed and slick, yet still earthy and warm, working with trusted colleagues in design and lighting, who combine to magnify the minutiae, to enlarge and enhance her understatement and precision, to inflate and concentrate the intimacy of a Sade set so that it fills a giant hall without ever going stadium. Rather than magnify what she is doing, she shrinks the room to her size so that everybody feels close.

Despite the visuals and the choreography, the giant screens and the big sound, it is still a simple Sade show. She is still largely still, the magnetic epicentre of attention. Making it all appear effortless, she doesn't do too much because too much would be too much, yet she is infinitely watchable. All eyes on those smiling eyes as she breaks into a grin during a duet with Leroy on 'Nothing Can Come Between Us' or shuts them tight to summon a final feline roar on 'Is it a Crime?' She'll bow down to Paul Denman in his bass solo on 'Smooth Operator' and put her arm round Stuart in recognition of years of brilliance.

The show doesn't deviate much from the sound of the records – it's on point, precise, sharp, yet warm and inclusive – because that is how she wants things to sound. Sade only deals in optimum. So what you get is the perfect Sade sound on those lovely Sade songs with the woman herself present to manifest the magic. It's a rare treat, worth a decade of waiting. It's proof positive that you do not have to go over the top to reach the top.

Chapter 14

Other Jazz Stories

I interviewed Miles Davis once. It didn't go well. Miles doesn't answer questions, he asks them, especially the one about whether a bad person can be a great artist.

Jazz is littered with fractured souls, the damaged and the driven, for whom this spontaneous, limitless yet near-impossible music provides an outlet. Their talent is tested and deconstructed every night up on stage, every solo a precipice, every career a smoke trail in the dark to be blown away by the next kid, the next sound, the next wave; jazz moves on. Throw in addiction and racism, exile and poverty. Jazz journeys rarely end well.

Miles to me is Picasso in a broken mirror, the most brilliant, restless, ruthless artists of their age; one painted in visuals, the other in sound. Neither were exactly exemplary human beings, especially in their shameful treatment of women, their shameful treatment of most everybody. But that does not detract from *Guernica* or *Kind of Blue*. Does not diminish the thrill of watching Miles on stage. He was Miles.

As a jazz fan there is an inherent, inevitable melancholy at the ones you missed. Jazz not only tells stories, it is in itself a story, a compelling narrative arc starting in fetid and fecund New Orleans and leading always to the next new thing. There are few left who caught those early chapters, but I met people who saw Satchmo and Charlie Parker and Thelonious Monk. I know a man who saw John Coltrane in unlikely Kilburn and Walthamstow, the only two places he played in London, and if I could travel to any time past in my city, that would probably be my destination. J. C. was a God-like talent, spiritual jazz made flesh, but Albert Ayler is my personal Holy Ghost and Holy Grail. Albert also made it to these shores and even played at my alma mater, the LSE, for a concert recorded by the BBC but never aired because it was considered too extreme for sensitive British ears. Another little Albert Ayler tragedy way before my time. He was floating in the Hudson River before I knew what jazz was. Jazz wasn't ever the same again.

I love the far reaches of this music, the way it challenges you with the discordant and the disconcerting. I can dig a good thrash, but I also love melody and simplicity; a tune is occasionally welcome, and beauty is never a bad thing. Free jazz all too often has a very high price, paid by the listener. I've spent too many nights watching self-indulgence prevail over shared pleasure. The term 'improv' is a huge warning sign. If it's good, it's jazz, and I'm a jazz fan.

I'm well aware that the music I love most is not everybody's cup of tea; sometimes even for me it leaves a bitter taste, but then every now and then it will be absolutely revelatory. I've learned a lot about the human spirit watching jazz. The creativity, the spontaneity, the way the individual can soar because of the strength of the collective. I've seen Ornette Coleman dancing gently to 'Lonely Woman' and Pharoah Sanders getting it on and banging a gong while yodelling. Those are memories which make me smile every time I summon them up. If the creator does indeed have a master plan, I'm glad it included those two.

My personal odyssey started with the Crusaders, funk and fusion, which I still love, and then travelled backwards. The second review I ever wrote for the *NME* was Ella Fitzgerald and Oscar Peterson at the Royal Festival Hall in 1979. After my Spandau piece, the *NME* asked me who I wanted to review, and I picked Ella. It might not seem like a particularly radical move now, but back then, when every other rock writer was obsessed with the Gang of Four and the Fall, choosing to sing the praises of the *grande dame* of scat singing was pretty daring for a twenty-year-old would-be hip music writer.

Of course, I wrote that Ella was fabulous because she was. Fabulous, majestic and charming, commanding the hall with her authority and dexterity, her tisket and her tasket. It was a proper education to have witnessed one of the undeniables, albeit at the back end of her career. But even back then, while acknowledging her magnificence and musicality, I knew I was actually more Billie than Ella. Emotion over technique, soul over sheen.

I've always preferred my jazz deep-blue, daring and dark. So I was less than impressed by Oscar Peterson. He was a technically gifted pianist, of course, but too slick for my personal bent, simultaneously florid and arid, and I said so. Looking back, I was perhaps both a little brave and extremely arrogant to be criticising such a master, but if you are to have any critical faculties, you have to get to know what you like. And you can't like everything. I never got to dig Oscar Peterson, whereas Bill Evans . . .

Jazz is a constant process of discovery and at that stage I didn't know I liked Bill Evans, didn't know that the man who might be the greatest pianist of all time, the most lyrical, magical and moving (and among the most horribly addicted), played regularly at Ronnie's, and I could theoretically have just about seen him. Watching Bill Evans play 'Waltz for Debby' in a small room is a miracle I never witnessed. I can mourn the ones that got away, like a weary fisherman, but also celebrate the fact that I caught some big names back in the day, or rather the night. Jazz belongs to the night.

Art Pepper could well be a contender for worst human being ever to blow a horn. His autobiography *Straight Life* is a litany of misogyny, racism, crime and callousness, a horribly compelling, staggeringly candid portrait of a bad life well and truly lived. In between long prison stretches and frequent fist fights, armed robberies, and endless opiate blackouts, he somehow played the toughest yet tenderest alto sax imaginable. And I saw him as an old guy, ravaged but defiant, hair dyed boot-wax black to match his soul, bearing many scars, unbowed and unflinching yet capable of creating the very sweetest, gentlest melodies imaginable. He blew a tune called 'Our Song', a ballad so enveloping and luscious, so seemingly heartfelt, that it haunts me to this day and continues to make me wonder how such beautiful music could emanate from such a dreadful man. Jazz poses many questions.

There was something about those clean-cut California boys. Stan Getz was almost as bad as Art Pepper, another gun-wielding, misogynistic drug fiend with a terrible reputation. When he had a heart operation in later life, fellow jazzer Bob Brookmeyer famously asked, 'Did they put one in?' Ronnie Scott, whose life as a club runner was made hell by Getz's charmless demands and sour demeanour, made an entire comedy routine out of Stan's rudeness. But he kept booking him – after all, this was the man who blew that solo on 'Girl From Ipanema'. And when you heard it played live, life was momentarily weightless. All sins forgiven.

Chet Baker wasn't much better. He worked with Pepper and Getz, scored and used with Pepper and Getz, three products of the same West Coast scene, who preferred smack to anything and anybody. Chet was a user in every sense, a shameless, selfish drifter, who floated from seedy tenderloin to seedy tenderloin, copping, playing, copping, moving on, leaving chaos and heartbreak in his wake. But he was also one of the most beautiful young men ever and, even as a ravaged old man, one of the most beautiful players on any instrument in any genre. So we loved him, even if he seemed immune to love.

Chet, with his diabolical habits, was blessed and cursed with the looks and the tone of a host of angels, so people let him get with away with it. Sing us a song, Chet, and we'll forgive everything. I saw Chet sing a couple of songs in Covent Garden with that bruised choirboy voice of his, weary and stoned, riddled with pathos and pain but entrancing and otherworldly. His singing was kind of magnificent, kind of wrong, swinging gently, swinging sadly, soft and junk-sick. Watching this human shell whisper sweet words was thrilling and disturbing. But his playing was astonishing.

This wreck of a man, looking for all the world like a worn-out old street addict, his fine features deformed, his mouth a mess, his trousers stained, his dignity shot, until he put a trumpet to his lips. Then he became an angel once again, all cheekbones and charm. It's like he only became complete when the mouthpiece touched his mouth.

Jazz is so compelling because it is the most direct art form, instantaneous and unfiltered, a straight line to the soul, and what emerged from this broken man's essence was unique. His tone was frail at times, just missing the mark, bending at the edges, wayward but still wonderful, at others clear and concise, always just behind the beat, yet absolutely on point. His music had a lightness of touch, an ethereal levity which made it and him and us soar to the seedy heavens.

Perhaps we were hearing what Chet was feeling on his intravenous speedball cloud, the sound coming straight from his ruined veins. All the chaos, disorder and disaster of his life quietened, made sweet and soft, made into melody. Untrained, unable to read music, Chet blew straight from his dark heart and shattered every heart in town. I'm very glad I saw the man before he fell off a ledge in a cheap Amsterdam hotel. Gladder still that I never got to know him.

I got to know Dexter Gordon, at least for a few minutes. It was one of those midweek, late-night second sets in Ronnie's in the mid-eighties, before they did the club up and did away with 3 a.m. finishes. Long tall Dexter was on something of a final flourish, having starred as himself in Bertrand Tavernier's fine movie *Round Midnight*. So the earlier session had sold out, but now, in the wee small hours, there was a wee small crowd present. I'd stuck around because I had a proper crush on the girl behind the bar, a smart and sophisticated French woman with dark hair and dark eyes that I was staring hopelessly into at the old back bar in the far corner.

I knew I had no chance with the woman, but the whole scenario just suited my battered romantic soul. It was far too late on Wednesday night in Soho, the lights were low, and Dexter was playing low and bluesy while I swooned over a far-too-cool-for-me Parisian beauty. It felt like a scene from a jazz movie, the soundtrack slow and easy, the focus soft and blurry. No one could play slow and easy like Dexter, deep down in the bottom register with his resolutely old-fashioned style, and his tone like honey and whisky. He stuck pretty much to ballads, with that lazy, sentimental lilt of his, as if he were specifically serenading my fruitless yearning.

Then halfway through a half-hearted but still heartbreaking solo, he laid his horn to rest and ambled graciously over to the bar where I was sitting, and perched his long frame on the stool next to me. And when Dexter sits next to you, you know you've been sat next to. He lit up a cigarette, which you could still do in those different days, while the band up on the stand just kept on playing; brushes scraping over skins, the bass walking a line, the piano vamping gently away. Filling time till Dexter returned.

'Good evening, Mr Gordon,' is the only thing I really

remember saying, but I offered to buy him a drink and I seem to recall he had a bourbon. I don't remember a single word he said, but the sound of his voice, so like the sound of his saxophone, resonates still. It was a full, rounded African American voice, cultured and profound, mahogany-rich, yet burred with the traces of a life lived, a sonorous patina of jazz habits. Dexter had also been to bad places, paid his demon dues, but his voice and his presence carried no trace of badness, a sophisticated, learned voice from a big gentle man. It sounded a lot like love.

And I presume we talked of jazz and Paris and movies. I know we talked slowly for many long minutes, and I looked over to see the band desperately glancing at us, trying to keep it up, wondering when the main man would return to the stage, but Dexter didn't seem in any hurry. It's hard to imagine Dexter Gordon in a hurry. So charming was this giant that the usually *froide* French girl behind the bar melted and gave us both another round free, which he finished off with a flourish before thanking us both, nodding and finally wandering back on to the stage, picking up his tenor sax and continuing the tune without missing a beat, like that sweet hiatus had never happened.

But it had, and it remains one of the loveliest little vignettes of my many hours in jazz clubs. Sitting with Dexter was like sitting with C. L. R. James, like sitting with Zeus maybe, if he drank whisky. Bad men can make good music, no doubt, they can make good company too, in a bad way. But Dexter seemed like one of the good guys, and jazz has those too. I've been lucky enough to get to know many musicians over the years, and the jazz men and women – and thankfully now there are more and more of the latter – are the best. Not motivated by money or fame, lacking rock'n'roll egos or showbiz vanities, they are purely musicians, and usually impure joy. And they live by night. If you ever have a night out in Soho with Guy Barker or Ian Shaw, be sure to call your insurers.

Another Soho night from the mid-eighties which is lodged in the memory had a very different energy from Dexter's dreamy sojourn. It was that year's visit to Ronnie's from Art Blakey and his Jazz Messengers, who were back with the latest roster of young talents passing through the academy. Blakey by this stage was an avuncular little white-haired man, still a titan on the kick drums and a taskmaster as a bandleader, but genial company with a rasping, smiling voice and a huge, wrinkled smile. We were introduced backstage before the gig and he seemed thrilled that a young London journalist was so interested in his music. Little did he know what was to come.

Blakey himself had a malign side to his story — as a younger man with a bad habit of his own, he apparently introduced many an impressionable recruit to the dubious delights of getting high. Some didn't make it out to the other side, including Lee Morgan, the sharpest and coolest of all the trumpet Messengers. His life was ended by a bullet from his lover's gun when she could no longer stand his chronic using, another tragic jazz story. Lee Morgan played high and fast; his crystalline solo on 'A Night in Tunisia' is a monument to hard bop at its very toughest, a brilliant, brittle torrent of notes with a jagged Levantine edge. An unlikely dance track.

But in London in the mid-eighties, jazz dance was a big underground scene. The DJ Paul Murphy, who ran his now legendary jazz rooms at the Wag and the Electric Ballroom, had cultivated a crowd of young Londoners, mainly black kids from Tottenham and Brixton, Ladbroke Grove and Peckham, who danced a furious, feet-flashing, quick-stepping, body-spinning dance to the most ferociously out-there jazz and Latin sides. And it so happened that 'A Night in Tunisia' by Blakey was one of the top tunes on that scene, and so it happened that many of the best dancers, including the faces from the street troupe IDJ (I Dance Jazz), had bought tickets to Ronnie's to see Blakey's band of Messengers.

Ronnie Scott's is of course a seated venue and one where the music is taken seriously; sagely nodding heads and polite applause are usually the most energetic sign of a good gig and an appreciative audience. And when the Messengers emerged, with their diminutive master sitting on his drum stool, and began to play to a sold-out crowd, it seemed like another normal night at Ronnie's. But at some point, two or three numbers into the set, Blakey called 'A Night in Tunisia' and those distinctive opening notes blasted out. That was the signal.

All around the venue young Londoners, attired in their 'up West' best, suddenly leapt from their seats and began performing their exuberant, lightning steps; twirling, dipping, and strutting with the ferocious beat, fast and indeed furious displays of youthful jazz joy. I believe Ronnie's had never seen the like. And I looked at Blakey and the man almost dropped his sticks as his grin became broader than Broadway and the already breakneck beat speeded up even more, cracking rim shots ringing round the room and the trumpet solo soaring as the young dancers whirled and shimmied.

After the show I spoke to Mr Blakey briefly and he was beside himself, beaming; never, he said, in all his years had he seen an audience anywhere in the world do that. This music, so often seen as po-faced and pretentious, was taken back to the bordellos and ballrooms from which it first emerged. I was excited too, convinced that only in London, with its fabulous club culture and subculture, would that have happened. To see those amazing kids dancing made an old drummer very happy. It was 'A Night in Tunisia' to remember.

Another unforgettable though slightly uncomfortable night in Ronnie Scott's occurred in the next century, on Monday 8 August 2011. The date is important because it was the night that London was indeed burning, the riots which began in Tottenham leading to conflagrations and confrontations all across town. And it was also the night that there was a power cut and a black out in Soho.

Matthew Halsall, a trumpeter from Manchester, was the man we'd gone to see, perhaps my favourite British player of the era with a lovely ethereal tone and a band of relentless spiritual explorers, including a fiery and fluid tenorist called Nat Birchall. Before the gig I was sitting with my jazz mate Rob Ryan in the Bar Italia, watching it kick off in Croydon, Enfield, Lewisham; windows gone, cars overturned, flames leaping on the big screen at the back where they usually show Serie A. It was clear that the London mob, hoods up, inhibitions down, had been unleashed and there was a razor-sharp edge in the air as we walked across Frith Street.

The room was agitated with rumour as we waited for the band, tales of sedition and pillage, talk of a column of *sansculottes* heading from the flaming *banlieues* towards the West End intent on looting, larceny and maybe murder. It was against this febrile backdrop that the band emerged and began playing their deep, healing jazz. Two numbers in, the opening notes of Alice Coltrane's monumental 'Journey in Satchidananda' filled the room, the apogee of spiritual jazz, the anthem of tranquillity, when suddenly all the lights went off and the amplification died.

To say that it was eerie is a massive understatement, and a frisson of fear filled that venerable venue. For a few minutes nobody knew what was going on – had power lines been intentionally cut, were we under attack, was this the work of the mob? I went to the front door to see what was happening outside, and all of Soho had been plunged into black, a medieval blanket of darkness spread across the streets, while a police helicopter hovered menacingly overhead.

Back inside, candles came out to provide flickering light and the management announced that there was indeed an unexplained power cut over the whole of Soho, but the band would play on acoustically. I don't think anybody left; instead we settled in and turned up our ears as the harpist plucked the opening notes of 'Journey . . .' yet again. The world outside had gone awry, but the healing force of this music calmed all, made the dark night magical and bright with hope. London was burning, but the flame of jazz kept us all safe.

Loving jazz and learning about jazz has taught me many life lessons. Taking risks is crucial – the music does not progress without risk-taking; diving into the unknown doesn't always work, but every now and then it will result in something wonderful, spiritual, something like *A Love Supreme*. Tradition and modernity are not opposites – all the best new jazz has come from people who knew and respected and indeed cherished the tradition; they absorbed the past to create the future. Miles knew Buddy Bolden just like Picasso knew Velázquez. We move forwards by understanding where we have come from.

Above all, being a jazz fan has taught me that the more you invest, the more you get back – cultural karma. You have to learn about jazz, read about jazz, study its sleeve notes, its history, collect the records, understand the personalities, the progression, the lineage. No other form of human endeavour – apart perhaps from cricket and the *corrida* – offers as little to the untrained ear or eye. If you don't know what is going on up on the bandstand, then it can indeed seem like a cacophony, but once you understand the story, it all falls into place.

And Miles has a place in that story like no other. I can't say Miles Davis is my favourite musician – there has always been something cold and distant about his music – but I have no doubt he is the most important musician ever to play jazz, arguably the greatest musical genius of his century. And I was lucky enough to see him play live. I was unlucky enough to interview him.

From today's perspective you would imagine that Miles Davis in 1984 was a huge star that would easily sell out major venues.

His star has not waned one inch since his death and in books and biopics he is universally portrayed as a giant and a genius. But back then, he struggled to fill the Hammersmith Odeon and his record company were desperately trying to drum up media interest. (I saw Curtis Mayfield in a half empty Dingwalls at about the same time, and David Bowie failed to fill medium-sized halls with his Tin Machine). So they arranged for me to meet Miles the day after the show for a feature in *The Face*.

On stage Miles was live evil, the dark magus, silent and dismissive, his back turned to the audience, crouched over a keyboard, pulsing daubs of electronic noise, using his horn sparingly but cuttingly, like a sound sabre, a star fighting his own wars. He was brilliant because he was Miles, with all that entails – his aura could have stopped the traffic on the Westway – but the material was pop and hip-hop. Until it wasn't. Until he decided to let it flow.

Over the rumble of a subterranean bass, he picked his way through a solo as piercing and unsettling, as sad and lonely and lovely as any sound I've ever heard. He played with a mute, which only served to magnify the plaintive melancholy and majesty of his voice and he reminded everybody present that he was indeed the one. And then he turned his back again.

I had to interview him next day.

Of course I was nervous and excited at the prospect of meeting the great and terrible man, and I arrived a little early at the West London hotel which Mr Davis had chosen as his base. I was ushered into a corridor and told to wait outside the room until I was invited in. So I waited and I waited, and then I did a whole lot more waiting. An hour went by, and my nerves only increased with the waiting. I remember asking an assistant when he would be ready and received only a shrug. Two very slow hours went by sitting in a hallway and I was on the verge of leaving when, finally, the door to the room opened and I was ushered in.

The curtains were pulled tight, and the large suite was steeped in darkness. Mr Davis was lying in some kind of striped pyjama ensemble on a four-poster bed propped up on elaborate brocade pillows, and all around the room were dark men, some in dark glasses, a retinue of helpers or followers or acolytes whose stares as I entered the room were as sharp as a Miles solo. Nobody spoke. Not a word. So I did.

I certainly can't recall in any kind of detail what I blurted out, but it was something along the lines of what an honour it was to be there, how I was a huge fan and what a thrill it had been to witness Mr Davis live last night. Miles listened to this but did not look directly at me; instead he pondered for a few seconds, then spoke directly to one of the men by his bedside. His voice was quiet and coarse, a sibilant bark, rasping and curt. 'Tell him to fuck off.'

Chapter 15

The Man

We need to address the Van Morrison question.

Back in 1974 I watched a show which was revelatory, which has stayed with me to this day, which I still talk about to anybody who will listen, and I wasn't even there. It was a film of Van Morrison and the Caledonia Soul Orchestra live at the Rainbow, which was broadcast on BBC Two late one night. I think it was an *Old Grey Whistle Test* presentation and it was definitely one of the shows which became part of the classic live album *It's Too Late to Stop Now*.

I was fifteen at the time and sitting on my own on the sofa in my mum's council house becoming increasingly excited. It was partly the exuberant performance by a striking blonde-haired cello player called Terry Adams, swaying and rocking ecstatically to the rhythm while she wielded her bow, which stirred a young boy's blood, but it was also what the podgy balding bloke in the too-tight trousers was doing.

I'd never seen or heard anything like it; this man with an intense, hypnotic voice, sometimes harsh, other times velvet-soft, but always soulful, was singing in an incantatory, almost mystical style. He kept repeating phrases, repeating phrases, repeating phrases, stopping suddenly, stuttering, wailing, roaring, whispering, like he was perhaps possessed, like he was some kind of fundamentalist hellfire-and-brimstone pastor saving souls on an East Belfast street.

His eyes closed, his plump face reddened, the sweat glistening on his comb-over, sinews tightening, fists clenching; during one particularly thrilling section his little legs suddenly kicked up in the air in a startling, comical fashion, almost splitting his jeans or his difference. He was ungainly yet magnetic, lost in a dream executing all this in perfect time to this near perfect band. What a performance. What in heaven's name do you call that?

I said that I've talked about that live show and the accompanying album ever since and one day I talked about it backstage after a show to Ivan, the man himself. I told him that my life was changed by watching that performance and that *It's Too Late to Stop Now* is still the greatest live album ever released. He listened intently, which is not always the case with Van, and said, 'Do you think so?' I reiterated that I did indeed think so, I was sure so. 'Well, there's more where that came from,' he said, 'I must look into it.'

And indeed he did, releasing two whole new volumes from the same tour (including a wondrous version of 'Snow in San Anselmo') and a DVD of that inspirational 1973 Finsbury Park show, all of which just proved yet again that it is one of the highlights of twentieth-century music and one of the gigs I would most love to have been at. I've been at many, many Van Morrison shows since, I've introduced him on stage a number of times, and I still cannot fully answer the Van Morrison question. But first let's talk a little about live albums as a genre.

Is it fair to say that most of them are not very good? That Faces album is a good example of why they are not very good. The looseness, the messy, boozy, loveable live-ness of that band on stage was a massive part of their appeal. They were a bunch of groovy geezers having a real good time, which was fine when you were part of the party, but later, in the cold light of day, just sounds a bit of a mess, especially when compared to the much crisper studio versions.

It seems to me that most bands divide into one of two camps: those who try to make their live shows as much like the records as possible, who aim for a kind of onstage perfection, and those who change everything up, who make the live versions noticeably different – looser, wilder, longer, funnier, funkier, jazzier, rockier . . . If it's the first, then what is the point of a live album, and if it is the latter, they had better be really damn good, and really well recorded, to make it work on your hi-fi at home.

Van is certainly in the latter category; he changes it up every time and he wasn't just good on that 1973 tour – he was magnificent, at the very peak of his unequalled powers. And what's more, that band, or orchestra, of his, with its full string and horn sections, was equally superb, capable of going with his every twist and twitch, shadowing his incredible use of dynamics to punch it up and smooth it down in a single phrase. Great musicians who were so well-drilled they hit every spot, yet so well-oiled they could slip and slide at will. Tight as fuck and loose as hell. And it is joyous to listen to. Even Ivan sounds like he's having fun.

It's Too Late to Stop Now still ranks as my all-time favourite live rock or soul album. (Live jazz is a bit different because jazz is designed to be different every night; it is improvised music and most studio recordings are pretty close to being recorded live anyway, so there is not so great a distinction.) But there are other fine examples of the form.

Bill Withers *Live at Carnegie Hall* is another monument, made so splendid by Bill's incredibly engaging onstage persona, his stories and asides, his introductions and elaborations. He extends 'Grandma's Hands' from a slight two-minute tribute to a joyous, rollicking visit to the church. He tells a tragic and moving tale before 'I Can't Write Left-Handed', which might just be the greatest anti-Vietnam war song of them all and yet does not appear anywhere else. He holds a note during 'Hope She'll Be Happier', which goes on so long you can feel the audience holding their collective breath. He is a great human being as well as a great musician, and you fully get that on *Live at Carnegie Hall*. Donny Hathaway is another commanding soul performer perhaps best heard on his live outings.

Sinatra at the Sands, where the Basic band swings so hard it makes you dizzy. Traffic's *On the Road*, the sound of a brilliant band falling elegantly apart in front of your ears. Most of *The Last Waltz* by The Band, but most specifically the incredible version of 'The Night They Drove Old Dixie Down' with the horn section directed by Allen Toussaint and Levon's unbearably raw vocals. Patti Smith is also raw, raucous and imperiously poetic on *Teenage Perversity and Ships in the Night*, the only bootleg I ever bother to play.

Bob Marley live at the Lyceum, Johnny Cash live at various prisons, the Allman Brothers *At Fillmore East*, taking rock'n'roll as close to spiritual jazz as it will ever get. I even love a couple of live albums by bands I wouldn't otherwise listen to: Thin Lizzy *Live and Dangerous*, where the dangerous charm of Phil Lynott shines through, and the sadly beautiful Nirvana *MTV Unplugged in New York*, which brings me close to tears every time I hear it.

All of those records are great because they are all by truly great artists, absolute *nonpareils*, at their absolute peak. (And please don't tell me to put the Who *Live at Leeds* in that list – it is an overblown, stodgy, leaden mess.) Those are the best live albums because they are by the very best bands. And *It's Too Late to Stop Now*, by that awkward little bloke from Belfast who defies genre, is the very best of the lot. So, is Van Morrison great live?

I didn't get to see Mr Morrison for many years after that life-altering televised experience as a teenager. I started collecting his records – *Hard Nose the Highway* and *Veedon Fleece* are both underrated masterpieces from that period, but punk came along, and even though his original band Them had been about as close to proto punk as you can get – Patti Smith's 'Gloria' is a glorious homage – he got sidelined in my mind. But I never forgot the power of that TV show.

I can't precisely recall when I first managed to make it to a Van Morrison gig, which probably points to the fact that I was a little underwhelmed. But equally I cannot keep count of the number of times I have seen him since – certainly dozens of times, which undoubtedly points to the fact that there is something very special about the man they call 'the man'. What is it about Van Morrison?

I get rather nervous telling people to go and see Van Morrison play live, and he still plays live a lot. Van doesn't come cheap, especially if you see him in a small venue, and you really need to see Van now in a small venue, as his shows in later life have become more and more intimate, internalised, smaller, no high kicking or ecstatic cello playing, no wild exhortations or declamatory gestures. I also get nervous because I know what is going to happen.

Van Morrison has always been a very economical performer. If you watch the film of him at Finsbury Park in 1973, even then he had a large wristwatch on his left arm, worn over his shirt so that he could keep exact track of the time. He now never plays a moment more than his contracted ninety minutes, rarely does an encore, often doesn't communicate with the audience, rarely plays more than a couple of his 'hits', and even then grudgingly, and fills the show out with old blues covers and repeated blows upon his saxophone or harmonica.

His reputation as a curmudgeon is sadly well-deserved, and he can come across as a grumpy little old bloke, hiding beneath a hat pulled down to cover his sweaty pate, doing the absolute minimum before taking the money and running. Which he literally does at the end of the show, leaving the band up on stage for the crescendo while he's out the back and away. He will murder 'Moondance' just for the fun of it. He will drive you mad as you yearn for him to sing 'Caravan' but he does 'Symphony Sid' instead. He will rant irrationally about Covid restrictions or some other bugbear. All that is true. And yet. And yet time and time again I go, and I urge you to go too. So why? What is it? That is the Van Morrison question.

The first thing to say is that of all the ageing rock'n'roll knights, Sir Van's voice has held up by far and away the best. Compared to his fellow illustrious Sirs: Rod, Elton and Mr McCartney, his vocal cords are in amazing shape. Pliable, pitch-perfect and profound, he can still reach down to the depths and soar to the heavens. Perhaps that economy has served him well. As has his decision to stop drinking years ago. I dread to think what Van was like drunk.

So he's in amazing vocal shape, though Van's voice is not always a pretty instrument. He carries the harsh cadences and brusque insistence of the staunch Protestant streets he came from, like Ian Paisley with his ever more raucous NO, NO, NOs. Rarely sweet, his delivery is nonetheless incredibly soulful, rich and textured, and also still lithe and supple, and what's more, it feels totally authentic. Sir Van still sings it like he means it, channelling the smouldering embers in his complex psyche.

What about his notorious lack of communication and badinage on stage? Well, what about it? Van is not there to muck about; once he steps up on stage, he is in his performing tunnel; he has his allotted ninety minutes and he is going to use it to do what he does best, and small talk is not what Van does best. Occasionally, if he's in a particularly good mood, he will acknowledge the fans, but that can just break the spell. And Van weaves a spell.

He is a deadly serious musician; in fact, I've never met anybody more serious, more knowledgeable or more obsessed with music. It is all he really talks about, all he really cares about, and I suspect all he has cared about since he first explored his father's record collection as a kid and fell in love with Ray Charles and Charlie Parker, Muddy Waters and Mahalia Jackson. He is up there with them and very much sees himself as part of that continuum. And anybody who plays with him had better come up to scratch, which is why he has such terrific bands and such a terrifying reputation in the industry. If you talk to him and you know your stuff, he can be fascinating, but he does not suffer musical fools gladly.

Getting to know Van a little, and I suspect you only ever get to know Van a little, I have begun to understand him a little more. He is a dreadfully shy man, self-conscious and socially awkward. He is also deeply sceptical after a life lived in the shark-infested waters of the music biz, always suspecting the worst, and indeed imbued with that profound Ulster Protestant defensiveness and insularity. He builds barricades around himself.

He can be occasionally funny, but even that can be awkward, and one incident backstage involving Miami Steve Van Zandt and a vacuum cleaner still makes me wince. He can be terribly demanding, once insisting that he would not go on unless the apple pie and custard in his rider appeared in his dressing room before the show. He is not easy company. Eggshells are everywhere.

He is also, amazingly, after a lifetime spent on stage (he was in Them at just fifteen), still nervous before every gig. I was about to introduce him for the first time at the Royal Albert Hall a few years ago and I was feeling a touch of anxiety about stepping out onto that most hallowed dais. I assumed Van would be blasé, but absolutely not, he was literally shaking with terrors, which is another reason he gets into the performing mode and does not let it slip. He is uptight because he needs to keep everything tight in order to do it. And boy, can he do it. But what is it exactly that he does?

This is where we need to talk about *duende*. This is where we need to talk about flamenco and bullfighting. This certainly isn't the place to go into the many legitimate and complex moral questions around the ancient Spanish practice of slaughtering six brave and beautiful bulls in a public arena (*la arena*, by the way, is simply Spanish for sand, the enclosed sandy circle where matadors walk to do their bloody job). But we cannot understand *duende* without involving bullfighting and we cannot understand Van without discussing *duende*.

Bullfighting, or more accurately the *corrida* – the act of dancing with and then dispatching wild bulls – and its close cultural cousin flamenco, are the two aspects of Spanish life (and death) where the concept of *duende* is most pertinent. Literally the *duende* is an elf, or a sprite, an exterior being or spirit who descends upon a performer, inhabiting them, inspiring them, taking control of their soul, and raising their game, so to speak, elevating the art to supernatural levels, lifting what they do above the realms of mere human endeavour.

To the Spanish it is a form of possession affecting the person up on stage or in the arena. But it also affects the audience, for we too will become instantly aware that the *duende* has arrived, collectively we will feel its force, know that we are all in the presence of this intense, intoxicating imp. Here in Britain, we might say there is magic in the air, call it a magic moment. Silence and excitement will enrapture us, our skin will tingle, our hairs stand up on end. That is the sign of the presence of the *duende*. That is very important to understanding Van Morrison.

In flamenco, it is what elevates a singer or dancer above the ordinary, makes them reach down into the recesses to bring forth the passions within. Flamenco is a dark art, brought forth only at night, and if you have ever been in a scruffy bar in, say, Seville, Cádiz or Jerez in the early hours of a sultry Andaluz night, you might have experienced something like this.

It usually begins with knuckles rapping upon a table, in a rhythmic pattern, and others then join in with *palmas*, hands clapping softly together, creating ever more complex poly-rhythms. Then a soft, guttural wailing emerges, an oriental, otherworldly cry from inside a man or woman sitting in a corner, and the room falls instantly silent. They know. We all know. Eyes closed, the singer will ululate, and the audience will concentrate, transfixed as this ancient sound swells and grows, becoming insistent and urgent, painful and powerful, ecstatic or tragic, filling the room with emotion. *Olés* and exal-tations will follow from those who are aware that we have been joined by the *duende*.

It is the same in the *corrida*, where a matador in his suit of lights will very occasionally be raised above the bloody mortal-ity of his task to reach extraordinary heights in his deathly dance. But only rarely. The *duende* does not deign to appear too often. It is also important to note that a person, a performer, does not *have duende*; it is not a character trait or a quality. If you meet Van Morrison off stage, he is not a charismatic man; he will not appear remarkable or mystical. But more than any other performing artist I have ever seen, he knows how to summon the *duende*.

Here we must talk about Curro Romero. The comparison between these two men from different worlds, but both noted performers, is truly remarkable. Curro, like Van is a short, stout slightly ungainly-looking old fellow with a low centre of gravity, but a high sense of self-esteem. But then he is not alone in thinking he is one of the all-time greats. His bronze statue sits proudly outside the Maestranza, Seville's imposing river-side bullring. He is retired now, but every time he appeared in that exalted arena, in a career which spanned over four decades, it was completely sold out. Seville loved Curro; he was the local hero and usually he was useless.

They say that early in his career he had been more consistently good at his bloody craft, an elegant and creative man, but was always known as an *artista*, an unpredictable, temperamental *torero* who relied on the inspiration and intervention of the *duende* to perform at his best. When it did not arrive, he simply went through the motions, caring not a jot about the reaction of the crowd. Take the money and walk.

Later in life – and he continued appearing well into his sixties, much later than almost all other bullfighters – that inspiration became less and less frequent, and he became more and more useless, a fat old bloke who could do little right. Yet every time he appeared the ring was *no hay billetes,* not a spare seat to seen. They came just in case the *duende* did.

Occasionally he would show the briefest flourishes of his former brilliance, a half-pass here, a graceful twirl there, just a hint of genius, then nothing. Shameless and useless, he would literally be booed off the sand after disappointing the full house yet again. Yet time and again they came, just in case, and then one year, after a long fallow period, this portly old bloke walked slowly onto that sand once again, always upright and serious, just like Van, and the *duende* decided to arrive.

As the wild bull charged across the ring and Curro picked up his big, pale red cape and took the first steps towards his roaring adversary, so the whole arena, those many thousands of patient people, knew instantly, instinctively that it had happened. The magic had arrived, and a giant intake of breath was followed by a profound hush as this ungainly old man became suddenly young and beautiful again.

For pass after sensual, elegant, death-defying pass, he danced a slow *paso doble* with this giant bull, leading him across the ring and back again in a series of flowing, effortless, moves, each one followed by rousing ¡*Olé!*s that just grew stronger and longer with every movement. Pandemonium. Nobody present could tell you how long that series of passes by Curro Romero in Seville actually took, because he stopped all clocks, suspended time. Supernatural indeed.

That night Seville celebrated its hero just as passionately as they do their other favourite resurrection every *Semana Santa* (Holy Week). They say that what Curro did that day was religious, it was fundamental. That's what Van does. If you're lucky.

You have to accept that when you go to see him now, you are not going to get that energetic, effervescent, young, high-kicking Van. It's too late for that now. He is a portly old bloke conserving his energy and watching his watch. But – and it is the biggest 'but' in showbiz – he might just be able to summon the *duende* sufficiently to give you that time-stopping, heart-stopping moment or two. And believe me, that will do.

Does Van Morrison really rely upon some form of spiritual possession to produce his best live work? He is a dweller on the threshold of transcendence and a seeker after earthly rapture; he understands the power of reaching deep and letting go, of talking in musical tongues. But I've seen him enough times now to know that it is a well-practised routine whereby he chooses one number, usually at the climax of the set, during which he will concentrate all his energy, draw upon all his skill and experience to go beyond. To take it to the heights.

It doesn't always happen, but when the mood is right and the fates align, he takes the music right down and takes us on a spiritual journey. A simple hypnotic phrase starts to dominate, repeated and repeated, twisted and elongated, which is his way of summoning the djinn within. 'In the Garden' with its refrain of 'No guru, no method, no teacher' has become one of his chosen vehicles for this display of intense introversion. If he calls that tune, the band are alert to his every nuance as this incantation swells and grows, getting louder and softer, more and more intense. Long-time Van watchers know that he is now in the moment, and we are in the presence: it is visceral, palpable, thrilling, exhausting and arresting. This is what we came for; this is why we will come time and again. Is it *duende*? Well, it's Van.

And the answer to the Van Morrison question is always yes.

Chapter 16

Changes

What is the most musical city on earth?

I guess it depends upon what type of tunes you are after. Maybe Vienna, with its whirl of penguin orchestras and rococo concert halls, or Berlin with its barrage of beeps and beats ricocheting around all those techno clubs full of black-clad robo-dancers. I'm told that Lagos is one big boom box, with every variety of Afrobeat enlivening the streets, and Kingston, Jamaica is definitely Jamdown: reggae, dancehall and dub providing the rhythmic pulse. Havana sways constantly to *son cubano*, Buenos Aires trips the light to tango and Mexico City, with its ubiquitous mariachis in big hats and tight trousers, is a fabulous cacophony of competing sounds on every corner.

New Orleans is perhaps the most concentrated musical town of them all, with jazz, blues, funky brass, zydeco and Cajun in every bar on every ornate block in every colourful quarter. Just don't go during spring break. New York is, of course, an incredibly groovy Gotham, offering everything from jazz to Latin, hip-hop to rock from the Lincoln Center to the Bowery Bar, and it was the first place I ever travelled to in search of sonic adventures. But even Manhattan and

fashionable Brooklyn can't compete with dear old dreary
London town for the incredible scope, the staggering variety
of music on offer. London has it all.

On an average night in my city, you can hear music of every
shade, from choral recitals in city churches to ska-punk in the
back rooms of boozers. There are gospel choirs and gay choirs,
piano bars and music pubs; you can see all-female Afro-jazz in
a former hairdresser's in Dalston, ferocious free improv in a
club just up the road and old-time ragtime in a restaurant a few
doors away. There's English folk, Irish folk and Albanian folk,
Americana, pop, indie, grunge and electro in venues of every
kind in every borough, every night.

There are classical orchestras and string quartets in solemn
auditoria, opera in Covent Garden and Holland Park, huge
stars in huge stadiums, famous acts in elegant theatres and local
kids on open mics. There is cumbia and rebetiko, fado, salsa,
samba, bhangra and Qawwali in their host communities. If you
fancy a dance, there are sultry milongas, whirling ceilidhs and
booming jump-ups. You can be entertained by r'n'b, r'n'r,
EDM and the LSO.

When it comes to venues, you can take your pick from the
Albert Hall, the Festival Hall, the O2, the Barbican, Ronnie
Scott's, the 100 Club, the Brixton Academy, the Shepherd's
Bush Empire and whatever the Hammersmith Odeon is called
this week. And that's just on an average night. Factor in the
Notting Hill Carnival, the London Jazz Festival, the Proms,
Wireless, Meltdown, the Fleadh, Camden Rocks, All Points
East, Lovebox, Hyde Park, On Blackheath, On Hampstead
Heath . . . On just about every day and night there is some
kind of event or festival. And yet I regularly find myself com-
plaining that fings ain't what they used to be. Nothing in
London is what it used to be. Maybe it never was.

Much of this is, inevitably, about the fact that I am not what
I used to be either: young, that is. As much as I still love live

music and still go regularly to gigs, I tend to prefer the slightly more sedate spots where I can bag the best seat in the house and catch the last train home. My appetite for late nights with noisy bands in draughty rooms, the raucous and the riotous, has inevitably diminished. But then so has the number of places where you can experience the thrill of live music at its most raw, while the cost has just gone up and up.

The analogies with football are again close. The people's game was a predominantly working-class sport, where kids could easily afford to attend their local team, stand on huge open terraces, join in the singing and the surges, get subsidised specials to away games, and feel the life-affirming thrill of commitment, community and the craic. It was rough and ready but cheap and thrilling. Not anymore.

In the seventies, I went to watch QPR with my cousin Ian, who is the same age as me, on our own from about the age of eleven or twelve and at away games not much later. We went to pretty much every home match and saw our team at all the major stadiums in the land, and bought a pie and a programme, all on the meagre proceeds of pocket money and a paper round. (No, we didn't live in a cardboard box, we both lived in decent council houses like almost half of London's population in pre-Thatcherite days.)

Compare that with a day out now at the Arsenal, say, in their plush but soporifically bland new home, where you're not going to end up with change from fifty or sixty quid for an experience which won't come close to the visceral thrill of standing on the North Bank or the Clock End taunting Tony Adams with carrots. With comfy seats and big screens, it is like watching a match in an airport lounge, and you pay club-class prices for the privilege. Even lower down the leagues, it is no longer a cheap day out.

The corporatisation and commercialisation of football has totally changed the experience of being a fan and denied that experience almost entirely to most working-class kids. And I fear the same thing is happening to music. Yes, you can still see young bands in old pubs for a few quid, but the prices at any of the major venues for any of the major acts have become horrific, and the hundreds of pounds you need to shell out for a facile 'VIP experience' at somewhere like the O2 is obscene. Roxy Music played there recently and charged £700 for the top tickets. Bryan Ferry can't even dance.

The smaller, cheaper, grittier, and to my mind better, venues are the ones which have been disappearing at an alarming rate, and with them the bands to fill them. Soho was once awash with great, grimy places to watch music; every other basement or garret had a club and a band of some kind in it, and now, apart from the two long-established jazz stalwarts, it is almost totally bereft. Dining in restaurants has replaced dancing in basements and Crossrail took out a swathe of venues, small and large.

My kids rarely go to see bands – they can't afford the big tickets and never got into the habit of watching groups lower down the pecking order. And as the audience shrinks and the venues close, that means there are fewer and fewer groups coming through. The big-name acts today are pretty much the same as they were ten, twenty or even forty years ago. The Stones and the Who still topping the bill is rock'n'roll bed-blocking.

Or perhaps you would rather watch wholesome family entertainers like Coldplay at Wembley Stadium with a fireworks display thrown in for a thrilling finale. Not so much 'Yellow' as beige. To stand on the pitch at Wembley to watch Elton John, the Beach Boys, the Eagles *et al.* in 1985 cost £3.50, which, adjusted to inflation, equals roughly £38 today. A similar ticket for Coldplay and fireworks cost £98. And for that you actually have to endure Coldplay.

Where are the contemporary equivalents of the groups I

saw in pubs and clubs as a teenager: the Clash, the Jam, Ian Dury and the Blockheads, Madness, the Specials, the Pogues, or for that matter, a generation later, Blur, Oasis and Pulp? These were fantastic bands with big, passionate followings, international renown, but playing in small and medium-sized venues at reasonable prices. But the days of such outfits with fire in the belly, and such venues with sawdust on the floor and a stamp on your wrist, seem to be largely over. Where have all the noisy boys and girls with guitars gone?

Instead we have reverted to a glam, photoshopped world of committee-composed, computer-programmed, autotuned pop which is not designed to be played live but watched on a screen and downloaded on a phone. I admit I was never much of a fan of much pop music, never got ABBA or Take That, don't buy into Dua Lipa or Sam Smith, don't see the appeal of shiny but shallow Saturday-night karaoke acts, even if they do have a catchy tune and a pretty singer.

Pop is only ever going to be a catch-all music, an exercise in instant gratification. Whereas I know I take music too seriously, invest too much in it, but then I came of age in a time when music really mattered, when you defined yourself by the records you bought and the bands you saw. I diligently kept a journal from about the age of twelve to fifteen in which I noted every record I ever played at home on our family hi-fi. One day my older brothers wrote in it that I had played a Bay City Rollers record and I was dismayed, ashamed in case anybody saw this and believed I was capable of such appalling apostasy.

My later teenage years were defined by the Clash, by an almost religious faith, and I've never really lost my proselytising zeal for proper music. I know other people, perhaps more sane and sensible people, can just enjoy pop music for what it is. But following impassioned acts who also made great popular music like the Specials, the Jam or Blur, required commitment and repaid you with an intense, life-shaping experience. But where are their equivalents today?

Perhaps perversely, the fact that there are so few blistering young rock and pop bands playing live sets to set the teenage pulse racing, no new contemporary youth-culture equivalent of mod, punk, two-tone or even Britpop to inflame the heart and fill the halls, is one of the reasons why there is such an extraordinary multiplicity and diversity of live music on offer in London today. The lack of lads and lasses with guitars and slogans, or even synthesisers and silly haircuts and a trouser tribe to call their own, is partly why we have so much great young jazz, folk, Afro-beat, broken beats and every other beat imaginable.

There are just as many committed, impassioned, inspired young musicians as there has ever been, but they are not forming or fronting rock bands. And if they did, where would they play? Any kind of coherent scene needs a home, and finding a home of any kind in London is tough indeed.

The London rock'n'roll scene in the late fifties first percolated up in the coffee bars of Soho. Pub rock started in old Irish boozers in North London; punk began in gay clubs, strip clubs and fleapit cinemas in the West End. New Romantic emerged from Billy's, a seedy Soho pick-up joint, and the Blitz, a Second World War-themed wine bar in Covent Garden; Britpop coalesced among the run-down drinking dens and back-room kebab shops of Camden Town. All of those have pretty much gone.

Gentrification, redevelopment, stricter licensing laws, pub closures and the killer blows delivered by Crossrail have taken out so many of the musical Petri dishes where these scenes germinated. Youth culture is like fungi – it grows in dark, dank places, but in an age when the lights and lenses of mobile phones are everywhere, and Instagram provides immediate illumination, nothing has time and space to flourish. Punk was years in the making, bubbling away in back rooms before it exploded. New Romantic was a secret scene long before it hit the charts. That can't happen now in this age of instant Instagram exposure.

Scenes can still emerge. A few years back I found myself watching a very young female saxophonist called Nubya Garcia and a ragtag collective of fearless young jazzers in the Total Refreshment Centre, a windowless warehouse behind a car wash in E8. My hand was stamped as I went in, beer was served in cans from a trestle table to a crowd of cool-looking kids of every hue, talking a dozen languages. The atmosphere was hip and clandestine, the music was infectious and free. I danced like I was back in the Wag. This was one of the highlights of twenty-first-century gig-going for me. Something was stirring in the murk.

Joyous, exciting, improvised music without boundaries, this scene took in dub and Afro, funk and soul; it sounded like London looks and it restored my faith in my city's continued creativity. Nubya and Shabaka, Moses and Zara, Femi, Theon, Kamaal and Cassie: such perfect names for our glorious agglomeration of all nations; these kids – tomorrow's warriors for musical integrity – made people dance, and that made me smile. Jazz is always either dying or reviving and this lot were full of life and love.

The Total Refreshment Centre was a great venue showcasing a terrific young scene with a real buzz about it, reminding me rather of Soho nearly three decades before, where I'd seen Courtney Pine, Working Week and Animal Nightlife, a former iteration of young London's love of jazz. Then Hackney council shut it down – something to do with licensing laws. Everything to do with a staider, more bourgeois city.

Nubya has gone on to bigger things, touring the world with her band, playing a jazz prom at the Royal Albert Hall, no less. But you can't get to the Albert Hall unless you have the Total

Refreshment centre in Dalston or Steam Down in Deptford to polish your chops in. London is an eternally creative and resourceful city, and new venues are always springing up in unlikely places, but nothing has really come along to replace the much-loved institutions we have lost.

Younger musicians, whatever their genre, need the Marquee in Wardour Street, or the Astoria or the Wag, the Nashville, the Clarendon, the Palais, the tattooed 12 Bar Club, or the fabulous Rainbow in Finsbury Park. The list of the lost would take up a large chunk of this book — great venues all gone. Most of the places where I watched music as a youngster are long gone, and they are genuinely mourned and missed. Of course new ones have come along, and some of those are fantastic, Earth, a nicely raw, derelict old cinema in Dalston, is just one example. But others are less encouraging.

Recently we have seen the edgy, organic warren of bars, recording studios, clubs and music shops in haunted St Giles — once London's Tin Pan Alley, once a grimy grunge enclave, rich with the patina of decades of outsider creativity — reduced to a gaudy rock'n'roll parody. A digital corporate fantasia worthy of Dubai has sprung up in the chasm caused by Crossrail, complete with a glitzy punk-themed hotel and a hideously bling thing called 'Outernet London — an immersive entertainment centre'. This glorified amusement arcade, full of giant screens and interactive advertising hoardings and some carefully curated graffiti, is all owned by a company called Consolidated Properties. It ain't rock'n'roll and I don't like it.

Great music rises up from the gutter; it cannot be imposed from above by developers or local councils. The venue which sits in the bottom of the Outernet, is at least in part supposed to replace the Astoria over the road, the run-down, loved-up former pickle factory where my brother Reggie had his stag night and we danced in the Centre Point fountains opposite. This is where I saw Big Audio Dynamite, Blur, the Black

Crowes, and the Beastie Boys, and where I didn't see Nirvana.

The Astoria and the seedy, dodgy club beneath it, up the alleyway and down the stairs, were the epitome of the live London experience; right in the heart of town, rough, real and raucous, home to so many gloriously abandoned nights lost in music and debauchery. The Astoria was the equivalent of the Old Den at Millwall, whereas the Outernet is like the Emirates Stadium with added bling. And it wasn't just the Astoria: so many of the old haunts have gorn, their ghosts banished, the silence shaming.

I am happy to watch music in comfort at my age, but even I do not want to feel like a night out is part of some corporate machine. London is still the greatest, most musical city on earth, and I have great faith in its innate creativity, but I do fear for its rock'n'roll soul.

Chapter 17

Learning Latin

There are two faces I cannot escape. They are everywhere: muralised, immortalised, painted by anonymous people in a kind of religious fervour; stencilled icons who live on on concrete and stucco, in bars, barber's shops and bus stops, two faces of pain and beauty. Two vocalists who filled the collective soul by singing of our shared woes and joys, who suffered for our sins and died for our delectation, only to become immortals on walls. Two of my own musical heroes.

In Camden Town, which for so many years was my own town, scruffy and proud of its rock'n'roll story, Amy is omnipresent, her beehive adorning any spare space. You can do an Amy Winehouse mural tour of Camden, including the one by the Portuguese corner shop I saw every morning when I took my coffee, the one by my bank, the one by the pub, the shrine by her house. This wayward Jewish girl has become a sort of secular patron saint of Irish Catholic Camden.

Amy's instantly recognisable visage staring back from those NW1 walls is a shorthand for a community displaying rebel solidarity, for battered, tattooed pride. Here we worship this genius girl who sang of lickle carpet burns and dodging rehab,

burned at the stake of tabloid prurience, our very own Joan of
Dark. Here we side with the outsider. It was one more reason
to love Camden Town, one more reason to feel melancholy
walking its streets, one more reminder that never again will we
hear her astonishing street-smart, wise-girl words over a lilting
rocksteady beat or see her unbridled smile as she shimmies and
shakes.

In Andalucia, the deep south of Europe, where I lost my
heart and found a home so many years ago, they have their
own local vocal icon to worship, their own tainted saint, called
Camarón. It means 'shrimp', and the little giant is present in
grand plazas and twisted alleys, in two-bit fishing towns and
dusty hill-top pueblos, his ravaged, bearded, beatific face is all
over the place. Camarón was all over the place.

Wherever you travel in that blazing, mythic land, you see
him in murals, friezes and especially statues, bronze monuments, many with overtly religious overtones, a new Romany
Jesús del Gran Poder. Always that lined and vivid visage, with
his curly, leonine mane every bit as recognisable as Amy's high
hair. You can buy larger-than-life-sized effigies of Camarón in
garden centres.

Throughout Andalucia you see him, but especially deep,
deep down in the province of Cádiz, which I call my other
home. Down there in the sweltering delta of the Rio Guadalquivir, where Africa hovers in the distance and rhythmic
handclaps hang heavy in the burning air, he is worshipped.
This was his birthplace, and also the birthplace of the Romany
blues they call flamenco, the music he possessed, and which
possessed him. Here where the ululating, guttural sound of
this dark and ancient song reverberates, you will see Camarón
de la Isla time and time again. And thankfully I saw him live
before I saw him in effigy.

My love affair with Spain began as a schoolboy, besotted
from afar by stirring stories of the civil war and the dark art of

the *corrida*, I was entranced by blood, honour and sand. Then when I finally went there in my teenage years, I was mesmerised by those merciless blue skies and bone-bleached white towns, by that austere, passionate culture. I fell in love.

I moved to Barcelona in 1986 when I was twenty-six, escaping from a lost love affair and seeking a romantic dream. The Catalan capital was the happening place, but I had no idea how different Catalonia is from the other Iberia below. The music there was club music, nocturnal electronica in industrial spaces like the famed Otto Zutz, as the hedonism of the post-Franco party exploded.

They called it *La Movida*, the movement, and it made the 1980s a great – if tiring – time to be in that terrific town. There was an exuberant collective exhalation after years suffering under the suffocating shroud of fascism. There was a heady whiff of freedom in the air, which meant Barcelona was exciting and exhausting, a blurry nocturnal whirl, thrilling, haughty and hedonistic. But it wasn't really Spain.

For nearly two years I lived in that elegant, sophisticated, occasionally constipated city. Barcelona is a beautiful European town, blessed by mountains and sea, truly glorious before it was choked by tourism and obsessed by Catalanism. But I began to realise that all my romantic notions of Spain were a long way south of there. I don't remember seeing any live music in the Catalan capital, bar a couple of visiting British bands, until one night I stumbled over Andalucia in a bar in Barcelona and first heard the wail.

There is a large expatriate Andalucian community in Barcelona, who moved there during the hungry years after the civil war, trying to escape the wretched poverty of their parched homeland. Like the mass movement of African Americans from the Deep South of the United States to the industrial towns of the north. Among those migrating were Romany communities who took their music and their mores, their fiestas and their flamenco with them, only to be met with the same old racist prejudices. Just one more striking similarity between flamenco and the blues.

One night, a Catalan friend who knew his homeland well said we should travel out to some distant suburb, way beyond the fashionable city, to hear some live music. We met on the Ramblas at about ten, but rather than hurry out, we ate and drank and talked as Spaniards do, until it was already past midnight before we got into his old car and headed God knows where.

When we arrived at wherever it was, this ramshackle suburb did not feel like that cool designer city we had just left. It was run-down and dishevelled, vaguely menacing, and we parked up in what passed as a plaza and began to walk the shabby streets trying to find I knew not what. I did know that we were going to see flamenco, so expected castanets and polka dots and all the florid tourist clichés, but this seemed like an unlikely setting for such a show.

I remember my friend sticking his head in a couple of bars and asking something in rapid Castilian (no Catalan spoken here) before finally we ended up outside a nondescript place with a few religious knick-knacks in the dusty window. We had found it, but what was it?

It looked like a typical working-class watering hole with an old TV in the corner, and some congealed cold tapas in a glass case. But it was the *peña flamenca*, and that word *peña* is one you need to know. It sort of means meeting place, a bar where like-minded souls, often musicians, gather, a hangout. You get football *peñas* based around the love of a club, bullfighting *peñas* for the fans of the bloody *corrida*, but this was a *peña* dedicated to flamenco. They exist wherever there is an Andalucian community, and they all look pretty much the same.

Black-and-white photos adorned the walls, shots of dark-looking men in dark suits and white shirts, a few buxom women with big seventies hair in fancy frocks, and some faded pictures of bullfighters too. There was a green-and-white Andalucian flag (the same colours as Islam for Al-Andalus) hanging at the back of the room, where a small, raised platform, with just a couple of woven-backed chairs on it, was sitting empty. There were perhaps a couple of dozen people present, drinking and smoking around tables.

We planted ourselves at a table, ordered a beer and waited for something to happen, but I didn't really understand what that might be. I still thought of flamenco as a style of dance, all stomping and stamping by lithe lotharios and moody señoritas, but nobody in this room looked particularly athletic or likely to leap about. They were small and worn and mostly quite old, though there were a few youngsters, even a couple of kids present. It felt like a social club on a council estate where the most musical treat you might expect is some badly warbled karaoke.

Instead, we got a rhythmic rapping of knuckles upon a table from one of the men, which was clearly a sign that something was about to start. Others joined in, using their fingers and palms to create complex percussive patterns on and off the beat, before the still-seated, knuckle-knocking man started to sing.

Accompanied only by this flesh tattoo, he made a series of sounds which to my ignorant ears was somewhere between a cough and a yodel, an impassioned, deeply melancholy wail, which emerged in bursts, shorn of any comprehensible lyrics or even melody. Like he was summoning and uttering pure emotions. As he reached deeper inside, closing his eyes, opening his heart, there were soft *olés* and encouraging comments from others in the room. I was amazed.

At some point a guitar appeared, played by one of the locals with incredible dexterity, left hand running up and down the neck, while the right slapped and twanged an intricate strumming beat, fingers drumming on the soundboard. Maybe half a dozen people in the room had a go at this improvised, spontaneous music, some renditions sad and dark like the first, others unbridled, spirited and lusty.

At one point some rudimentary foot-stomping occurred; a middle-aged lady stood on that stage and displayed her dancing wares, adorning her strident steps with flirtatious flicks of her hem. An old man joined in, dancing with her with a big smile on his face. It was ribald and funny, lots of cheering and laughter, but mostly the night was full of this sombre, alien, oriental vocalising, which reminded me most of the muezzin calling the faithful to pray. They call this *cante jondo* – deep song.

I have no idea if the people performing that night were any good. Having since seen many such improvised flamenco evenings in humble Andalucian bars and *peñas*, I would guess they were capable amateurs, invoking the home they left behind, but they had a huge effect upon me.

When I become fascinated by a new music I dive in deep, do my studies, read as much as I can, seek out records, drench myself in the music and the mythology. (It's the same with sport. I've had periods of being obsessed by boxing, baseball, cycling and even a brief flirtation with sumo). And the moment you start to find out more about flamenco, you come upon the name of Camarón de la Isla. His name is the most prominent, the most revered of them all. Though that is not really his name.

José Monje Cruz was known as Camarón, or shrimp, because of his diminutive stature, not much more than five feet tall in his Cuban heels and much of that was his ebullient shock of auburn hair. Born into a prominent but poor Roma family in San Fernando, an isolated pueblo on an isthmus (hence *de la isla* – of the island) just outside of Cádiz, he was singing for pesetas at bus stops by the age of eight. By the time he was a teenager there was already widespread recognition that this shrimp was a phenom, a fine guitarist and the very embodiment of *cante jondo*. Flamenco incarnate, wild and gifted, charismatic and troubled, he was the Maradona of this ferocious but always marginalised music.

Flamenco and the *gitano* community, which primarily creates it, hold a unique and complex, often contradictory place in Spanish culture. On the one hand flamenco is central to the Spanish sense of self; along with bullfighting, it is a clichéd but still accurate representation of these fiery, intense people. Yet it is also looked down upon as the music of the poor, dark-skinned souls of the south, the Roma who have always been an outcast caste. Camarón, too, was regarded with deep ambivalence.

His voice was a sacred cry, an age-old siren call which could reach back across continents and ages, a howl to attract and repel, deep in the shadows yet blessed with a blinding lightness of touch. It was pure soul music. Yet the purists were upset by the way he took flamenco and fused it with jazz and rock, modernised it away from its sometimes obstinate obscurity. He was a rock star, and conversely the puritans hated him for his wicked ways, his brandy, heroin and cocaine, his prodigious smoking and womanising, his excess and his wantonness. His most famous song was 'Soy Gitano' – 'I am a Gypsy' – and he unapologetically was.

Camarón was somewhere between Elvis Presley, Jim Morrison and Johnny Rotten with a dose of Edith Piaf and Billie Holiday thrown in. Universally recognised as Spain's greatest ever singer, he had teamed up with first Paco de Lucía, and later Tomatito on guitar, to create a huge body of work, which revolutionised the form and brought it back to the very front of Spanish consciousness.

The young, who had previously turned their backs on flamenco, loved Camarón, bringing a whole new generation into the fold. I too adored him, especially the earlier, purer *cante*, and loved watching old videos of Camarón performing, one of the most charismatic men ever to stand on a stage. But I couldn't get to see him live.

By the time I had discovered flamenco, its greatest star was largely inactive, mired in debt to the taxman and addictions and scandals of every kind. His life had taken a toll and although still only in his late thirties, he had the worn-out and seriously weary looks of the serially self-abused. So I went and saw other flamencos.

People often ask me how and where to go and see live flamenco and I explain the word *peña*, then shrug and wish them well. Flamenco, like blues in Memphis, like *son* in Havana, reggae in Kingston, is everywhere and nowhere, It's in the ether – you hear it coming out of car doors and apartment windows, you hear it on the Levante, the burning wind which blows from the Sahara in hilltop white towns, but try to go and see it . . .

There are nightly flamenco shows called tableaus in big towns; advertised in hotels and restaurants, held in threadbare old theatres. These tourist tableaus are easy to dismiss, but they are actually where the pros ply their trade. Camarón starred in a tableau in Madrid for more than a decade and the performers are usually top notch, certainly worth seeing, but because the show is a bit showy and the crowd is invariably touristy, the *ambiente* and *afición* can be a bit perfunctory.

The biggest-name artists, both musicians and dancers, appear in theatres and concert halls like the stars they are. These *grandes figuras de flamenco* are a big draw, and seeing Diego el Cigala or Estrella Morente in an elegant theatre in Seville or London is wonderful, but it will be the same show wherever they go: slick, sharp, everything choreographed, lacking the immediacy and intensity of this improvised music at its most beguiling.

There are also major festivals throughout the long summer

in many Andalucian towns and cities, where you can see the whole range from tacky to tormented, maestro to amateur. Jerez is often seen as the epicentre of flamenco life, and their annual jamboree is one for the aficionados, but I also watched sublime *cante jondo* in a ruined castle outside Tarifa in a crowd full of surfer dudes. You can get lucky.

If you are very lucky you will be invited to a *gitano* wedding or celebration, where the music will ebb and flow throughout the day and night. Flamencos come from specific families, often dynasties of performers. I once spent some very long, very inebriated, occasionally awkward, but absolutely fascinating time in a gypsy house built around a ramshackle patio, in a town called Villajoyosa, very near Benidorm, but a million miles from the tourist Spain.

It was home to a sprawling *gitano* clan who came and went over time, bringing food, drink and narcotics, paying tribute to the elders, paying little attention to the outsider in their midst. Music was a constant; they sang and they played, and they clapped and they danced. Everybody, from small kids to gnarled grannies, every single member of the extended family covering four generations, took turns to perform It was like watching an intense, evolving history lesson. It was only when the wild teenage son tried to sell me some heroin that I felt the need to leave.

I was lucky to have witnessed such intense flamenco in its natural setting and you may get lucky too. You can just chance upon it, as I have done occasionally at what I thought was the end of a long hot Sevillano night. You turn a corner, hear some music, and just know the night is about to get considerably longer and hotter. Enter that bar to hear the wail rising from the back of the room, the *olés* emerging from the crowd, and just go with it. If ever you chance upon flamenco late at night, and it is always late at night, do not spurn the chance in exchange for an extra hour in bed.

As I say, you may get lucky, but more likely you will have to do what we did on that Barcelona night; you have to ask, and trawl and hope. First rule is never before midnight. Flamenco occurs in the dreaming hours, often when musicians have finished other jobs. Second rule is wait. If a place looks likely, and they all look pretty much the same – the photos, the memorabilia, perhaps the small stage with two or three chairs, a guitar or two lying around, a few slightly shady, unshaven characters – chances are it will happen. But this is a spontaneous, improvised, unpredictable music and if the muse, or the *duende*, does not deign to appear, then just drink the brandy and drink in the atmosphere and try again; another bar, another *peña*, another night.

Searching for flamenco can be frustrating, but it can be incredibly rewarding, and that pattern is the same for many other forms of Latin music. I have a real passionate love affair with the music of the Spanish and African diasporas, and hunting for the rhythm has taken me round the world, got me into some scrapes, got me some great memories.

I have been frustrated in Havana searching for salsa and *son*.

It is easy to get the tourist version, in every bar and lobby of every hotel, which is usually pretty damn good anyway, but trying to go deeper can lead you on some adventures. Clandestinely climbing fifteen flights to a crumbling apartment in an old art deco block just off the Malecón in the middle of the night was one. There was a whole band crammed into this tiny flat in the Cuban version of an illegal rave and lookouts posted to make sure the police didn't turn up and arrest us all.

When I became obsessed by tango, I headed to Buenos Aires in search of flashing bandoneons and nearly came a cropper.

Tango, like flamenco, is perceived here as primarily a dance form, and watching great *tangueros* with their flicks and twirls, their limbs sensually entwining is mesmerising – it takes two to tangle.

Elegant afternoon *milongas*, or dances, in grand old Buenos Aires ballrooms where the men wear fine suits and the women wear the men out with their spins, hooks and slides, are just phenomenal, worth the journey alone. But I had become captivated by the tougher, darker, denser music of *tango nuevo*, a potent mix of tango, jazz and classical first popularised by the great Astor Piazzolla, and had it in my head that I could find a bar or club where I would see that live.

Piazzolla is up there with Miles Davis and Fela Kuti in the pantheon of musicians who singlehandedly changed their sonic world. Dramatic, operatic, cinematic, the music of Piazzolla and his followers is extraordinary; brooding and poetic, a lot like the elegant, faded city which inspired it. Buenos Aires, the great misplaced European metropolis so far away, is one of the most cultured, melancholy, and absorbing places I have ever been. It is sexy and sad and occasionally dangerous.

I went to La Bombonera to watch Boca Juniors play and have never known passion and terror like it; Millwall away at the old Den was tame by comparison. I tried to find tango – born in bordellos and tavernas – in its seedy, backstreet birthplace and found instead a glittering threat. Stupidly naïve and trying to follow my musical nose, I ended up in bad company, seeking good music in bad places and nearly paid a high price to a man with a blade, before a steadfast *tanguero* took pity on the stupid gringo and saved my mortal soul. Thankfully, I lived to see Astor Piazzolla.

Just a year before the stroke that killed him, Astor Piazzolla played with his tango sextet at the now defunct Wembley Conference Centre. It was an odd, cold venue, clinical and distant, better suited to business conventions than this throbbing, sensual music. So all I really saw of the great man was a distant, seated, balding fellow in a sweater, with his head tilted to one side and a squeezebox on his lap. But what I heard was phenomenal. It was a whirlwind of swooping grandeur;

'Libertango' and 'Adiós Nonino', some of the most startling, heart-stopping, breathtaking music ever made.

This was the sound of migration, of loss and yearning, mixing Mediterranean melodies with dark New World rhythms and a keening melancholy for former lands. Piazzolla took this, and with all his ruthless innovations and midnight-blue creations, became known as the Tango Killer. He absolutely slayed me that night, his swirling melodies making my brain and my soul leap and twirl.

Mariachi in Mexico is the opposite of tango; it is relentlessly upbeat and absolutely ubiquitous. You do not have to go looking for mariachi: it will seek you out wherever you are. Go to a restaurant, enter a department store, walk into a hotel, board a bus or a boat, and there will be a band on board; turn a corner and there will be scores of men dressed in their tight-fitting, fancy regalia playing their hearts out. Mariachis are musicians for hire, booked to play at events or just to serenade your lover, when you pay them by the song.

In Mexico City simply head to Plaza Garibaldi and the whole square is jammed full of mariachis with Elvis hair and comical hats, guitars and trumpets for hire. It's the most surreal carnival, but it isn't only in the big cities. The loveliest serenade I have ever heard was outside my hotel in the tiny verdant square of San Miguel de Allende, where a fellow guest paid the mariachis to play for his lover on the balcony above.

But the most amazing mariachi performance, perhaps the most incredible musical vignette I have ever witnessed, came in the wee small hours in a wee small, sleepy town called Jerez de García Salinas, in the dusty heartland of Mexico profundo, deep Mexico. This is cowboy country, and Jerez is a one-horse town, where, instead of horses, the cowboys – in all their finery, their Stetsons, their jeans and their boots – ride bicycles. Cowboys on bikes.

I was staying in the one hotel in town and couldn't sleep, so

I got up and went out for a walk in the dark of the night, just before dawn. I walked up the main street and was amazed and intrigued to hear the mariachis playing in a cantina at this unlikely hour.

I poked my head inside to see a scene so bizarre and enchanting I had to find out more. In this old-time spit-and-sawdust bar there were five or six mariachis lined up, looking exhausted and playing a ragged ranchera ballad, completely out of time and out of tune, to an audience of one cowhand, who was standing at the bar drinking. I ordered a drink and asked the bartender – who did not look happy – what was happening.

'He came in here with the mariachis, just before midnight, when we were about to close, and he has paid them to play the same song over and over again ever since. His girlfriend left him last night and this was "their" song.' And as I looked over, this forlorn cowboy was sobbing gently into his mescal as the band played on and on and on.

I thought that might be the most sad and beautiful musical moment I would ever witness. Then I saw Camarón.

It was 1992 and a promoter friend of mine had coaxed the maestro out of his stoned, narcotic retirement. He had visited Camarón where he lived with his sprawling tribe, and told him that as Spain's greatest singer he had to go out and play to the people. 'But I sing for *my* people every night,' was one of his responses, saying that he performed to his large circle of friends and family in the traditional Romani way.

He also drank, and smoked eighty cigarettes a day, and used every drug known to mankind. He was in a bad way, but he wasn't overly keen to get clean and get back out there. 'You must understand, when you are a *gitano* it is hard to find a reason to *do* anything,' was another of his responses.

But he was finally convinced to get into rehab, get himself in better shape, and get back on stage where he shone, even agreeing to go and play in New York, where he famously met, did not recognise, and did not please Mr Quincy Jones after the show. Quincy had seen the show, was amazed by the talent of the man, and had come backstage to shower Camarón with compliments, but unfortunately the feeling was not reciprocated.

I saw him closer to home in a sports hall in Madrid, the city he had called home for many years, and the turnout was incredible. The Gitano community, sporting big Camarón hair and bright, wide-lapelled suits, chunky gold jewellery and high Cuban heels were there in numbers to see the chosen one. I thought at the time that it was like the Highland clans gathering for the return of Bonnie Prince Charlie, here to see the once and future Gypsy king.

The atmosphere before he came on stage, way later than late, was a kind of reverential fervour mixed with a fear that he might not make it at all. Restless and agitated, the disquiet rose in volume until suddenly José Monje Cruz was helped on stage by his faithful guitarist Tomatito, and a silence descended the like of which I have rarely experienced. It was sacred and it was scared – how will the maestro be?

Without speaking a word, he sat in his chair, closed his eyes, and summoned a mournful incantation which ripped the place apart, tore through every heart, a sound so ravaged and desperate, so anguished and yet defiant. I have no idea what he sang, barely understood a word, cannot remember one tune, but I know I was in the presence of no ordinary greatness. No other human being could have made those sounds, could have communicated such pure, unfiltered emotion so eloquently, so powerfully, so softly. The tears of tough men flowed down the walls like rain.

It felt like a privilege and perhaps a penance to have to endure such beauty, and I think most people there on that final night left the hall shrouded in both exaltation and melancholy, the closest I have ever known to the ecstatic pain of the Catholic faith. We had indeed been in the presence of the one.

And when, less than a year later, aged just forty-one, Cama-rón de la Isla, the Romany shrimp from poor San Fernando died of lung cancer, the entire nation became masters of lamentation: they sobbed and wailed and mourned. A hundred thousand people attended his funeral, his coffin draped in the blue-and-green Roma flag paraded through the throng, desperate for one last glimpse, while the official flags of Spain all flew at half-mast.

Spain had lost its greatest ever singing son, one they never really cherished before he died, because of his race and his roots. But Spain loves death more than life and so it was with Camarón, whose legend began as his life faded away. After his death, his status as a wholly holy man just grew and grew: he became a martyr and a saint. That is when the murals and the statues began to appear. That is why I was so glad to have seen him in the flesh, live. Even if only just.

Chapter 18

Two Drummers Drumming

Q: What do you call a person who hangs around with musicians?
A: A drummer.

There are certain concert-going conventions that rarely change. On your way to the show, a shady bloke talking out of the side of his mouth will say repeatedly, in a loud whisper, 'I'll buy and I'll sell. I'll buy and I'll sell,' in a cockney accent wider than the Holloway Road. That always makes me smile; it's part of the build-up to the event, a form of affirmation, proof positive that you have a scorching ticket in your pocket. I have a lot of time for old-school scalpers – they have occasionally served me well and if you know how to do a bit of business and have the bottle to leave it late, you can almost always get in and maybe even get a bargain in the process.

I've known a few touts over the years, blokes I've seen at every venue in London, from Wembley to Wimbledon (and some who worked World Cups in Japan and Germany, and Springsteen tours around the world), and they usually have great stories and splendid nicknames. My favourite was 'Harry

Round the Corner', so called because if you asked any of his team for a ticket, they would tell you to go and see Harry round the corner. Of course they are dodgy – they're direct descendants of Flash Harry and Stan Flashman, street anglers working the margins, but no one is forcing you to hand over a monkey for a pair of briefs. To my mind they are infinitely preferable to the faceless 'ticket agencies' employing bots, bulk-buying seats and flogging them at extortionate prices online.

Once you get inside the venue and head for the bar, no matter who is playing, there will always be a phalanx of bald blokes in jeans and Harrington jackets buying voluminous rounds and talking at high volume. While blocking your path to a drink, they will noisily compare notes on the set list of the last seven gigs by this particular artist and try to outdo each other in naming obscure B-sides they want to hear that night. If it is a Paul Weller gig, the entire audience will be like that.

But you needn't rush to get a drink and take your seat, as the show will rarely start on time. Artists are always late, and (with a few exceptions) the bigger the artist, the later they will be. Backstage, the manager will be fretting about curfew penalties, haranguing and herding his errant charges, while somebody, usually the lead guitarist, will be fussing and preening in front of a mirror – divas come in all kinds. Proper divas come on very late indeed – half the audience at the Festival Hall had left by the time the wonderful but wayward Cassandra Wilson finally made it on stage.

But of course, keeping 'em waiting is also an intentional ploy by the artist to build up the atmosphere, get the audience hyped up, get the handclaps going, stoking the excitement and anticipation. It is a fine line, though, too late and the audience will begin to get seriously pissed off and spend most of the night looking at their watches worrying about the last train home. But get it right and you get that magical moment when the slow handclaps turn to applause and roars as the house lights go down and the journey begins. It still sends chills.

Some bands come on to a particular piece of grandiose recorded music and whirring lights, like overwrought wrestlers in WWE, which always worries me slightly. It's sometimes a sign that we're in for an evening of flash and bluster. If you go too big too soon, how do you build it up from there? A great concert is a narrative arc, which progresses and reveals itself through the night. Personally, I prefer a silent amble on stage, with perhaps a little bow by the star and a sullen stare from the bass player, and then straight into a corker. The first tune always sets the scene.

Once they're in their stride, introducing the band on stage is the job of the front person, but whooping hysterically at the name of the bass player or percussionist is the job of the strange, probably American person a few rows away. Why is there always a raucous dork determined to make their presence known at every concert in the world?

Whooping and hollering, clapping, and shouting in general is not to be encouraged while the song is going on, as it is bound to happen in that carefully planned lull just before the crescendo, when some silly bugger will shout out inane nonsense, thereby destroying the magic of the moment and the musical momentum. Also, calling out time and again for your favourite song between numbers is inevitably a futile task, especially at a Van Morrison gig.

Shouting AALLRIIIIGHT with a Californian twang for no apparent reason, probably doesn't occur as much as it once did, but then the famed hippy dancer 'Jesus' doesn't take his clothes off and shake his maracas anymore, and far fewer people sit on the floor of standing venues smoking dope than they once did. In the seventies there was that strange crossover period when sixties flower-power mores and seventies punk

behaviour collided, usually at the Roundhouse, where this culture war was played out every Sunday afternoon.

There would literally be the long-haired, flared-trousered
lot sitting on one side of the room being stared at disdainfully
by the pogoing safety-pin brigade on the other. This uncivil
war went on until the spiky-haired hegemony prevailed and
the loon pants were banished. Suddenly no more waft of patchouli oil, but far too much gobbing.

Another generational change has occurred in gig-going eti-
quette in recent years. The ubiquity of mobile phones used as
torches, text machines, tape recorders, cameras and movie
cameras is now so entrenched that it is a natural part of the process for many. I watched a gig recently where the guy standing
next to me texted a running commentary to his mate throughout the show. Others filmed it all. Quite who ever watches that
stuff back I have no idea, and it sometimes seems churlish (I can
definitely do churlish) to ask people to stop filming. But when
you can't see a thing except the back of a wall of phones, surely
you have every right to politely request them to desist. One of
the reasons for loving Ronnie Scott's is their prohibition of all
such devices. Bob Dylan also demands that all phones be put
away for the duration. Good on you, Bob.

I honestly don't get the motivation to reach for your mobile
during a show. To really enjoy a live event to the fullest, you
need to be absolutely in the moment, in tune, fully absorbed
by what is happening on stage, and filtering it all through a
phone is a major distraction. I suspect once we get over the
thrill of new technology, people will stop being so obsessed by
their gadgets.

'Idiot dancing' was once a big thing, a spontaneous and
deeply embarrassing twirling and flailing of limbs, totally out
of sync with the music, usually executed by skinny white
people, often with their tops off. This made something of a
return during the rave years, when those elevated by ecstasy

found their inhibitions sufficiently reduced to execute a few elaborately inchoate routines in the aisles in their bucket hats. But even for those not so inebriated, there is always the question of 'to dance or not to dance'.

Obviously, it depends on the band and the venue. Watching Light of the World or Incognito at the Jazz Café is made for moving. Brit funk, or any kind of funk or reggae in a standing venue, is meant to be a boogie night. When the Average White Band hit the opening notes of 'Pick Up the Pieces', you had better pick up your feet. But dancing at seated venues has a number of pitfalls.

Usually, it's a pair of girls who start the uprising, and then maybe a show-off couple who can execute a few well-practised steps, who move out to the aisles to facilitate a more elaborate routine. There is always that pivotal moment when enough people have got up out of their seats to jig about that you either have to join them in a little half-hearted dad dancing or look like an absolute curmudgeon who can't see over their heads anyway. But if the whole place rises too soon and a ballad follows, you get that embarrassing choice: do we stay standing up and sway self-consciously or sheepishly slope back down to our seats?

I have rather got over being told to get up, stand up by the artist up on stage. Shouldn't that be a spontaneous thing? Shouldn't the audience decide whether or not they want to rise as one? The same goes for standing ovations, which have a kind of momentum that is hard to resist, even if you are not entirely convinced that was the greatest show on earth. I have been known to sit intentionally rigid with my arms folded across my chest to pompously signal the fact that this is not, to my educated ears, a standing-ovation-level performance, but more usually I'll at least join in with the clapping. Most shows are decent, and this is supposed to be fun, after all. But I will not, cannot, encourage drummers.

Does anybody really like drum solos?

Again, I have to provide a jazz proviso here. I've seen Art Blakey and Brian Blade, Elvin Jones and Jack DeJohnette, Steve Reid and Rashied Ali. Wizards with sticks and brushes. I recently watched a seashell-adorned Chicago shaman called Kahil El'Zabar entrance a room full of people with just a tiny handheld thumb piano. It was a percussive masterclass, a truly moving African echo. I like those sorts of drummers.

Witnessing one of those masters of metre and clave take a solo is to witness a Time Lord in action – they can speed up and slow down the very molecules in the room with a confluence of mathematics and art. Rolling thunder or hazy mist, mallets or brushes, their playing is precise and profound, rolling around the kit and around the beat, playing in between the pulses, making silences count, constructing an exquisite little essay in rhythm, talking the complex language of the drum while making it all look easy. Keeping our attention by keeping it short, dynamic, musical.

Jazz drummers are great to watch; keep your eyes on the minutiae of their movements, the flick of the wrist, the nod of the head as they keep it tight, keep it cool, masters of understatement, making every action count, every snap and shot. Everybody knows they can really play, so they don't need to show off. A stripped-back kit with just a snare, a tom-tom or two and a couple of ride cymbals in the pocket drive it on, just the occasional flourish, always keeping time.

These are hardened rhythmaticians: they can do syncopation, counterpoint, polyrhythms, paradiddles and all that malarkey, so they do them sparingly, economically, wonderfully. They are not show-offs. They are not Keith Moon.

The most preposterously flamboyant drum solo of all came during an Earth, Wind & Fire show at Wembley in the mid-seventies when during the obligatory solo, the entire drum riser suddenly levitated, rose up in the air and turned upside down with Ralph Johnson defying gravity while still flailing and funking away. It was all part of their elaborate Afro-futurist sci-fi staging, including a vanishing spaceship, a floating pyramid, and a set of shiny tinfoil jumpsuits. To this day, those of us who saw that show still talk about that drummer's stunt.

But your bog-standard drum solo is really only good for a trip to the bog. If you knew it was coming, you could plan your escape, you'd be out of your seat and into the latrines or the bar before the spotlight operator could shift his attention to the man (or very occasionally woman) behind the kit. But invariably the obligatory drum solo sneaks up on you and you have to sit there while this tuneless parade of bangs and bongs, thuds and thumps gets louder and louder, ever more point-lessly percussive, ever less musical. Completely divorced from the song they've just been playing.

The sheer wanton showiness of drum solos, the look-at-me vanity of them, is part of what makes them so tiresome. It is simply an excuse for the least famous, least fanciable, least wealthy member of the band (they rarely write tunes, so never get any royalties) to work out all their grievances by hitting and kicking things. Keep the drummer happy by letting him loose for five minutes while the musicians have a fag.

As well as being boring and occasionally bleeding painful to listen to, it's also ugly to watch as this sweaty bloke with a mad grin, often with a naked torso, flails about maniacally, limbs flying in all directions, hair everywhere. And he won't stop. Most drum solos would be bearable and maybe even enjoyable if they were half the length, but once they've been unleashed, it is almost impossible to get them to desist. Enough is enough.

Just when you think that interminable solo is coming to its logical conclusion and he's going to bang the bloody gong and we can get back to the music, some silly bugger in the audience cheers and claps, and we're off again on another round of pointless noise. Why do they do it, why encourage them? I've never met anybody other than drummers who actually enjoys drum solos, so who is it that whoops and cheers every time this terrible racket and ritual occurs? If we could all agree to stop egging them on, the gig-going experience would lead to much less tinnitus.

But just to prove that I do not have anything against drummers per se (it's just their solo excesses) my two favourite live sightings of musicians both involved sticksmen.

Perhaps two of my favourite musicians ever were sticksmen, and they never took solos.

Charlie Watts was the most elegant man I have ever encountered, straight, no chasers. With his Savile Row suits and his handmade shoes, this truck driver's son from Wembley was the absolute epitome of the ever-dapper music man about town. I asked him once what he did on his visits to London from his Devon stud farm, and he said, 'I take a Turkish bath and I visit my tailors. And that is tailors plural – you must always have two and you tell them both the other one is better.'

The other thing he did was watch jazz. I saw Charlie in Ronnie Scott's on a number of occasions in the eighties, when he was in his late-night druggy phase, sitting quietly at the back, digging the scene. And I also saw him play there with his jazz band a decade or so later, one of the most joyous evenings ever.

It's time for an admission here, I have never seen the Rolling Stones live. By the time I could have done, they were playing stadiums, and besides I never quite forgave them for nicking Ronnie Wood from his rightful home in the Faces. I like some Stones records, I recognise that they are an institution, and in retrospect I would love to have seen Charlie Watts behind the kit, unfazed by the hullabaloo and brouhaha, doing exactly what a great drummer should do. I never saw the Stones, but I did see Charlie Watts walk along Frith Street, which was probably better.

It was the night I was due to go and see the Charlie Watts

jazz band and I was in Soho a couple of hours early, so plotted up outside the Bar Italia with an espresso or two to wait for my mate and watch the world go by. I was lazily gazing across the street when suddenly this apparition floated around the corner from Old Compton Street and the world turned to slow motion. When I think of it now, it is like a scene in a Scorsese movie, shot in vivid technicolour, a swooning saxophone playing, the focus entirely on this one figure as they glide effortlessly through the throng.

I swear it was glorious. Mr Charlie Watts: loafers, flannel trousers, a crisp polo shirt worn beneath an immaculate checked sports coat, striding purposefully but economically towards his night's work, holding a pair of drumsticks as the street just flowed by. It was a picture of perfection, the ultimate Soho moment, a vision of urban élan and I think I was the only one who noticed.

Later that night I saw him at work, doing what he loved most, that Mona Lisa smile of his as he sat deep in the pocket behind a brilliant band and just drove this machine forward. Although he couldn't drive a car, Charlie had a fleet of vintage motors because he loved the look of them. This band was his favourite vehicle of all. And he never took a solo. The jazz that night was far from cutting-edge, not really my style, but boy, the man behind the kit had style.

I never saw the Stones and I never saw The Band. But I did see Levon Helm. If musical drummers are an exception, then singing drummers are rare as hens' teeth and people who can do both as well as Levon Helm is a club of one. Sadly, I never witnessed him sitting behind a kit, playing in that sweetly neat and tidy style of his, all wrists and fingers, shoulders hunched, head swaying gently while leaning forward into a vocal mike as if reaching for a sound, that keening, southern sound, the bruised but softly defiant voice of a lost – or at least losing – America.

I have watched film of Levon playing and singing so many times that I know every mannerism and every movement; I also know that if I stare at or listen to Levon Helm for too long, I will start to weep. There's a duet he recorded with John Martyn, 'Rock Salt and Nails', which sets me off within a few moments, the sound of two men singing truth, their emotional entrails exposed for our entertainment, trading blows, blows they have received, Levon in his ethereal Delta drawl, John with his soused Glaswegian slur.

It is too beautiful, a masterpiece of abstract expressionism to equal Rothko's Seagram murals in its celebration of the light that shines within darkness. The song begins on the banks of a river. Which is exactly where I saw Levon.

I was doing a journalism job for the *Observer Magazine*, a travel feature about a journey down the Mississippi from the source to the sea. It was fascinating in parts, but also dull and occasionally disturbing as we meandered through two-bit towns scarred by poverty and racism. This was the deep dark South and the often-ugly past kept reaching up from the undergrowth in places like Vicksburg and Natchez, where wars are still being quietly fought.

I spent one night in a tiny town in Arkansas called Helena, which was about as close as you'll get to the birthplace of the blues and has a fine little museum dedicated to that foundation music. It was also close by the birthplace of Levon. I was having breakfast the next morning in a desultory diner, hard by the levee, the high bank which holds back the mighty Mississippi, the levee which features in so many Southern songs, indeed in songs by The Band themselves.

As I was eating my grits (I wouldn't advise it) and biscuits, I saw the thin, angular frame of a bearded man ambling along the levee, and thought I recognised him straight away. I immediately asked the man behind the counter if that could possibly be the greatest ever singing drummer, and 'yes' was all he said.

I opened the door of the diner and just watched. There's no story, really – nothing happened, I felt no desire to go and disturb him, didn't really have anything to say to the man, and didn't want to spoil a perfect moment. This was Levon Helm on the levee, right by the place he was raised, Levon Helm, the sound of that sad America just walking by the timeless Old Man River. It was the history of a continent. It was the greatest solo drummer ever.

Chapter 19

Twenty-First-Century Boys

I had a punch up with Paul Weller's mate, and Madness tried to run me over.

I saw the Jam oftentimes in their early days and, as I've already said, was never really convinced. Madness somehow escaped me live until much later, but I was equally sceptical about the whole 'Nutty Boy' thing. Indeed, I also stupidly dismissed two-tone, which in retrospect was an incredibly important cultural movement, because it was wearing the wrong clothes and came from the wrong place (Coventry), but also because it was backward-looking at a time when I only had eyes for the future. I'd grown up with ska records, Sta-Prest and pork-pie hats and didn't feel the need to revisit them. Bring on the synthesisers.

Punk was a rigorous and unforgiving finishing school, and I still suffer (if that is the right word) from some of the prejudices ingrained in true believers; still cannot stand prog rock in any form, don't trust hippies, not mad on Elvis, the Beatles, or the Rolling Stones. (Actually, I quite like the Stones.) Until quite recently I would not tolerate long guitar solos, and I struggle with pop music.

So, the Jam and Madness, both quintessential British pop
bands of the very best kind, were not allowed to enter my
world. I was deaf to their brilliance. Which makes it even more
telling that my two most memorable gigs of the twenty-first
century were by Madness and Mr Weller. I guess I grew up.

I got to know the Maddy bunch way before I ever saw them
play. I interviewed the band on a few occasions in the eighties,
invariably for magazines, which closed down directly afterwards. (*New Sounds New Styles*, *Flexipop!*, *City Limits*) and they
were terrific, if mischievous company. Trying to herd that
mob into some semblance of sanity was not easy. But by then I
had to admit that they were the most incredibly creative clan,
and that unbroken string of hit singles and videos which lit up
that decade was among the greatest ever made.

Then, when I moved to Camden Town in the nineties, they
became neighbours, and I would see Suggs in many of the local
watering holes, always well dressed, always excellent, eloquent
company. We began to talk of shoes and Soho, Clerkenwell
and titfers, share stories and become pals. I would sometimes
meet Suggs and his mum, a proper West End character, in the
French House, where they would always raise a glass and a
smile. London legends.

I first saw Madness perform up in Finsbury Park, where
they created an earthquake, literally, 33,000 fans stomping
their way to 4.2 on the Richter scale, but because of my aversion to outdoor gigs and the fact that they were miles away, I
was mainly in the pub over the road, so I have little recollection. The next time they invited me to the Hackney Empire to
see their show for the album *The Liberty of Norton Folgate*, a brilliant piece of cockney Edwardiana, all music-hall references
and bowler hats in that fabulous Frank Matcham theatre.

They were terrific, but my abiding memory is the fact that
this was my little baby girl's first gig. Maude was nine years old,
and she decided that she wanted to go to a pop concert, so we

sat together in an ornate box as she watched the show and then did a precipitous little moonstomp during 'Baggy Trousers'. Alfie's first gig was Big Audio Dynamite when they reformed for one tour, and we went to see them in their all-conquering homecoming show at the Shepherd's Bush Empire. Alfie had met Mick Jones before, because he sits behind us at QPR, and he was enthralled when the crowd started chanting Rangers songs; I think he assumed that would happen at every gig. He was also amazed and maybe appalled by the fact that decrepit old blokes his dad's age still get up and dance like idiots at concerts.

The Madness concert which really did it for me was not even officially by Madness and I nearly didn't live to see the gig and tell the tale. I was walking down Parkway in Camden Town, just opposite the Dublin Castle, early one evening, having popped out to get some provisions. I stepped off the kerb just as a car swooped backwards into the space I had just entered. With a screech of tyres and a squeal of terror we collided, but thankfully I managed to bounce off the back of the vehicle, no harm done. The driver jumped out to see what had happened and we both burst out laughing.

My attempted assassin was Lee Thompson, the sax-playing Madness stalwart, who apologised for having nearly done me in and invited me to see them play later that night over the road in the pub. The band were celebrating their twenty-fifth anniversary by returning to the place it all began. Under the pseudonym of the Dangermen (very apt when Lee is driving), they were playing a secret gig at the Dublin Castle, doing all the songs they first performed there a quarter of a century before.

As close to a sauna as the back room of a pub can become, the heat generated by a couple of hundred mainly bald, rather lardy middle-aged blokes crammed into a tiny space, waiting for their heroes to come on could have topped up the national

grid. Then the arrival of the aforementioned dangerous fellows, walking through the parting crowd like a band of old
boxers, themselves all a little portlier than they once were,
just added to the heat and humidity. It was the steamiest
room I had been in since the Marquee in its seventies heyday.

The tiny stage was creaking and overflowing with flesh, some
of it rather wobbly. Fezzes balanced on balding pates, they
delivered a set of venerable and jaunty old ska classics, joyful
three-minute masterpieces I had first heard on a Dansette in
1969. I still had most of these songs on seven-inch singles my
brothers collected and still knew almost every word of the
lyrics. I realised there and then that these Madness men were
the epitome of a savvy, funny, proudly working-class London
culture that stretched back from youth clubs to music hall, via
football terraces, Irish pubs and West Indian blues. That was
precisely the culture I had grown up with too. I knew I was in
kindred company.

Rapscallions and rascals they may be, and there are certainly
high jinks in their presence, but they are also the embodiment
of that lineage reaching back through punks, skinheads, rude
boys and mods to the teenage Victorian costermongers who
adored Marie Lloyd. And when they played 'One Step Beyond',
you could hear the cheer in Kentish Town. I danced. God knows
I danced.

After the gig we reconvened in another rough-house Camden
boozer round the corner for an old-fashioned lock-in, which
carried on deep into the next day. Alcohol was taken and the
hangover created was savage and structural. But I only have
wonderful memories of that night, the serendipity and spontaneity but also the celebratory nature of it all. In an after-hours
session in an NW1 pub, I had long rambling conversations with
the band reflecting on musical lives remarkably well-lived and
a body of work well worthy of the pride they displayed after
a quarter of a century. I just wish I had taken notice earlier.

The worst hangover I ever acquired came after a marathon session 'interviewing' Shane McGowan and the rogues from the Pogues. It started in the Crown in Cricklewood, one of the last of the great Irish institutions on the Edgware Road, and carried on for days. We went from pub to pub to shebeen to squat, and at one point I was physically carried to the next whiskey bar by Spider Stacey.

Unlike Madness, I recognised immediately that the Pogues or Pogue Mahone as they were originally called (it means 'kiss my arse' in Gaelic) were a work of genius. The genius in question was of course Shane, who sold me a white-label copy of their first-ever single from the record shop he worked in on Hanway Street. 'Dark Streets of London' captured so much of the rich and tragically romantic feel of the London Irish experience that I could not stop playing it over and over.

I'm not Irish, but growing up in North-West London, I was surrounded by Kellys, O'Keefes and O'Donnells, and I knew that Mr McGowan managed to encapsulate the complexity and contradictions of their lives, as both proud Londoners and sons and daughters of the Éireann Isle with amazing clarity. Pints in Ward's Irish House, punch-ups at the Galtymore, hurling on Paddington Rec and mass at Our Lady of Hal. I'd been to enough rumbustious Irish dance halls to relish the rousing up-tempo Pogues numbers like 'Sally MacLennane', or 'Streams of Whiskey', but it was always the tear-and-beer-soaked ballads I loved the best.

I saw the Pogues live many times, including the aforementioned bizarre launch party on a boat on the Thames for their debut album, *Rum Sodomy & the Lash*, where my congenital motion sickness saw me throwing up even before the Jameson was unleashed. On dry land they played the Wag, the 100 Club, the Mean Fiddler and the Hammersmith Palais, they played memorable gigs in the stalwart company of the Dubliners, including one historically hedonistic Paddy's Day at the National in Kilburn, and every time they created an incredible atmosphere.

The band were wonderfully ragged, just the right side of collapse, and you have to be a very fine musicians to pull that off. Shane, to me, is one of the greatest lyricists of our time, sentimental without being syrupy, poetic without being pretentious. But his slide into alcoholism and addiction was hard to watch. Amazingly and thankfully he is still with us, and I just hope that he is happy inside his head. The Pogues provided me with a barrel full of pleasure.

Paul Weller very publicly gave up drinking a few years ago, but I never really knew him when he was on the sauce. For years we managed to studiously avoid each other, even though we moved in overlapping circles. We were both involved in Red Wedge in the eighties, both at many of the same clubs and events throughout that decade, but never spoke.

There was a fracas at Steve Strange's club at the Camden Palace, involving journalist Paolo Hewitt and myself, which ended up with insults being traded and punches being thrown. It was all silly stuff and nonsense between two factions, about an article in the *NME*. Nobody was hurt, no harm done, but Paolo was seen as Weller's man, while I was embedded in the Spandau camp, and as a result there was a lingering animosity. As a result, I never saw the Style Council, even though I thought they were a major upgrade on the Jam. Never kept up closely with the twists and turns of Weller's career, liked the occasional tune, but never realised or acknowledged just what a phenomenal musician, writer and performer he is.

Then he wrote me a letter. It came after the publication of *The Way We Wore*, my memoir about growing up obsessed with threads. In an act of enormous humility and generosity, Paul penned a handwritten letter saying how he had read the book and it chimed so completely with his own story that we should surely forget any differences. He passed this note to me through a mutual friend, and I was so taken by his honesty and touched by this gentlemanly gesture that I wrote right back.

Since then we have become friends – not bosom buddies, but luncheon mates, capable of intense discussions about the merits of Alden loafers and J. Simon sweaters. We share a love of the late suedehead, Budgie/Faces style of 1971–2, we talk of schmutter and barnets, and the heartbreaking melodies of Ronnie Lane, but he rarely discusses his own music. He is a taciturn, internal man, a doer rather than a talker, which means that he is still one of the great enigmas and one of the great rarities. How come, unlike almost all great songwriters, Paul Weller just gets better and better?

In recent years I've seen Mr Weller play two very different shows, one at the Forum in Kentish Town, where he came roaring out of the traps like some sort of punk greyhound, lean and swift, propelled by two drummers and a vehemently rocking band. Much of the set was songs I didn't know, played with a ferocity I didn't recognise, and yet it was engrossing, pulling you in with its power. And just occasionally the opening notes of a number would register, and an extra roar would arise.

That show was exhausting and thrilling and the last section, when he ran through just a few of his hits from every stage of his career, was sensational. Quite where those levels of energy come from is hard to fathom, but that other question, about the continued brilliance of the songwriting, is even tougher. And when he played with strings at the Royal Festival Hall, the mystery became almost mystical.

I have a sort of spiritual link to the Royal Festival Hall. My father was a steel erector who helped rebuild London after the Blitz. Because he died when I was only six, I have very few memories of my time with the man, but one of them is of visiting the RFH and him proudly pointing out where he had sat on girders at the top of that fine mid-century modern

building. He was proud to have been part of it, and I am proud
of him every time I visit.

I love it there, love the carpet and the balconies, the view,
and the foyer. Love the bold post-war socialist ambition to
create a people's palace. And on the night that Weller with
strings was about to take place, that foyer was like a modernist
Who's Who. Except for the Who.

Normally Paul Weller gigs are chock-full of middle-aged
blokes in jeans and trainers with market-stall Harrington jackets a go-go, but it seemed as if everybody was aware that this
one was a bit special, so had made an effort to look their uptown
best. Faces everywhere you looked, whistles for the men, lots
of immaculate women – many more than you get at most
gigs – pocket squares, silk scarves, splendid footwear, proper
polished shoes. London turned out, well turned-out. The
Woking boy may not quite be a Londoner, but he encapsulates
a certain uptown, West End working-class style. And just
standing in the RFH foyer amid such sartorial rectitude was
the perfect start to a memorable evening.

You can hear for yourself what the night was like, as it has
been captured on a live album, and it is one of the rare good
ones, a very good one. But being there surpassed even that.
Weller, wearing an ice-blue sweater adorned with a line of love
beads was seated throughout, with a stripped-back band alongside him and an orchestra behind. There was little or no direct
communication with the audience, as it wasn't needed; the
bond between audience and artist had been forged years before
and was entirely non-verbal. We were here to hear what he was
going to do in this setting, and it was fascinating.

Subtle, thoughtful, beautiful. There's a whole string of
words I could use to describe the sounds we heard that night,
and all of them would stress the elemental, understated majesty of the music and, indeed, the whole event. It was the
epitome of mod: it was clean and cool, but it was also supremely

soulful, a man at the height of his powers curating his music and laying it out in as elegant a way as possible. Despite the full string section and horns, it was Weller stripped right back to a series of sumptuous melodies and lyrics. His voice was strong and rich, mellow and resonant. It felt like a rare peek into his soul.

There were many moments to delight: a tango rhythm here, a bossa nova there, that gently swinging Style Council tune you had forgotten, that Jam song transformed. And then he did 'You Do Something to Me', the opening notes creating a gasp and a swoon from the audience, a song so lovely it filled that venerable hall with something like love. Weller did something that night to all of us.

I think what has made that concert stay so vivid in my mind, so affecting to this day, is the fact that it showed a way. Paul is a man just a year older than me, the audience was largely grown-ups of a similar age, yet there was a thrilling communion and a sense of togetherness, a tangible feeling of unity, which gets so much rarer as we get older, more distanced, more alone. Weller proved there's hope for us all on this grand evening, dignified and fine, yet deep and mature. It was live music at its most life-affirming.

Chapter 20

The Old Joanna

Every time I look at that beaten-up old upright in the corner of the radio studio where I broadcast, I think of Chas Hodges. We've had some extraordinary artists sit and play at that piano: Dr John, Glenn Frey, Allen Toussaint, Georgie Fame, Jamie Cullum – who is a fantastic live performer as well as a charming chap, by the way – and Lonnie Liston Smith playing a truly awesome, acoustic 'Astral Travelling'.

We've had hosts of others with guitars and violins and cajones, one band who used the bin as a drum, Joe Brown with his little ukulele, Ian Dury with his blistering Blockheads, Gregg Allman with just an acoustic guitar and an elastic band around his hair. We've seen amazing debuts – Joss Stone and Norah Jones –and some tragic farewells: Jeff Buckley and Ian Dury. But that studio, and in particular that piano, belonged to Chas.

The piano was saved from a skip when BBC Radio London moved from our old HQ on Marylebone High Street. Made by Laurence and Nash, it is one of the last survivors of a batch built specifically and uniquely for the corporation and it surprises almost everybody who plays it. Jamie Cullum offered to buy it from us the first time he ran his fingers across it. None of them are seduced by its looks – it resembles something you'd see in a run-down boozer – but not too many pub pianos can have been played by such an illustrious line-up, and they all sing its praises. It gets tuned regularly by a charming Polish chap, or at least it did until Covid; the lack of live artists in my studio, which has gone on for years now, has been a real blow. The silence from that shabby brown box a shrill reminder.

I think it was my colleague Simon Lederman who spotted that this old joanna was about to be thrown away and asked if we could take it with us to our new home at Broadcasting House. Back in Marylebone, we had a strange set-up where bands would play down in a basement studio and I would watch them on monitors. But in our new Portland Place studio, artists would be right in there with me, the piano no more than four feet away. It meant I could really see them at work, watch the hands, feel the muscularity and the musicality, see them swing. Jools Holland loved showing off on it, demonstrating different styles with that broad smile and deadpan South London delivery. Ian Shaw made me laugh time and again while sitting at it, and made me cry when he first played a song called 'My Brother'. But Chas Hodges bashed and caressed and cajoled that piano more than any other artist. And I miss him more than anyone.

Chas and Dave are precisely the kind of performers that 'serious' music journalists cannot take seriously. Perhaps they do not know that the two of them were among the finest session musicians in the land, both playing everything from bass, guitar, banjo and piano, from jazz to funk to old-time rock'n'roll. Chas was taught piano as a teenager by Jerry Lee Lewis himself and could play the meanest pumping boogie-woogie this side of the Killer. But he also played those songs my mum sang.

My mum loved Chas and Dave. I told Chas so once, and after that he never failed to ask after her – that's the kind of fellow he was. He was also the most complete music fan I think I've ever met. He loved talking music and loved playing it even more. If ever there was a gap in the schedules, we could just contact Mr Hodges and he would come and play for the fun of it, either with his mucker or on his own. They never got paid, often had nothing to promote, but knew there was a good piano, a positive host who dug what they did, and an audience listening who adored every note. The response to Chas from the listeners was always overwhelmingly positive.

Seeing them live in concert was so like the parties and weddings and wakes of my youth. My Aunt Glad played pub piano around Shepherd's Bush and I knew every word of every one of those old-time tunes. Chas and Dave were a bridge between that wartime generation, with their songs of hope and fortitude, their ribald knees-ups and their lachrymose ballads. They were also an affirmation of the value of a working-class London identity, singing in 'our' accent, using 'our' vernacular, making our everyday almost mythical by rendering it as song.

In an individualistic, economically driven age, when the qualities of communality and continuity, along with the very idea of class identity, have been derided and devalued, they were an absolute tonic. The sing-along simplicity of Chas and Dave masked a profound sophistication, a nourishing of our deep roots.

They put on a top show, a proper beano, whether it was at the Albert Hall or the Dog and Duck. It was live music as a tribal bonding exercise, a cross-generational belting-out of our collective songlines, the tunes which bind us together. But the best I ever saw of them was the last time they played together in my studio, at that piano.

I'd heard rumours that Chas was not in great health, but he was his usual upbeat, unshaven, dishevelled self, asking after my mum, cursing his beloved Spurs, and settling straight into our old joanna. Dave was with him, playing a ukulele if I remember correctly, and they were premiering a new song they'd written called 'Wonder Where He is Now?'. Chas was always a chatty chap, but on this occasion he took an unusually long time prefacing this song, telling us all what it was about, how it was the story of an old fishing friend he'd lost touch with and thought about often. Never mawkish but unashamedly sentimental; I have often wondered if Chas was really telling us something else too, that the song was equally about him. The journey he was about to make.

This wonderful, gentle ballad about a couple of mates by the old canal is full of idiolectic old London constructions, which instantly made me think of my old mum. It is a fantastic song, a great swansong, and although it is only with the hindsight of Chas's death shortly after that final performance that the full weight of the lyrics struck home, I can honestly say that there were tears shed that day. It was a fine farewell to a friend.

Ian Dury also played his last set in our old studio. It was nearly two decades before Chas's passing but only a short time before the man who brought us 'Plaistow Patricia' and 'Billericay Dickie' finally left this city. It was a very long time ago, but I still recall being nervous when Ian entered the studio for the pre-session interview. Partly it is because I was such a fan; *New Boots and Panties!!* is one of the all-time great records and I had seen Ian and his mercurial band play live so many times. I was also wary of swearing, which was a near-capital offence on BBC London at the time, plus I knew that Mr Dury had something of a reputation.

Although by this stage he was an alternative national treasure, a much-admired punky poet laureate, Ian was known, even by those who loved him, as a difficult bugger. He was cantankerous and unpredictable, with a relish for embarrassing and bullying interviewers, so I had something of a sleepless night before the day of the show. It was back in Marylebone, so the band were setting up down in the basement while Ian came into the studio to talk. And it became instantly obvious that he was not a well man. He was subdued and appeared weary, far from the ferocious force of nature who had once played a gig at the Ilford Odeon so mighty that the dance floor collapsed.

He talked wistfully and gently tried to summon some of his famous witticisms but was clearly not at his best, and I remember thinking that my fears had not only been unfounded, but that I would rather have enjoyed jousting with a fully functioning Ian Dury. He went slowly downstairs, dragging his leg behind him, to play a song called 'Mash It Up Harry', one of the standout tracks from the new album they were promoting.

I could only watch the band on the monitor, but even at that distance, for a mere local radio broadcast, the change in Ian once the music started was extraordinary. He wrapped a hankie round the mike and, somehow, he summoned up a performance of brio and energy, vim and vigour, spurred on by that great ensemble of his, the bassline pumping away; he was hollering and writhing, gutturally guffawing and driving the tune with a maniacal zeal. I could almost feel the force coming up through the floor. He mashed it right up. It was the restorative power of rock'n'roll made manifest. It was why Ian was such a star. And then he was gone.

Jeff Buckley wasn't such a star when he appeared on my show. He only became properly famous after his death, and I have to admit to paying little notice when he turned up in Marylebone for an interview and a live number or two. I knew little about him except that he was his father's son and I assumed he'd ridden to what prominence he had on his dad's coattails. I was also sceptical because the artists most likely to be a pain (other than Ginger Baker, of course) were young American acts on the way up. They tended to demand this and that, bring in stroppy sound engineers and pushy PRs, behave like spoilt brats, and I feared this moody indie-kid would be one of those.

He wasn't, of course – he was a fantastically talented singer with a unique voice; he was also extremely handsome, which is really all I remember, that he was far too good-looking for his own good. Or at least I think I remember – there is no record of his performance, no date, no set list, nothing recorded online. And given that there is an almost obsessive interest in every note he ever sang, that's very odd. Jeff Buckley definitely appeared on GLR (Greater London Radio) in 1994, singing 'Grace', and you can listen to that online, his extraordinary vibrato leaping out at you. But there is no trace of him appearing on the Robert Elms show.

I think he sang 'Hallelujah' – certainly I can hear that in my head, and it is amazing, a spectral masterpiece – but I am not sure it happened, nobody is; it's as if he wasn't really there, an apparition, which, given the way his tragic death occurred, is somehow apt. A ghostly voice just floating by, somewhere in the ether.

Gregg Allman was most definitely there, in the studio at Broadcasting House, promoting his last album, *Southern Blood*, itself a mordantly melancholic affair, ethereal and shrouded in swamp mist. He came into my studio with one of the great rock'n'roll mythologies preceding him and a long mane of flowing white hair trailing behind. I was more than a little in awe of this legendary Southern singer, and although he looked old and pale, when he opened his mouth to speak it was like someone had poured molasses over moonshine, with some grits thrown in. Sonorous and soft, drenched in Jacksonville sunshine and spiced with bad, bad habits. He was super-polite – I could have listened to him speak for days – and the interview went well, but he was here to play.

He had another musician with him; they both carried acoustic guitars, and without any kind of sound check, they just picked up their guitars, Greg wrapped a stray elastic band round his hair and tied it into an impromptu ponytail, and began to sing and play. It was as if all the ghosts of the Delta had got together to emerge from his mouth in a lazy drawl which was atmospheric and wounded. It was a proper hair-on-the-back-of-the-neck moment, a sonic summation of all those drug-drenched, poor-boy, Allman Brothers blues. It was mesmerising, and after he had finished playing, Mr Allman invited me to go and see him play at the Barbican and what's more, insisted that I come backstage to see him before the gig.

I was completely made up at the thought that Gregg 'Laid Back' Allman was my new mate, and I invited an old friend to be my plus-one and to come and meet the great man with me. We got through security just fine – my name was indeed on the list – and we made our way through the warren of corridors to the dressing room where my new best friend awaited. We knocked on the door and entered, and indeed there was Gregg Allman getting ready to go on stage. I introduced myself and my plus-one and he politely said hello, while looking at us oddly. Within about thirty seconds it became apparent that he had no recollection whatsoever of who I was, didn't remember me or my name and probably had no recall of playing in my studio just two days before.

On stage, though, he was great, delivering a 'Midnight Rider' for the ages in what was to be his last ever London appearance.

I will always remember Gregg Allman. Which is itself unusual; thousands of artists have appeared on the show, and I cannot possibly recall them all. People often come up to me and say they were on my show a few years back and I have no memory of meeting them. I'm not being rude – it's just impossible to retain all that.

Having a great voice helps, and I don't just mean a singing voice. Tony Bennett didn't sing for us, but came in the studio for an interview and charmed everybody in the building with his impeccable attire and manners. He called me 'Sir'. Tony Bennett, with his old-time Italian New York accent and old-time courtesy, called me Sir. Wow.

Lou Reed, also a New Yorker, did not have such winning ways; in fact he was grumpy and guarded, and clearly not happy to be there. The interview started in a really stilted fashion, his answers terse and his demeanour defensive. Until, that is, I mentioned Ornette Coleman's soundtrack to *Naked Lunch,* and he was off. He immediately loosened up and began to enjoy talking music; we rattled through tales from *Street Hassle* and *Metal Machine Music,* and it occurred to me that he was really like Van Morrison. Prove to Lou Reed that you knew what you were talking about and Lou would respond positively.

Something similar happened with Linton Kwesi Johnson. He was apparently peeved with the BBC in general over some perceived slight and made that immediately clear. I was crestfallen; this is one of my all-time heroes, and I was really excited to finally get to talk to him. Even if he was in a bad mood, that voice, blimey that voice, just made me weak at the knees. Ever since boyhood expeditions to the General Smuts pub on the White City estate to drag my granddad out of the saloon bar for his tea, I have been enamoured by Caribbean accents. The bar there would be full of dapper men from Trinidad and Jamaica, drinking stout and playing raucous dominos and I loved the musicality of their hubbub.

Linton was like a learned, erudite and at first rather stern uncle, if your uncle had the richest, most rhythmic baritone Jamaican accent. This time it was mention of having interviewed C. L. R. James, which made L. K. J. soften a little, though only just a little. He is a serious fellow, and when the time came for him to recite a poem for us, it was as if a bombshell of brilliance had been let off in the room. The words just exploded with rage and sagacity, the sound of generations of resistance and fight encapsulated in the vocal cords of this slight, greying, serious man from South London.

Perhaps the most intense atmosphere ever created in the studio came when two sisters arrived to sing for us. And if you know their story, you might understand why it felt so acute and edgy to be there with both of them. Shelby Lynne and Allison Moorer are both excellent contemporary American country singers, the album *I Am Shelby Lynne* is one of the greatest of modern times, and Shelby had appeared on the show before, so I knew she could be private and prickly. But I also knew that she had a terrible, scarring back story, which she shared with her equally talented younger sister.

When they were teenage girls in Alabama, their alcoholic father had shot their mother dead, then turned the gun on himself, all in the presence of the young sisters. Since then, they had both turned their trauma into music, both lived large, sometimes lurid lives, but had never recorded together, and shared an understandably complex relationship.

When they walked into our little studio together it felt like electric currents were reverberating around the room, like these two strong magnets were simultaneously attracting and repelling each other. It may just have been my perception, but it felt like finally singing together after all these years was both necessary for their wholeness and healing, yet incredibly painful and powerful, some kind of seismic psychic shock which they were about to share with us.

I think Allison played the piano while Shelby was on acoustic guitar, but to be honest, the whole performance was a mesmerising, compelling blur of tangible, palpable tension. The song they chose to play was Bob Dylan's 'It's Not Dark Yet', a hauntingly sombre ballad, and it was indeed dark, the deepest, darkest blue, as their kith and kin harmonies – as close as DNA can be – intertwined around Dylan's stark and moving lyrics. It is commonplace to describe a good performance as 'spellbinding', but in this instance it was exactly that, like some musical necromancy had occurred, a tortured communing between these two troubled sisters, which shook me and many listeners to the core. It was a very special, very spiritual, and starkly memorable moment.

As was Glenn Frey performing 'Desperado'. That song has become a stone-cold classic of a kind of yearning American mythology, a 'Knocking on Heaven's Door' or a 'Willin'', a John Ford film of a song. It is one of the monuments, and when the co-writer was in our studio, I had no idea that he would be willing to sing it for us. We talked about various solo projects he was involved in and touched a little on the fact that I had been an Eagles fan since Wembley 1975.

We got on to the fact that many of those classic Eagles albums, defining moments of West Coast Americana, were in fact recorded in the deep South-West of London, in leafy, dreary Barnes, of all places. He winced a little remembering the food on offer in London in the 1970s. But he smiled when I told him that the piano he had been looking at in the corner was tuned and ready to go. He played a song from one of his solo records, and then asked would we like to hear 'Desperado'. He also said that he had never performed this solo at a piano in public before and wasn't sure how it would sound.

Well, I can only say it sounded majestic, marvellous, bloody moving. From those opening notes it was sublime to sit there and hear the whole thing stripped right back by the man who created it, a massive beaming smile on my face and a huge thank you to Simon Lederman for having saved that old joanna. I was very sad when I heard that the charming Glenn Frey had passed away a couple of years later. Rest easy, Desperado.

Dr John has gone too. He didn't come in as often as Chas Hodges, but whenever he was in town, Mac Rebennack, the Night Tripper, the Gris-Gris Man, the Voodoo Hoodoo Man, good old Malcolm, would come in to talk to us. And every time it would follow the same pattern.

Dr John is in competition for greatest-ever speaking voice with only one person, and that was his near neighbour, Tony Joe White. There is something about the Louisiana accent which is incredibly attractive to my ears. It's a slow, thick syrup of sound with an alluring, behind-the-beat musicality and an almost hypnotic softness. And those two musicians both had speaking voices which you would buy tickets to hear.

Dr John's conversational voice was pure New Orleans, all swinging second-line funerals and Mardi Gras patois, gruff and tuneful, like a great, late night in a Faubourg Marigny bar. While Tony Joe was a swamp fox from down below the Deep South in Cajun country, where ancient French and Spanish inflections mingle with a deep bayou-boy twang and his low-down baritone tones. He sang for us, but it could not compete with the pure joy of hearing him speak. Dr John only ever came in to talk, and he always ended up doing so much more.

Every time the good doctor was in the house, invariably to play at Ronnie Scott's, we were told by the PRs that he would not under any circumstances play live. He'd arrive adorned in rings, bangles and amulets, wearing a hat and shades, carrying his gnarly voodoo cane, growling his Big Easy vowels. And every time he would see that piano and somehow be pulled inexorably over to it.

One of my favourite memories of all the hundreds and hundreds of live performances over the years on my show, on that battered old joanna, was by the man who wasn't supposed to play live. Dr John gave us a remarkable, impromptu, illustrated history of Crescent City piano styles, all the while providing a running commentary in his glorious twang. There in the studio with us were Professor Longhair and Fats Domino, James Booker, and Jelly Roll Morton; we had stride and boogie-woogie, barrelhouse and phonk; we had a glorious musical history lesson delivered by a man who had been there and back, lived the music which started it all. Here were the roots of jazz and blues and funk and rock'n'roll embodied by this grisly old guy on our battered old piano. The same piano, the same spirit Chas Hodges played. Just occasionally I think I have the best job in the world.

Chapter 21

The Axemen Cometh

'You're my guitar hero.'

It was an impromptu Joe Strummer ad lib, which became enshrined in the lyrics of 'Complete Control', the Clash's blistering third single. This was Strummer's gently teasing response to a short Mick Jones guitar break, delivered with a big smile, a slight sneer, and a huge dollop of irony after Mick stepped forward to play his staccato, thirty-second solo. Joe would look across at his bandmate and playfully admonish him for playing the rock star and playing too many notes, while simultaneously acknowledging that Mick Jones is actually a terrific guitarist. The message was 'punks don't do solos'. But that was a good one.

The elaborate, extended guitar solo, reverberating with fuzz and feedback and screaming, screeching, testosterone-filled runs, was a feature of all prog-rock and heavy-rock performances. Usually delivered by a bloke with over-tight trousers and long frizzy hair and involving lots of exaggerated writhing, grimacing and theatrical finger movement, the geetar solo is a recurring rock'n'roll cliché, and a big part of what the punks were rebelling against.

It was a sign of inflated egos and theatrical excess and an exaggerated reverence for technique over feeling. Putting guitarists up on a pedestal was also a symbol of the axe-wielding, phallic, macho, rock-god, star-system bullshit which punk intended to overturn. Plus, most of them were shit. Rick Derringer, for God's sake?

Punk was all about economy and a certain puritanical disdain for over-elaboration and show-off virtuosity for its own sake. 1970s rock-god guitarists were preening Cavaliers, while punks were definitely Roundheads. And I've always known what side I am on in that civil war. I still struggle to 'get' Jimi Hendrix, I do not understand the reverence for Clapton and Page, and cannot tolerate the bombastic Joe Satriani, Brian May, Joe Bonamassa school of too many notes, too little soul. Mick Jones is a genuine guitar hero compared to those guys. I like Jim Hall too.

So it is very strange and quite awkward for me to admit that the two most beautiful and memorable songs I have witnessed being performed live in the twenty-first century both featured long, complex guitar solos by magnificent guitarists. Am I growing soft in my old age, has something terrible happened to my taste or is there something different about these solos and these guitar players?

Before I come on to those two, and they have both played live on my show, and both played solos for the ages, I want to talk about some other guitarists who made a major positive impression over the years.

Back in those barnstorming, barricade-building punk days, Tom Verlaine of Television and Bob Quine from the Richard Hell band were favourites of mine. They were both from the New York art-house school of angular, atonal guitarists, very different from their punky British counterparts, but also nothing like the standard American cock-rock exhibitionists. This was a scene born of the Velvet Underground and Patti Smith poetry readings, Andy Warhol, and William Burroughs; it was essentially neo-beatnik and so appealed immediately to my jazz ears.

Some of the most memorable musical minutes of the entire punk era for me came when watching Television perform the mercurial 'Marquee Moon', with its intertwining guitar parts ricocheting off each other; hypnotic, gossamer runs spiralling upwards before obliquely cascading with rough-hewn garage-band energy towards an astonishing crescendo. Tom Verlaine's carefully chosen notes are like phosphorescent shards tumbling down upon us. Like lightning striking itself.

As a teenager who had already absorbed and adored John Coltrane, I not only got it but felt like it was an affirmation of the fact that you could wear bondage trousers and still like complex, profound, beautiful music. Transcendent was a very hippy word I would never have used then, but it was, it was transcendent. It was also frowned upon by some British punks, who hated its arty pretention, and indeed it was one of the fault lines between those who would go on to grow mohicans, scrawl 'Crass' on the back of their biker jackets and beg on the King's Road, and those who would jettison the scene once it became crass. Punk may have come from the gutter, but Tom Verlaine's guitar was aiming at the stars.

A few years later, in the early 1980s, I spent lots of time in New York, mainly night-time; an insane nocturnal whirl of clubs and after-hours clubs and after-after-hours clubs, often ending up in the splendidly named Save the Robots, some-where below the Lower East Side. In this period the scene known as 'No Wave' was exploding all over downtown Man-hattan, and it was a musical maelstrom with gigs to go to every night and my name on every guest list. It was dinner at mid-night with August Darnell and breakfast at midday with the hookers in the Meat Packing district. It was fun.

No Wave was essentially a collision between post-punk,

funk and jazz, personified by skinny white boys taking lots of drugs and taking terrible liberties with dance music and the jazz canon because they couldn't actually play very well, but could make a joyous racket. Out of that culture clash came some great music from largely forgotten bands like Konk, Liquid Liquid and ESG, some great, very messy gigs and some very bad hangovers.

James White – or James Chance or James Siegfried – and the Blacks were the ultimate embodiment of this unlikely fusion, and its main man, a splenetic, chaotic, sometimes near-catatonic sax player and shouter remains one of the most compelling acts I've ever seen. A bizarre blend of James Brown, Ornette Coleman and Johnny Rotten, his tastes fitted so closely with my own that it felt like they had been manufactured just for me and my prejudices.

Watching James White and the Blacks at the Mudd Club or Danceteria murdering 'Heatwave', while contorting himself in a fury of St Vitus' dance moves, screaming like a banshee and blowing wincingly off-kilter alto was one of my ideas of heaven. When they did a genuinely harrowing version of 'King Heroin', it gave an insight into his private hell.

Watching him a few years later in London at a venue called the Venue in Victoria, it was clear that the hellish side of his persona was winning, as he stumbled around the stage and disappeared for long periods, like a zombie with a saxophone, yet he was still ghoulishly compelling. Many years later, when he resurfaced, I was still so excited to get a chance to see Mr Chance again that I got a speeding ticket rather than be late for a show at a tiny venue on the Holloway Road. It was worth it, as all the hellfire and fury of his performance was still there, and he had matured into a truly exceptional avant-garde sax player.

That period in New York was scary and thrilling, edgy and dodgy, a psychotropic L-train ride through a collapsing metropolis peopled by beautiful freaks and fabulous misfits. I was barely in my twenties, writing for *The Face*, on the make and on the guest list, so I plunged head-first into this maelstrom of great music and art, and great arty music. And discovered another fine guitarist.

The other band who spearheaded the New York No Wave scene of the early eighties were the Lounge Lizards, an achingly hip collection of Manhattan nocturnalites playing their warped, ironic version of film-noir jazz. They were the talk of the town, and they featured one of the most charismatic characters I've ever met, some of the coolest gigs and another one of those detached but switched-on downtown guitarists.

John Lurie on sax was the bandleader, and if you've ever seen any of the films he starred in for Jim Jarmusch, particularly the splendid *Stranger Than Paradise*, you'll know that he has a laconic magnetism all his own. He was a kind of thrift-store Bryan Ferry, all cheekbones and tuxedos, with a brilliantined quiff and a brilliant tone. Seeing the Lounge Lizards play at a party in a SoHo loft with Jean-Michel Basquiat and Keith Haring, Debbie Harry and Chris Stein milling about was like walking into one of those arty downtown documentaries of the time, a proper crash course for the ravers.

The Lounge Lizards, for all their pseudo amateurism, were rather good: John's brother Evan played fine, Monkish piano, John could handle his horn and they looked terrific in a louche, threadbare approximation of forties style. But it was Arto Lindsay, another pale, thin, bespectacled, angular figure hunched over his guitar, which he played in an equally oblique fashion, who really caught my attention. Discordant but deeply musical, melodic and jarring, the sound he made was so far removed from rock'n'roll as to be a different language.

Arto Lindsay was more Albert Ayler than Eddie Van Halen, capable of skronking dissonance, but also lilting beauty, a sweet player, and I've followed his career ever since. I've seen him live in small clubs and followed his solo sessions via the internet during Covid, and never been less than amazed at his continuing creativity. He became a collaborator with Tom Waits, which is perhaps the ultimate seal of approval.

I was convinced that No Wave was the next big thing, that the fun I was having in Manhattan at the time would translate into worldwide success, and I became a proselytiser for ZE Records et al. But it never ended up much more than a foot-note and a collection of hazy memories.

From freezing squat parties on Delancey Street to soirées in Park Avenue mansions, the whole city was a playground. There was some great music made in New York in the early eighties, an incredibly fertile scene, but it was made to be seen live, didn't really translate onto record. It was drug-fuelled, decadent, genuinely dangerous and infinitely thrilling to a boy from Burnt Oak.

It is no coincidence that London and New York were both at their most febrile and fecund when both cities were skint and in the depths of economic decline. Because it meant that there were cheap squats and apartments in the heart of the city for youngsters, artists, writers, musicians to live in, and scores of places for bands to play right in the centre of town: old dis-used warehouses, lofts and industrial units in SoHo or Soho, which could be colonised and turned into clubs or venues. Punk and everything it spawned was born of bountiful decay.

While I was swanning around New York, milking my Eng-lish accent and making the most of my links to *The Face*, I also saw another couple of live events but didn't think much of them. One was watching one of the waitresses from Dancete-ria leap about and mime to a demo she had recorded with the DJ Mark Kamins. I might even have been in the DJ booth at the time, as I had wangled a gig spinning a few tunes, even though I am spectacularly cackhanded and my speciality was playing the wrong side of the record at the wrong speed.

Anyway, this girl with a ra-ra skirt and badly dyed blonde hair cleared some space on the floor and made a proper exhibition of herself to a pop disco tune. That's the last we'll ever hear of her, I thought. When she turned up at the Camden Palace in London a few months later and did the self-same thing, I was even more convinced that this Madonna character should go back to being a waitress.

Missing out on the biggest female artist of her age was a minor mistake compared to the other live acts I dismissed in New York in the early 1980s. It was at a club called the Roxy, on a night curated by a fellow Brit, a girl known as Ruza Blue, or Kool Lady Blue, to give her her street name. A friend of Malcolm McLaren, who worked in Vivienne's shop in SoHo, she is something of an unsung hero of the music which was about to take over the world. She was the first person to take hip-hop down from the crumbling tenements of the South Bronx and give it a showcase in shiny, show-off Manhattan.

Afrika Bambaataa, Grandmaster Flash, Fab 5 Freddy, the Rocksteady Crew, they all appeared at this downtown club, spinning records backwards, spinning on their heads, painting graffiti, skipping Double Dutch and speaking double-fast rhymes over deconstructed old funk tracks. I thought the whole thing was kind of quaint and would probably be a novelty hit for a few weeks, but that the world would soon tire of such shenanigans. It all struck me as thoroughly unmusical, and rather parochial and juvenile. How wrong can you possibly be?

To this day, I don't love hip-hop, while acknowledging that it has been the most potent and important music of a generation, it is not my thing. I like my African American vocal music to be soulful and cool, deep and moving, Marvin Gaye, Aretha Franklin and Donny Hathaway. Bill Withers holding that note on 'Hope She'll Be Happier'. Rap always struck me as closer to hard rock or heavy metal than soul. It even featured guitar solos.

At the time when I first saw those kids from the Bronx burst into life, I already loved Gil Scott-Heron and The Last Poets, understood the precedent for outspoken spoken word, set to music. That was serious civil rights stuff, the African American experience of racism and oppression made angrily manifest, but I saw all this hip-hoppy rapping with rhymes about 'ladies' and 'Mercedes' as a superficial street craze that would not last. Hip-hop was doo-wop without the harmonies.

I certainly did not for a second think that this scene I was witnessing in New York in 1981 would take over the world, so gave it little credence and sneered at its bright colours and backwards baseball hats. At the same time, I also turned down the chance to buy a painting by Basquiat. If I ever offer you a tip on the horses, you know what to do.

Folk music is another musical form I struggle with, particularly finger-in-the-ear English, warm-beer-and-flat-vowels folk music, of the kind much beloved by people who favour socks with open-toed sandals. Admittedly it is hard to imagine John Martyn sporting such footwear, although he may have been the greatest British 'folk' artist of his age. Unfortunately, by the time I interviewed him in the late 1990s, Mr Martyn had already lost a leg due to his chronic alcoholism, which rendered him a bloated, sweating, shivering shadow of a man as he sat in my studio desperate to leave and get to a pub.

I felt terribly sad seeing him in this sorry condition, a giant reduced. I already knew that he was one of the greatest ever maverick British singer-songwriters and guitar players. I'd seen this big, unruly, trouble-loving fellow live on several occasions and always been in awe of his soft, slurred, touchingly melancholic vocals and his uniquely dynamic guitar style, all echoplex and dubby delay.

One night at the London Palladium back in the mid-1980s,

before his lifestyle had taken such a savage toll, I watched him seduce that sumptuous room with what he described as 'songs of misery and despair' to the point where the girl I had taken with me, who knew nothing of his music, was a blubbering wreck. Big, rollicking, street-fighting, yet oh so gentle John could do that.

But loving John Martyn did not make me a convert to folk music. Gillian and Dave did that. When the debut album by that unknown American folk/country duo landed on my desk in 1996, it was the interesting black and white, retro styling of the cover which caught my attention. That was a photo of Gillian Welch in a forties-style dress, a wan but strong looking figure, seemingly from a different, darker age. And when I listened to it, the music took me to distant Appalachian valleys and a far-off, long-lost Depression America of the imagination. I started playing it immediately on my show.

Her singing was chillingly correct, a coalminer's daughter of a voice, plangent and insistent, a keening call simultaneously young and new, and as old and weary as the hills. The overall sound was sparse and austere, monochromatic and intense. Their voices together had a sombre edge, but it was also the guitar playing which really made me sit up and take note. That strange, mesmerising guitar playing.

I've already written in this book about watching Gillian Welch and her finger-picking partner Dave Rawlings in the disconcerting company of David Cameron and his wife. That was a good gig, only partially marred by the people present. But the greatest gig I saw them play, and perhaps the greatest guitar solo I've ever seen and heard was in a deconsecrated church in Shoreditch. That numinous building was the perfect setting for a solo to shake the mortal soul.

It is a good time here to talk about authenticity, because when that first album burst out, there was quite the debate about whether this remarkable, likeable couple were genuine or not. Neither of them claimed to be high-mountain hillbillies; they are both middle-class, university-educated city kids. But they are also both absolutely committed musicians, dedicated to preserving, but also advancing the kind of deep American roots music they fell in love with. It is studied no doubt, a learned language, but then absorbed so fully into their being that it is never pastiche. They know it and they mean it.

Authenticity is not about where the artist is from, it's about where the music comes from. Joe Strummer was no less authentic as a punk because he was the son of a diplomat who went to a private school. Spend a second with the man, even just watching him up on stage from afar, and you knew he meant every moment, that he lived it, that his soul was totally engaged. Gillian is the same.

Strangely, the comparison that springs to my mind is August Darnell. The man is a Shakespearean scholar, a multilinguist and an Ellingtonian authority, and I once saw August, as his alter ego Kid Creole, get on a Ryanair flight at Gibraltar airport in a full lemon zoot suit, carrying three hatboxes as hand luggage. He is so steeped in the sound and style of 1940s Harlem swing that he lives it every day and plays it every night up on stage. And the same is true of Gillian Welch and Dave Rawlings with their very different chosen America.

They have appeared on my show four or five times, and they never step out of character, two impeccably dressed travelling musicians with a guitar each, one old, trusted microphone and a perfect set of manners. Their whole ethos is so stripped-back and low-tech that there is no fuss at all. They stand together either side of a single mic and sing and play, and this almost supernatural symbiosis occurs: they become one with each other and with the song, a telepathic unison of purpose as they fully inhabit this bleak, beautiful musical terrain of theirs.

You might be able to tell that I rather like Gillian Welch and her partner. I also like Dave Rawlings Machine, where the roles are reversed and he takes the lead in a rockier, more seventies style of music, while Gillian provides pitch-perfect harmonies in a Nudie suit. Their rendition of 'Ruby', an old time tale of a telegraph man live on my show was so wondrous I demanded a copy of it on CD to take home and listen to time and again, something I never do with music, which is live and of the moment.

Their masterpiece is the album *Time (The Revelator)*, the perfect fusion between their sparse old-time country roots and a baroque, almost gothic post-modernism. The seven-minute-plus title track with its oblique, mordant lyrics, cuss words, philosophical expositions and baffling tangents is a proper contemporary epic. It's a masterpiece driven by the imagery and the interplay between their voices, but also the momentum provided by her insistent acoustic strumming and his out-of-kilter, impressionistic guitar-picking, which doesn't so much gently weep as sob and moan and lament in the corner.

His guitar itself is worthy of note: a tiny old 1930s Epiphone rescued from a friend's garage, it is the antithesis of a rock god's axe; humble, brown, and seemingly insignificant. But watch him play it live, especially on 'The Revelator', especially that night at St Luke's Church, where they were just feet away and close to divine, and it is as near to a spiritual experience as this old atheist is ever likely to get.

He takes a solo three quarters of the way through 'The Revelator' and not a note that he chooses is one you would expect. While she keeps the circular rhythm of the song pushing forward, he takes us on this dissonant, sometimes uncomfortable ride with jagged jazz chords, spiralling out-of-sync phrases and sharp, sour notes; it is discordant, disconcerting and intriguing but above all intensely emotional as these unlikely sounds are strung together with a fluidity and a clarity which is molten.

Watching in absolute enthralled silence, a tension builds throughout the solo; it feels as though he is walking a musical tightrope, in danger of falling at any moment – where can he go next? His concentration is palpable, yet it also looks like this is perhaps some kind of out-of-body auto-guitaring, as if an external force is making him play in tongues. But with just a shake of his mane and a twist and wrench and wrestle of his Epiphone, having taken us all to the edge, he brings it to a strangely logical, deeply musical conclusion. He suspends time and then lets it loose. This was hairs-on-the-back-of-your-psyche stuff: how does he do that? Am I really hearing that stuff?

I can describe that solo in great detail because that event was filmed and so I can watch it time and again, and indeed I have, and thankfully it is almost as moving and magnificent as it was live. But only almost. A lived moment like that will stay with me despite the film version, not because of it. I can watch Bobby Zamora scoring in the ninetieth minute of the play-off final at Wembley on YouTube, or else I can close my eyes and remember what it felt like falling through space and into the arms of a demented stranger. Years of suffering vindicated.

That Dave Rawlings guitar solo made me feel that the world is still full of possibilities and surprises, that you ain't seen nothing yet and that even as an older man, music can shock me, transport me to a better place. It can make the world a better place. And I don't like guitar solos.

And I didn't know I liked the Tedeschi Trucks Band until I introduced them on stage at the Royal Albert Hall. Somehow this sprawling twelve-piece band, born from the ghosts and DNA traces of the Allman Brothers, had escaped my attention, probably because they play blues rock of the kind I had long dismissed as dead in the water. Long-haired Americans with long guitar solos and all that.

I really should have learned by now not to rely upon my prejudices, although on the whole they have served me quite well. You can generally judge a book by its cover – it's what covers are for – but I misread this one. By dismissing the TTB because of the way its lead guitarist looked, I had forgotten that there is always room in life to surprise yourself. Sometimes you have to say, 'This is not the sort of thing that I like. But I really like this.'

Which is exactly what I found myself thinking the moment the band started to play. I should have known before that. I went backstage to talk to Susan Tedeschi and Derek Trucks about how they wanted to be introduced, and there they were, with the rest of their sprawling outfit, musicians of every hue and age, all together, joking, laughing, no separate dressing room for the stars. And they weren't just polite to me, they were gracious and warm to this English guy they've never met, kind and genuine. But still I was sceptical.

I know that bad people can make good music, but is it possible for good people to make bad music? These were clearly really good people and yet I was not expecting to be bowled over by a blues-rock band featuring one of those feted guitarists, long hair in a ponytail and all. Then they started to play.

Yet again, despite the presence of a big, rumbustious band, organist, two drummers, percussionist, and numerous horn players, it is essentially the tension and interplay between her and him, Susan's soulful, husky vocal and rhythm guitar and Derek's fluid, sensuous slide playing.

They've also been on my show, and as with Gillian and Dave, there is a striking oneness, an intimacy between the two, true love-looks in their eyes, which absolutely informs the music they make together. It is the product of the pair.

The whole macho, alpha-male guitar-hero shtick is balanced out, softened, rounded, by the presence of a female partner in song. Perhaps I'm being soppy here, and it's not easy for an old punk to write this, but I believe that my two favourite pieces of music of the twenty-first century, my two favourite live performances, even the two greatest guitar solos, have come about because of love.

And it is during the song 'Midnight in Harlem' that you really feel the love. The first time I heard it, that night at the Royal Albert Hall, watching proceedings from a box, I'd already realised what a great band this is, but wasn't prepared for what was about to be unleashed. Perhaps the most beautiful, heartfelt, heart-wrenching ballad of its age.

Again, you can watch this on the internet – not the Albert Hall performance, but others which are spectacularly good. Indeed, this is the musical clip I have watched most, turning to it for solace, for joy and indeed to be reminded that the human spirit can soar. When I first saw them play live, I did not know the song at all, so don't remember it with any clarity, just a wondrous blur, a sense that something incredible was unfolding in front of my ears.

It starts with silence. Derek Trucks, not a showy man, moves to the centre and begins carefully, thoughtfully selecting a gentle tumbling of notes – Eastern, modal, like a raga, hypnotic and intriguing, something Mr Coltrane from North Carolina might have played. Then the band join in, but softly in a sweet soul vein, a Hammond organ pulsing with church intonations, a deep Southern groove with a loping, mournful bassline. Susan starts to sing in that grainy, textured voice of hers and it is a sad song, a 'bruised country girl goes to the city seeking solace' song, full of old men's shoes and needles on the ground, an American song.

As this lament unfolds, laden with layers of meaning in a multiracial Southern band, so it gradually, almost imperceptibly, builds momentum and at some point, his voice, as channelled through the strings of his Gibson, takes over from hers, and his serpentine slide-guitar playing tells the tale.

Still imbued with melancholy and regret, but also stoicism and strength, perhaps even hope, he gently leads us through a whole raft of emotions. Never brusque or showy, but loose and intense, everything channelled through those bending notes, the slide on his fingers tenderly caressing and cajoling the strings. I remember him stock still, concentrating, creating, letting this angelic music flow from within. He soars and swoops and he leads us from the Delta to the Hudson on a journey of compassion and revelation. It is a monument. It is a different, other, better America. It is a prayer.

Susan was standing to the side watching him intently, with something like awe, something very much like adoration in her eyes, while my own eyes welled up. Here was I, a grown man sobbing, thousands of concerts in, and a guitar solo, a bloody guitar solo, can do this to me.

Chapter 22

Staying Alive

QPR are top of the league. This doesn't happen very often, so it's worth noting. We have hope, which is always dangerous, but also intoxicating, Alfie and I have taken to going to every away game we can get to, realising deep in our shared DNA that this probably will not last. Enjoy it while you can; that dark and sodden night in Norwich looking for our kin and kind in a pub before the game. That mad scramble to get to Coventry or Stoke before kick-off, the balti pie at Blackburn, remember for ever the flying limbs for that last-minute winner, the sing-song sung on the train home, the raucous roar as we pull into Euston. UUUURRRRs.

I'm a grown man, my son is now a grown man, but none of that diminishes my appetite for the crush of a distant concourse at half-time full of the truly, madly devoted. I like the beer on the floor, the terrible food, the queue for the loos, the silly boys shouting and jostling, the old blokes from Ladbroke Grove and Northolt moaning and prophesying doom, the young kids with their dads wide-eyed at such wayward behaviour. I like seeing people I've known, but only in this context, only on a distant grotty concourse, for forty or more years, forty or more years mainly watching us lose. 'See you at Preston.' But today we are top of the league.

The privations of Covid have only sharpened my appetite for every kind of shared live experience and right now my diary is full. The London Jazz Festival is just around the corner and I've booked half a dozen shows, most of them pretty tough stuff. One highlight should be Neneh Cherry, who is part of a tribute to her esteemed father Don Cherry at the Barbican, which reminds me of my most embarrassing moment as a broadcaster. Early in her career I was unaware of her family history and so mockingly asked her what she knew about jazz. She looked at me, understandably askance, and said, 'Do you know who my dad is?' I do now.

I'm particularly looking forward to Matana Roberts, a river-deep alto sax player from Chicago, a poet and wise woman, who is exploring the sonic echoes of slavery in the Deep South; her music is disturbing and inspiring, occasionally harrowing, often beautiful and will make for an intense, intriguing evening. This is the sort of racket my wife threatens divorce over, but I find challenging, exciting and often truly moving. So much great stuff coming out of Chicago right now, I feel a trip coming on.

I've also got tickets for the Tedeschi Trucks Band at the Palladium. The thought of 'Midnight in Harlem' once again is mouthwatering, potentially eye-watering. I'm off to see Nick Lowe at Nell's once more; I could watch Nick Lowe most weeks and still get excited at the prospect. Rarely has charm and self-deprecation been backed up by so many great songs. Steve Harley from Cockney Rebel is doing a one-man show and he's a very entertaining man too.

I'm incredibly lucky, of course, because I can afford to go to so many shows. I still get a fair number of freebies and have friends in low places, but even if I had to pay for every gig, I would still prioritise live music, because it is the best way of reminding myself that I am still alive.

I felt alive and aware, but pretty damn old recently when I went to a gig in a tiny upstairs room, painted all black, in a properly scuzzy Chalk Farm bar. A band were on the bill called Safe At Any Speed, and their lead singer, guitarist and lyricist is a young man I've known all his life. Blake is a family friend and neighbour who has been obsessed by music since he was a small kid in Camden Town, and I've tried to guide his musical taste by proffering suggestions and discussing albums. For his eighteenth birthday I bought him six LPs on vinyl that I loved when I was eighteen, including *Horses* and *Marquee Moon*. So going to see him play in his band for the first time was both exciting and a touch worrying. What if they were rubbish?

Standing in line in the street before getting my wrist stamped was a culture shock in itself. Three times the age of most people present, I hadn't done this in a very long time, and the bouncers, who looked like they had served in a Serbian militia, studied me with some scepticism. Once inside, the place was cold and dark with graffiti all over the toilet walls and the lager was served in plastic glasses, presumably in case a fight broke out. It smelt like most of the beer usually ended up on the sticky floor and looked like many of the punters had recently graduated from posing school as they cast hopefully cool shapes around the room. It was great.

Then Blake and his band ambled on. He's a tall, blonde, good-looking boy with cheekbones in all the right places, and you could feel the little frisson of charisma as he plugged into his amp and cranked out the opening chords. It was fast and fresh and raw as all hell, a bit thrash, a bit grunge, but with some decent tunes poking through. This is a very young band in love with the Clash and the Velvet Underground (both albums I bought him) and summoning the spirit of a punky past, yet very much of today.

It was noisy and brash and rather sweet, and I felt a glow of something like pride seeing my young friend keeping the faith and the flame. That there are still eager young musicians making a terrific noise in smelly rooms in Camden is a source of great solace to me.

Writing this book, unleashing all those memories, has served to prove to me that live sport and music have been the great constants in my life; it started with 'ABC' and QPR and will probably end with ZZZs as I nod off at a game or a gig somewhere in my dotage. County cricket is looking increasingly attractive.

As I've got older, if anything my appreciation of music has got broader, deeper, less intense perhaps, less ecstatically proselytising, but more satisfying, rewarding. Certainly, I've become more emotional, more aware of what it all means. In fact, I've come to need live music more as other more hedonistic pleasures have receded, cannot bear the thought of living without a gig to look forward to.

The proximity to so much creativity is one of the main reasons for continuing to live in London. My wife and I have finally torn ourselves away from our beloved Camden Town and moved to the Barbican, where there is a world-class concert hall and theatre downstairs. Even if I'm not going to a show, I like to pop down and mingle, just feel the buzz of the crowd, the frisson of anticipated revelry. Share in the collective.

I also like to wander round the estate listening out for fragments. The Guildhall School of Music is situated here, and one of the great treats is hearing the students practise as you navigate round the baffling brutalist warren, see them carrying their instruments on their backs, glimpse them in their rehearsal rooms. A solo cello late on a dark night is one of the most hauntingly plangent sounds.

Up here in our eyrie we can see out over almost all our city, see London nestling in a bowl of distant hills, a patchwork of memories with a river running through it. There are five football stadiums within view, including Wembley Stadium in the distance, where I dodged Party Sevens and walked out on Elton; the Festival Hall, built by my dad, blessed by Paul Weller; Crystal Palace, where I saw Bob Marley blowing in the wind; and Ally Pally, where I once saw Siouxsie and the Banshees, missed the last bus home and had to walk all the way back to a squat in Warren Street. Sade played there too, just up from the fire station we squatted in.

In between those northern and southern extremes with their spindly towers like points of a compass, there are hundreds of humble, low-lying and therefore invisible-to-us places, where I have seen and heard musicians weave their spell. Pubs and clubs, municipal halls, discos, disused swimming baths, derelict warehouses, lofts, squats, shops, cinemas, theatres, railway arches, parks, gardens. London has always been and still is alive with sound and from high up and above I can map this city in music. I have a form of geographical synaesthesia, whereby when I think of certain parts of London, I hear very specific music.

South-East London is Squeeze playing in their backyard at the Albany in Deptford; North-East London is rockabilly bands — Stray Cats, Polecats and Rockats with upright bass and drooping quiffs. West London is owned by the Clash, breathing righteous fire over the Westway, but it's also Aswad, 'The Lions of Ladbroke Grove' grooving in Meanwhile Gardens, W10. The Edgware Road reverberates with penny whistles, bodhrans and pints of Guinness as the Pogues play on. Islington still shakes with the Thames Delta rhythm and blues of the Feelgoods and the Hot Rods, who regularly smashed the Hope & Anchor.

Leafy South-West London is almost silent, save for the laconic sneer of the Subway Sect on their home turf, while the East End is the joyous jolt of Asian Dub Foundation with their riotous mash-up of bhangra, dub and punk. Dalston is free-form jazz, Camden is Britpop, Brixton a blaring blend of roots and culture and drum and bass.

Soho, which we can see from our balcony only as a shadow beside Centre Point, a dark well of dreams, is a cacophony of all the music, all the memories, every band, every show, every night, each street with its own beat. Wardour Street is rocking, black leather in the Ship, cold sweat in the Marquee, with Lemmy grinning at the back. Dean Street is funky: Crackers, the Beat Route, Groove Records, where the old lady knitted. Meard Street is electronic and Teutonic Bowie and Kraftwerk deep in the basement of Billy's, while Berwick Street smells of cardboard and vinyl and sounds like the grumpy old git in Cheapo Cheapo, the record shop.

The musical epicentre of my Soho, Frith Street, is the boss sound of hard bop, full stop. I can hear the snap of the snare and the crack of the rimshot, the crystal blast of a trumpet, the siren wail of a saxophone. It is the sound of neon, burning-bright Bar Italia, the sharp suits of the modernists, the curling cigarette smoke, the svelte lines of Charlie Watts in his Savile Row floating like a ghost. It is jazz, jazz, jazz. My city swings like a pendulum and sounds like a movie soundtrack.

And directly down from our home in the sky lie the twisted and richly storied streets of old Clerkenwell, one of the most charismatic of barrios. It was here on the eve of the Royal Wedding, the star-crossed Charles and Diana one in 1981, that I watched Blue Rondo à la Turk, still one of the best ever live bands, in a ruined room up above an alley, at the top of a dark, decaying Victorian building. Halfway through the set, a massive John Wayne-style bar-room brawl broke out, chairs flying, windows smashing, all hell breaking theatrically loose, as the zoot-suited band spun and whirled to 'Klactoveesedstein'. Still makes me smile.

And so does a little boozer called the Betsey Trotwood. A typical old London pub named after a Dickens character, hard by a large block of Peabody buildings amid the throb of the Farringdon Road. It is a music pub, a small stage in the centre, piano at the back, always good tunes on the sound system and usually a band of some kind about to go on and play for the fifty or so people present. It is the root of all, the source of this great love. And I've been going back to my roots. My son says it's my Jake LaMotta moment.

On Sunday afternoons, once a month or so, we put on a show. I tell a few tales, do an interview or two, the man we call the Rock'n'Roll Routemaster joins some historical dots, and then Danny the Champ takes over. Danny George Wilson is a music man, more than just a player and a singer – he is drenched in music, and it was our shared love of the godlike genius of Ronnie Lane and Gallagher and Lyle, Lindisfarne and Frankie Miller, the seventies sound I dubbed neckerchief rock, which brought us together.

That music, which I first fell in love with as a fourteen-year-old Faces fan, is an urban, working-class folk music dressed in a waistcoat and a collarless shirt. These are swaying songs: simple, melodic tunes, with clip-clop *Steptoe and Son* basslines, unashamedly sentimental lyrics, with sing-along choruses but soulful vocals which reach back beyond the seventies and the youth of most people present to our mums and dads in their Sunday best, canoodling to a saloon-bar crooner and clinking bottles of light ale. It was our version of The Band, and it touches our collective roots.

And when Danny sings 'Debris' or 'Ooh La La', his mandolin-playing mate takes a short solo and Raz, the governor of the pub, leaps from behind the jump with his harmonica to join in, the whole place is as one with this wonderful music. Londoners singing the songs of their lives, sharing the melodies of our memories. At that moment, at the centre of this party, I am just about as happy as I have ever been, as in love with this music, with live music and its ability to unite us, excite us and make us feel. And that always feels good.

QPR are seventeenth in the league.

A Note on the Author

Robert Elms is a writer and broadcaster, based in central London. He started out as a journalist, writing for *The Face* and *NME*. He is best known for his eponymous radio show on BBC Radio London which covers everything you need to know about the capital, from architecture and clothes, to accents and great music.

Robert is the author of three previous works of non-fiction, *Spain: A Portrait After the General*, *The Way We Wore: A Life in Threads*, and *London Made Us: A Memoir of a Shape-Shifting City*, and a novel, *In Search of the Crack*.

Unbound is the world's first crowdfunding publisher, established in 2011.

We believe that wonderful things can happen when you clear a path for people who share a passion. That's why we've built a platform that brings together readers and authors to crowdfund books they believe in – and give fresh ideas that don't fit the traditional mould the chance they deserve.

This book is in your hands because readers made it possible. Everyone who pledged their support is listed below. Join them by visiting unbound.com and supporting a book today.

Max Bellhouse
Leigh Bellinger
Gareth Bennett
Dawn Benson
Steve Benton
Anthony Betts
David Bickle
Will Birch
Julia Biro
Gary Blay
Johnny Bongo
Nick Boorer
Richard Bowles
Richard Boyce
Chris Bradshaw
Paul Bratherton
Andrew Brignell
Steve Brine
Tim Bronock
Jason Brooks
Kirsty Brooks
Andrew Brown
Andy Brown
Carolyn Brown
Jeanie Brown
Jude Brown
Robert Mark Brown
Brian Browne
Steven Browning
Tim Browning
Ray Brumwell
Linda Brunette-Jacobs
Kevin Buck
Della Buggy

Paul Burden
Terry Burdon
Justin Burke
Nichola Burke
Patrick Burke
Nick Burkinshaw
Iain Burridge
Anna Burt
Helen Butler
Rachel Butler
Andrew Buurman
Sean Byrne
Jon Bywater
Steve Came
Roxy Camp
Dom Candon
Bob Cappa
Nick Carline
Paul Carpen
Fiona Carpenter
Colin Carroll
Lewis Carter
Steve Carter
Mark Cathcart
Clemente Cavigioli most
    loyal listener
Ronke Chalmers
Lily Chan
Martin Chillcott
Paul Clancy
Alan Clark
Peter Clark
Chris Clarke
Russell Clarke

Tom Cleary
Miles Clinch
Steve Cockle
Ted Cockle
Jason Collins
Kevin Collins
Michael Collins
Chris Colwell
Paul Comerford
Steve Cook
Keith Cooper
Tony Cosaitis
Damian Coughlan
Stephen Court
Robert Courtney
John Cowen
Eileen Cox
Alex Coxon
John Crawford
Jason Crimp
Adriano Cristino
Anthony Critchlow
Ken Crosland
Nick Crotty
Ciaran Crowley
Kellie Crozer
Anthony Cummins
Declin Daly
Christopher Damiano
Simon Dangoor
Timothy Daugherty
Brian David
Catherine Davies
Tim Davies

Phil Dawe
Rob Day
Stephen Day
Paul de Zylva
Justin Deans
Paul Spencer Denman
Alan Derry
Martine Derry
Paul Devaney
Alison Dickens
Keith Dickie' Finch
Alan Dillon
Mark Donald
Rob Drake
Dom Drew
Victoria Dry
Esther Dryland
Robert Duggin
Diane Dunkley
Jamie Dunkley
Brian Dunlop
Nick Durling
JoJo Dye
Mark Dyer
Wendy Edmonds
Gillian Edwards
Steve Edwards
Stuart and Michaella
   Edwards
Lee Eldred
Dr. Sebastiaan
   Eldritch-Böersen
Emma Ellis
Lee Emmerson

Don Esslemont

Sue Ettinger

Jonny Evans

Alex Everitt

Richard Fabb

Adam Fairbank

Paul Fenn

Jason Fenton

M Fisher

Alan Fitter

Mike Fitzgerald

Jennifer Fleming

Stu Fletcher

Kathryn Flett

Bob Flew

Jane Foran

Anthony Ford

Mark Forsyth Taylor

G Foskett

Stephen Foster

Martin Fox

Eileen Francombe

Bradley Franks

Marcus Free

Steve freestone

Andrew Frith

Gary Frost

Nicola Fuller

Harvey Gallagher

Tom Galloway

Tom Gally

Kate Gamm

Jane Garry

Freddy George

Julie George

Claudia Giacopazzi

Gary Gilbertson

Julie Giles

Charlie Gillan

Jacqueline Gillman

Lindsay Gilmore

Bernie Gleeson

Lucy Gomes

Rob Good

Mark Goodwin

Bob Grainger

Ed Gray

Darren Greene

Margaret Ann Greene

Lee Gregory

Jacky Griffin

Rachel Griffiths

Janet Grimes

Michael Grogan

Joe and Lindsey Guest

Stewart Gunn

Mark Gunning

Andy Gunton

Lee Guyatt

Gary Haigh

Kelly Haines

Clare Hamilton

Marcus Hamilton

Amanda Hammond

Spencer Hammond

Sara C Hancock

Wayne Handley

Anthony Hansen

Deborah Harding

Beverley Harper

Dominica Harringtonsmith

Johnny Harris

Neil Harris

Alan Harrison

Andy Harrower

Zara Hart

Ian Hartley

Emma Harvey

Eunice Hayes

Normski Hayes

Jonathan Haynes

Robin Hayter

Nick Hazeldine

David Henshall

Bob Hepburn

Edward Heppenstall

Justyn Herbert

Paul Herman

Nigel Hewitt

Mark Hey

Jacqueline Higgin

Iain Hill

Yasuhiro Hiraki

Paul Hobbs

Bronwen Hodgkinson

Karen Hodson

John Holliday

Janice Holloway

Paula Holt

Lindsey Hood

Karen Hookway

Andy Horton

Bryan Michael Hotston

Jes Howe

John Hubbard

Helen Hudson

Sandra Hughes

Amanda Hume

Neil Hume

Amanda Humphreys

Derek Humphries

Rona Hunnisett

Stephen Hunnisett

Alan Hunter

Elliott Hurst

Fiona Hutchings

Mark Huxley

Dave Illing

William Imeson

Paul Jameson

Jan

James Jenkins

Jenni

Samuel Jessop

Heather Johns

David L Johnson

Phil Johnson

Ian Jones

Joanne Jones

Kate Jones

Linda Jones

Paul Jones

Sara Jones

Steve W. Jones

Miles Jordan

Simon Joe Jordan

Jacky Judd
Chris Kamen
Arthur 'Deckard' Karczmiarz
Gary Kedney
Simon Kelly
Gary Kemp
John Kemp
Lee Kettle
Dan Kieran
David Kinchlea
Simon Kingham
Stephen Kirk
Jackie Kirkham
Jacky Kitching
Richard Knott
Paul Kramer
Kris Kubiena
Lee Lacey
Ross Laing
Dominic Lake
Kevin & Claire Larkham
Barrie Larvin
Peter Layzell
Mike Leigh
Mark Robert Lennon
Lynda Lester
Paul Lewis
Sean Liberty
Robert Lim
Cameron Lindo
Richard Linton
Robert Lipson
Tim Little
Annie Littleton

Susan Livingstone
Nikki Livingstone-Rothwell
Paul Lloyd
Steve Lomax
Kim Lovegrove
Nick Lowe
Franceska Luther King
Trudi Lyall-Mears
Kirsty MacDougall
Maximillian Hugo Macson
Trevor Madden
David Maddox
Yukiko Maekawa
Diane Maguire
Gita Malhotra
Karen Malivoire
Gerry Malone
Dennis Mann
Craig Manning
Pamela March
Daniel Markham
Paul Marsh
Andrew Martin
Bryan Martin
Ian Martin
Sarah Matheson
David Matkins
Wendy Maxey
Mark Mayo
Karen Mayze
Ian McArthur
Simon McAuley
Alison McBride
Aidan McCarthy

Jim McCluskey

Tony McConnell

Neil McConnon

Scott McCoy

Katherine McCutcheon

Marc Mcfarlane

Bridgid McGill MacSeóin

John McLaren

Gideon McLean

Nick McMahon

Alison McNally

Declan Meagher

Emma Medd

Erkin Mehmet

Steve Melhuish

John Micek

John Michie

Jon Midlane

Mike

Dominique Miller

Simon Miller

John Mitchinson

Steven Moe

Rachel Moffat

Richard Moody

Chris Moore

Eddy Moore

Mark Morfett

Lee Morrison

Peter Morrison-Bartlett

Simon Mottram

Kai Muxlow

Mark Nagle

Graham Nash

Carlo Navato

Elizabeth Nevin

Vas Nevrides

Alison Newell

Christopher J Newman

Delphi Newman

Jay Newman

Mark Norris

Peter Nowlan

Caroline Nuttall-Smith

Richard Nye

Steve O'Brien

Angela O'Connor

Bernard O'Keeffe

Sean O'Neill

Deb O'Reilly

David O'Sullivan

Karen O'Shea

Richard Ogle

Philippa Oldmeadow

Mandy Oliver

Peter Orr

Krystian Orszulik

Bob Owen

Lee Page

Mark Painter

Ajay Parekh

Steph Parker

Fiona Partington

Mark Pate

George Patterson

Tom Pattullo

Jeremy Pearce

Simon Peirce

Alan Pell

Barry Penny

Paul Pepper

Angie Phipps

John Phipps

Robert Pigram

Simon Pilcher

Marshall and Natalie Pillay

Justin Pollard

Tom Poole

Mary Portas

Spencer Power

Dave Prior

Nigel Proktor

Carlos Q

Shiv Quinlan

Tim Quinn

David Quirk

Michael L Radcliffe

Ian Rae

Tony Ramos

Liza Ramrayka

Karen Ramsey

Keith Ramsey

Lorna Randall

Angie Rawlinson

Marc Read

Gerry Reardon

Nick Reay

Paul Reedy

Neil Reeves

Greg Reid

Mark Reilly

Ian Rhodes

John and Sarah Riglin

Deborah Ripley

Marc Risby

David Roach

David Roberts

Johnny Roberts

Neil Robinson

Tim Robinson

Gabriela Rodriguez

Danny Rogers

Paul Rogers

John Rowland

Jocelyn Ruparelia

Stephen Rush

Gary Russell

Steve Russell

Ruth from Godalming

Robert Ryan

Lloyde Sargent

Alan Saunders

David Alexis Saunders

Mary Scanlan

Andy Scarr

Arthur Schiller

Shane

Angela Sharp

Chris Sheldon

Daniel Shields

Mark Shillito

Ian Shipley

Timothy Shyne

Lorna Simes

Charlotte Simons

Scott Sinclair

Siobhan

Brian Small

Adam Smith

Gail Smith

Graham Smith

Graham D. Smith

Laura Smith

Marcus Smith

Dean Smythe

Kyri Sotiri

Steve Southall

Paul Southerland

Julie Springett

Steve Staniforth

Julian and Monika Stansall

David Stelling

Martin Stenning

St.John Stephen

David Stokes

Andrew Stone

Jez Stone

Matthew Stroud

James Stuart

Andrew Stylianou

Chris Sutton

Jimmy Sutton

Ian Swan

Swimone I Swim A Bit

Julia Szepietowski

Frankie T

Danny Taggart

Ian Tamborini

Lynn Tanner

Jules Tatner

Jacqui Taylor

Neil Taylor

The Betsey Trotwood

Jens Thelander

Julie Thomas

Lindsey Thomas

Dominic Thompson

David Thornton

Jim Thornton

Lawrence Tildesley

John Tinline

Phil Togwell

Stephen Townsend

Ian Traynor

Sara & John Treanor

Jonathan and Debra Turner

Kim Turner

Jane Tuxford

Eleanor Tweddell

Jim Valenti

Mark Varney

Samantha Vocking

Simon Wady

Steve Walker

Teresa Walker

James Wall

Russell and Jan Walters

Brian Ward

Graham Ward

Jo Ward

Paul Ward

Lil Warren

Merwin Wass

Christine Watson

John Watton
Johnny Watts
Geoff Waugh
Steven Way
Andy Wears
Duncan Webb
Cathy Webster
Caroline Weeden
Sheila Weeden
Paul Weston
Kevin Wheatly
Robert White
Stephen White
Lucy Whitehead
Rebecca Whitehouse
Amanda Wilkins
David Wilkinson
Kevin Wilks
Mark Willis
Janet L Wilson
Dominic Winchester

Susan Winter
Ian Winton
John Wood
Jon Wood
Tim Wood
Tristan Wood
Rob Woolley
Steve Woolley
Alex Woolman
Anne Wright
Gary Wright
Sam Wright
Simon Wright
Debbie Wythe
Deirdre Yager
Amy Yankoviak
Clare Young
Barbara Zahora
George Zahora
Anthony Zweck